SYMBOL AND THEORY

*A philosophical study of theories of religion
in social anthropology*

SYMBOL AND THEORY

A philosophical study of theories of religion in social anthropology

JOHN SKORUPSKI

Lecturer in Moral Philosophy
University of Glasgow

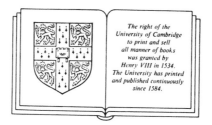

The right of the
University of Cambridge
to print and sell
all manner of books
was granted by
Henry VIII in 1534.
The University has printed
and published continuously
since 1584.

CAMBRIDGE UNIVERSITY PRESS

CAMBRIDGE

LONDON   NEW YORK   NEW ROCHELLE
MELBOURNE   SYDNEY

Published by the Press Syndicate of the University of Cambridge
The Pitt Building, Trumpington Street, Cambridge CB2 IRP
32 East 57th Street, New York, NY 10022, USA
10 Stamford Road, Oakleigh, Melbourne 3166, Australia

First published 1976
First paperback edition 1983
Reprinted 1986

Printed in Great Britain at the
University Press, Cambridge

Library of Congress Cataloguing in Publication Data
Skorupski, John, 1946–
Symbol and theory.
Based on author's thesis, Cambridge University.
Includes bibliographical references and index.
1. Religion, Primitive. 2. Symbolism.
3. Ritual. I. Title.
GN470.S57 1976   301.2'1   76-3037

ISBN 0 521 21200 6   hard covers
ISBN 0 521 27252 1   paperback

TO MY MOTHER

Contents

vii

CONTENTS

Part II Ritual action

CONTENTS

ix

CONTENTS

Preface

A book which deals with topics in two separate disciplines and with the relation between them stands in special need of some prefatory explanation. The main problem is usually that of setting limits on the area to be discussed and keeping within those limits; and the preface should indicate why the limits have been set where they have been. The difficulty is, I think, raised particularly acutely by the topics discussed here. The central topic – conceptions of religion in social anthropology – is, in one way, reasonably narrow and well defined. But the philosophical questions involved, concerning problems of translation or interpretation, the relation between actors' and observers' descriptions of an institution or social activity, the relation between belief and action, the possible bases for changes in concepts or beliefs and so on, ramify widely indeed: to the sociology of thought in general and beyond. Consequently if the discussion is to be kept to manageable proportions the need for drawing clear boundaries is particularly great.

The policy I have tried to follow is that of choosing a particular line of argument and following it through, taking into account the various methodological and philosophical issues at those points in the argument at which they become relevant. The central focus is on what is often called the 'intellectualist' conception of religion and magic in traditional cultures. I examine how plausible that kind of account can be made and how it relates to various philosophical issues involved in the understanding of traditional cultures. I also examine those alternative conceptions of the nature of religion and magic to be found in social anthropology which take the idea of symbolic meaning as their key interpretative concept.

Part I traces out and assesses the implications which these conflicting approaches have as to the meaning of 'ritual belief' and its relation to 'ritual action'. Part II analyses the concept of ritual, paying particular attention to notions of ritual as symbolic, and as communicative, action. Part III returns to the intellectualist account of 'traditional', or 'primitive', religious beliefs. It concentrates on the relation between scientific and traditional modes of thought, and on the way in which ideas from the philosophy of science have recently been used as a way of deepening the intellectualist comparison of the two.

The principle of following through the argument between intellectualist and anti-intellectualist – predominantly 'symbolist' – conceptions has dictated the limits set on each of these areas of discussion. And, of course, this book is a philosophical study, and so naturally concentrates on those issues which fall within a philosopher's competence. At the same time, one point which becomes clear in this discussion, I think, is that there is no sharp division in this area between philosophical issues and issues of general sociological theory. Moreover, constant disclaimers of sociological competence and cautious refusals to adopt anything so dangerous as an empirical thesis end in being merely tedious. The reader will recognise that this study is the work of a philosopher, not an anthropologist with fieldwork experience: if I have from time to time incautiously stuck my neck out in the wrong places, my head will be the only one to roll.

It will be useful to say something about particular decisions I have had to take about what to include and what to exclude.

(1) I do not discuss at all the structuralist analysis of myth, for two reasons: the methodological and philosophical issues it raises can in fact be fairly clearly separated from those questions about the study of religion and magic with which I am here concerned, and, on the other hand, they are complicated and difficult enough to merit monograph-length treatment on their own.

Some of the distinctions made in chapter 8 overlap with similar semantic ground covered in semiotic theory. (For a recent discussion in this vein see Leach 1976.) My own view of the conceptions of 'sign', 'symbol', 'index' and so forth developed by writers working from this angle is largely critical. But this book is not the place for an examination of their analytic tools. So I have simply backed my belief that an approach related to broadly 'Anglo-American' philosophy of language can cast a more focussed and better-directed light on the questions about ritual and magic with which I am concerned here, and have left comparisons to the interested reader.

(2) I do discuss the issue of conceptual relativism: but it has

been very difficult to decide whether or not (and if so, how) to treat the subject. On the one hand, from the philosopher's point of view, to discuss the 'problem of understanding other cultures' without any mention of relativism would be absurd. For the sociologist of thought, too, especially since Kuhn's *Structure of Scientific Revolutions* (1962), the comparative issues discussed in Part III cannot be insulated from relativist currents in the absence of an explicit discussion of relativism and its implications somewhere in the book. Finally, what in philosophy of science is often referred to as the thesis that theory is underdetermined by experience also has a completely independent source in the intellectualist tradition. Indeed it is fascinating to watch how Tylor's brisk and very offhand recitation of the blocks to falsifiability which explain the persistence of magical beliefs is developed by Evans-Pritchard into a much more serious and extended analysis of the 'circle' of magical – or 'mystical' – beliefs; how in turn this account, which originally was offered as marking a contrast with scientific thought, has more recently developed into a sense that *all* generalising systems of thought involve such 'circles'; and how this has finally led to relativist doubts about the possibility of explaining changes of overall belief in rational terms.

On the other hand, any serious consideration of a relativism based on the thesis that theory is underdetermined by experience inevitably leads into extremely difficult philosophical territory. "When formulated in a very abstract manner", Ernest Gellner has remarked (1968: 404), "I doubt whether the problem of relativism has a solution." Unfortunately the problem *has* to be formulated in an abstract manner, if one is to see how the underdetermination thesis needs to be conjoined with a particular approach in semantics, before it yields conceptual relativism – hence, if one is to have any real insight into relativism's philosophical presuppositions. The exploration of the conception of meaning – 'anti-realist', or 'verificationist', as I call it in this book – which this approach involves, and the question of its merit in relation to the 'realist' conception, are among the most fundamental and difficult problems in contemporary philosophy. Nevertheless it is on them that a solution to 'the problem of relativism' ultimately hangs.

The difficulty about whether or not to discuss relativism was, in short, that as with structuralism, a proper and extended discussion would take a book in itself, but that unlike structuralism, the issue of relativism has rightly been central in scholarly discussions of just those questions with which I am concerned. What I have done is to confine what I have to say about relativism and its relation to the intellectualist programme to an appendix which grows from the discussion of Tylor's blocks to falsifiability in chapter 1. The resulting discussion is compressed, and belongs much more to 'pure philosophy' than does the rest of the book, though of course I have tried to state the issues as simply as I can. A reader who is not particularly interested in the issue of relativism as it affects the study of other cultures' world-views may want to miss out this appendix. But I have tried to provide enough material for a reader who *is* interested in the subject to get an idea of where the nerve of the relativist argument leads, and enough for the philosopher to get his teeth into.

(3) Another problem of limit-setting concerned the issues discussed in Part II, which have been discussed in a somewhat related way in sociology, notably by writers in the tradition of ethnomethodology. Here the choice was between giving space to explaining how my discussion relates to that of the ethnomethodologists and how we differ on more general methodological issues, and, on the other hand, using it to show how recent philosophical work on the relation between convention, the actor's communicative intention, and the sense of a communicative act, and on speech act theory, can be helpful in analysing the character of what I call 'interaction codes' (chapter 6) and 'operative acts' (chapter 7). It seemed to me that it would be more interesting for the sociological reader to see this approach in action, rather than to read about its relation to another approach with which he was already familiar, and that for the philosophical reader too it would probably be more interesting to see familiar concepts and approaches applied in an unfamiliar context. There was of course a limiting problem on the philosophical side here also. For example, the analysis of convention on which I rely (D. K. Lewis') could have been set out and discussed in an explicit and extended way. But as with the other demarcation problems, the guiding principle throughout was to keep up the momentum of discussion between 'intellectualist' and 'symbolist' conceptions of religion, magic, ritual.

For criticism, advice and encouragement I am indebted to Dorothy Emmet, Fr Richard Farmer, Hugh Mellor, Howard Mounce, Roy Rappaport, Gareth Watkins, Bernard Williams and Peter Winch. Dr Mellor and Professor Winch examined the Cambridge doctoral thesis on which this book is based, and Professor Williams supervised it.

My greatest debt is to Robin Horton, who, in the course of a year's innumerable conversations and arguments at Ile-Ife, inspired my enthusiasm for the subject and made me see that intellectualism could be much more than a quaint relic of rationalistic Victorian simple-mindedness.

Parts of chapters 13 and 11 have previously appeared in Skorupski, 'Science and traditional religious thought', pts. I–II, III–IV, *Philosophy of the Social Sciences*, III (1973), no. 2, 97–116, no. 3, 209–31; and in Skorupski, 'Comment on Prof. Horton's "Paradox and explanation"', *Philosophy of the Social Sciences*, V (1975), 63–70.

J.S.

February 1976

THE FRAMEWORK OF BELIEF

1

The intellectualist programme

I am concerned with two – on the face of it, sharply opposed – approaches to religion. In this chapter I set out the first of these – 'intellectualism'; some philosophical issues which bear on it are discussed in the appendix. The other of the two approaches is the subject of the remaining chapters of Part I.

The initial conception

For the intellectualist the contrasted concepts of *tradition* and *modernity* mark out a systematic and deep-running difference between forms of religion – a difference in the aims, interests and felt rewards of religious life. When we speak of the 'traditional' culture of, for example, an African village or township, we are thinking of that culture just in so far as (among other things) it has been insulated from the explosion of scientific knowledge, the resulting leap in men's ability to control their natural environment and its consequences. Related to these differences, and contributing with them to the complex distinction between 'traditional' and 'modern', is the contrast between contemporary religion in the West and the religious thought traditional in such a village or township. So intellectualism starts with a claimed contrast between traditional and modern religion – the contrasting characteristics of which must then be set out, and will in turn require contrasting explanations. What will also be required, of course, is some account, consistent with these differences, of why we group traditional and modern religion together as forms of *religion*.

On the intellectualist view,[1] traditional religion pre-eminently takes the form of a cosmology whose basic explanatory category is that of *agency*: its pantheon of gods and spirits, whose actions have consequences in the perceptible world, can be invoked to explain why this rather than that event occurred; and it affords a means by which men, through influencing the will of the gods, can themselves hope to influence the course of events. Modern religion, on the other hand, has relinquished the explanation and control of nature to science, and restricts itself to other functions – here the account is rather broadly sketched – which religion has either always had or has gradually acquired. Religious – and also magical – activities in traditional societies, then, are to be taken by and large to be intended ways of bringing about desired events or avoiding feared ones; and the ideas which give them point are again to be taken literally as cosmological in character. What is more – and here we come to the distinctive feature of the intellectualist view – the explanation (at least in its main outline) of this cosmological emphasis is taken to be that traditional religious thought originates and persists as an attempt – not self-consciously experimental, but nevertheless to some degree responsive to experience – to explain and control the natural environment. Other aspects and preoccupations of religious life are then to be understood as building on the emotional and moral possibilities opened up by a cosmology based on the fundamental notion of personal agency.

Four stages of explanation

The sequence of explanation which this approach implies can be set out in more detail. Proponents and opponents are agreed in regarding it as the development of a tradition which Evans-Pritchard called the 'English' or 'intellectualist' interpretation of religion and magic.[2] For present purposes we need go no further back than the writings of Frazer and Tylor, though a proper intellectual history would refer to many other names (Spencer, Jevons and Comte, for example).[3] What these two writers have in common in the first place is something that looks like no more than an innocuous methodological platitude. "It is, I think", said Tylor (1866: 86), "a principle to be held fast in studying the early history of our race, that we ought always to look for practical and intelligible motives for the habits and opinions we find existing in the world." But when the implications which Tylor took this dictum to have are spelt out, they lead into an outlined programme of questions and blocked-out answers which in turn raise further questions and in this way dictate the direction in which explanation will go. The programme falls naturally into four stages.

The first of these, Stage I, starts with the question: Why do people in traditional cultures perform magical and religious actions? They perform them, said Tylor and Frazer, because they believe them to be means of bringing about ends which they seek. This they believe because – in the case of magic – they suppose that there are spells, actions and objects which, properly spoken, performed and used, will produce effects on weather, crops, game, the psycho-physical or spiritual condition of others or of oneself and so on; and because – in the case of religion – they suppose that there are spirits and gods, normally not perceived, but usually not in principle imperceptible. who are able to influence men's lives and their environment in favourable or unfavourable response to their behaviour – of which the spirits and gods are taken to be aware.

In many societies, people see themselves as members of a greater community to which some at least of these spiritual beings also belong; so that the complex web of reciprocal obligations which binds together the members of a community is thought of as woven also between, say, men, ancestor-spirits and gods. Hence men may perform religious rites, in accordance with the hierarchical obligations of such a community, as they perform ceremonious or formal actions in accordance with the hierarchical obligations of their human society. But within this ceremonial framework they also perform actions which they may conceive to be, for example, the striking of a bargain or an exchange of gifts with spirits or gods who have the power to influence their lives for good or ill – whether these are thought of as belonging to the wider spiritual community which so many religions postulate, or as being outside it.

This all naturally leads to the next question, with which Stage

II of the programme is concerned, namely: Why are these beliefs, which inform magical and religious behaviour, accepted? Why do people think spells and 'medicines' are efficacious? Why do they believe in the existence of unperceived beings who have goals, intelligence, the power to influence natural events and some sort of interest in human affairs? Here the intellectualist's uncontroversial first answer is that the believer grows up in a culture in which such beliefs are socially legitimate, and is socialised into them, just as we grow up in a culture in which it is accepted that the earth is round and moves round the sun, and are taught to believe it. And just as the number of people in our society who would accept the truth of, for example, the general theory of relativity exceeds the number who can understand (let alone explain) it, so people brought up to accept cosmological doctrines, religious or magical, may take them to be true even when they do not themselves claim fully to understand them. Obviously this answer is in itself only a first step. It does not explain how these beliefs, accepted in society, originated. Nor does it explain why they persist. The question of how accepted beliefs and attitudes actually change lies at the heart of any contrast between 'traditional' and 'modern', or 'closed' and 'open', societies. It is however a truism that in every society beliefs can fail to be retained not merely as a result of incomplete transmission, or because inefficient transmission allows their character to be gradually metamorphosed through an accretion of misinterpretations – 'channel noise' – but also as a consequence of positive rejection.

Hence there arises the question with which Stage III of the intellectualist programme is concerned: Why do people *go on* believing the religious and magical doctrines which give point to their rites? The answer which Tylor gave to this question was to be an influential one. Some of his reasons depend on the assumption that magicians have often been tricksters, carrying out conscious deceits. But he grants that "magic has not its origins in fraud, and seems seldom practised as an utter imposture" (Tylor 1891, 1: 134). There is then still a question as to why "honest but unscientific people" should continue "practising occult science in good faith" (p. 135). Among various other reasons he gives (such as the indefiniteness of predictions, the self-fulfilling power of prophecies, the fact that apparent successes always make a greater impact than failures do, and so on), four are worthy of note.[4] In the first place, magico-religious rites are often combined with techniques, such as planting seed, which effectively bring about the desired results. Then, on other occasions they are performed to bring about events, e.g. successive stages in nature-cycles, which would have occurred in any case. In the third place, where a detectable failure does occur, it can be ascribed to an improper performance of the rite. And fourthly, it is not supposed by the traditional thinker that results are fully determined by the rite. They are, rather, a function of a number of factors of which the ritual performance is only one. Other magical forces or spiritual agencies may always intervene. So where the rite fails to bring off a desired effect it is always possible to speculate that one or other of them *has* done so, even if one accepts the efficacy, *ceteris paribus*, of the rite.

These four points all concern what may be called blocks to falsifiability: each one describes a way in which facts and theories lose their potential for coming into direct opposition. There is no need to ascribe magico-religious believers' failure to see the falsity of their beliefs to illogicality: a good reasoner, supplied with a negated consequent, can only reason back contrapositively to the negation of the whole antecedent – if the antecedent is conjunctive in form, logic tells him nothing about which conjunct to reject.

This kind of account was taken up and greatly expanded by Evans-Pritchard in his *Witchcraft, Oracles and Magic among the Azande*, where he supplied the reader with twenty-two reasons why Azande fail to see the falsity of their 'mystical' beliefs. Again, these reasons are in effect offered in explanation of why a normal, rational person, brought up to accept the beliefs legitimated in Zande culture, could well never get to the point of rejecting them – why, as he says, the Azande "do not perceive the futility of their magic".[5]

There is an important difference among Tylor's four points. (It is reflected also in Evans-Pritchard's account.) The first two concern the traditional believer's *attitude* to the magical and religious beliefs received in his culture. The second two stem from the logical structure of those systems of beliefs themselves (see appendix). The first two blocks to falsifiability would be removed by an experimental approach: seed could be planted without accompanying prayers, sacrifices or spells; the frequency with which rain follows rain-making ceremonies could be compared with its natural incidence.[6] The 'could' here is of course a logical and not a psychological or sociological 'could'. it is precisely the absence of the attitudes associated with self-critical attempts at falsification of one's beliefs which the intellectualist perspective presents as a key characteristic marking off the 'closed' from the 'open predicament'. That the idea of making some sharp distinction between 'practical' (empirical) techniques and such 'mystical' (theory-laden) practices as divination, prayer, sacrifice or spell, of stripping the latter from the former and of making them separate objects of critical scrutiny, is not within the psychological and social limits of the *traditional* Zande's world – this the intellectualist may accept, assert and indeed build up into his notion of a traditional world. Thus he can accept that Zande 'mystical' beliefs are not *hypotheses*, in as much as a hypothesis is a belief held with a certain detached attitude – although, as we shall shortly see, he does claim them to be hypotheses or theories in the sense that they originally stem from and are actually put to the service of explanatory objectives.[7]

Tylor pointed to 'conservatism' and 'unreflectiveness' as two 'indices' of 'savagery'. Obviously the point needs to be worked out with some subtlety before it can be built into the distinction between tradition and modernity. It cannot be taken as just an aggregative remark about individual psychologies because, among other things, the testing of socially shared beliefs in modern societies is itself subject to a division of labour. Most of us, for example, no more test the efficacy of aspirin tablets than Azande do that of their medicines. It is true that we often have a general idea of what kinds of statistical test would be appropriate, but we take it on trust that they have been carried out – or at least that the analgesic efficacy of aspirin can be deduced from a general theory concerning its chemical composition which is itself well tested. This dimension of trust is not involved in Zande acceptance of magical substances – the testimony on which they rely concerns no statistical tests but expresses word-of-mouth recommendations conveying the kind of personal experience with which one person in our society might press some tablets on another.

Someone who wanted to carry out for himself the experiments

required to test aspirin properly would need to have access to technical resources, and preferably to a social organisation of a certain type and complexity which would allow him to recruit volunteer guinea-pigs – neither of which Azande have. Having established his results, he could give them a degree of permanence and publicity impossible in an oral culture by writing them down. Hence the technical and social preconditions of a 'scientific' approach – i.e. of detailed, recorded experimentation which, by being recorded, becomes shared knowledge, publicly recoverable and capable of being checked – are, or rather, were, absent in Zande society.

Reflections of this kind, however, take us only so far. They show that the contrast of 'traditional' and 'modern' is a contrast of institutions as well as attitudes, but not that it is *merely* a contrast of institutional preconditions. Although I am clearly talking of a continuum here, all the evidence indicates that there are differences in the degree to which inherited beliefs, attitudes and so on are, and are expected to be, questioned in traditional and modern cultures, differences striking enough to serve as the basis of the distinction itself. Traditional cultures are not full of would-be investigators frustrated by a lack of equipment, techniques and recruitable personnel. In placing such differences at the centre of analysis, and connecting them with the persistence of magical and religious beliefs, the intellectualist approach (though these points are still not exclusive to that approach) seems to be on firm ground.

The next step would be to map the ground out in more detail. For example, anthropologists often stress the lively scepticism which some of their informants display towards some medicine men as opposed to others, towards some supposed medicines as opposed to others and so on. The scepticism finds its place within a framework of traditionally legitimated ideas. Again we are often told of old men who have the time to think about such things and develop their own speculative elaborations on this traditional core of beliefs. "Vansina recalls affectionately three very independent thinkers he encountered among the Bushong, who liked to expound their personal philosophies to him. One old man had come to the conclusion that there was no reality, that all experience is a shifting illusion. The second had developed a numerological type of metaphysics, and the last had

7

evolved a cosmological scheme of great complexity which no-one understood but himself" (Douglas 1970a: 108). The phenomenon of a received core of beliefs coexisting with localised scepticism on the one hand and idiosyncratic speculative elaborations of a metaphysical or cosmological kind on the other is no less familiar in our own society. But the question for the anthropologist becomes: Under what conditions might localised scepticism about particular diviners develop into the rejection of a traditionally institutionalised technique of divination, or a personal cosmology become incorporated into the shared set of accepted beliefs? Outbreaks of mass enthusiasm such as the cargo cults or witch-finding movements, their occasions and the permanent traces they leave on the core of received beliefs, also deserve attention here.[8]

The proposed distinctions between 'traditional' and 'modern' discussed above, and initially suggested by Tylor's first two blocks to falsifiability, will be examined in chapter 12. The potential relativist implications of Tylor's other two blocks to falsifiability are considered in the appendix. But we must now round off the intellectualist's programme with its last stage, Stage IV.

The question here is: How do people come to adopt magico-religious beliefs in the first place? Again Tylor and Frazer agree on the outlines of an answer: such beliefs are hypotheses, perfectly reasonable given the accumulation of knowledge and techniques and the types of social organisation in the societies from which they emerge. Tylor, as Evans-Pritchard says (1965: 26),

wished to show that primitive religion was rational, that it arose from observations, however inadequate, and from logical deductions from them, however faulty; that it constituted a crude natural philosophy. In his treatment of magic...he likewise stressed the rational element...It also is based on genuine observation, and rests on classification of similarities, the first essential process in human knowledge.

"Crude and false as that philosophy may seem to us," says Frazer (1911, 2: 420–2; 1957: 347–8),

it would be unjust to deny it the merit of logical consistency...The flaw – and it is a fatal one – of the system lies not in its reasoning, but in its premises; in its conception of the nature of life, not in any irrelevancy of the conclusions which it draws from that conception. But to stigmatise these principles as ridiculous because we can easily detect their falseness would be ungrateful as well as unphilosophical...reflection and enquiry should satisfy us that to our predecessors we are indebted for much of what we thought most our own, and that their errors are not wilful extravagances or the ravings of insanity, but simply hypotheses, justifiable as such at the time they were propounded, but which a fuller experience has proved inadequate.

To recapitulate in bare logical outline so far: The question in Stage I, which initiated the intellecualist's programme, was: Why do people in certain cultures perform certain types of *actions*? The answer here took the form of imputing *beliefs* to the actors, which, if held, would give an understandable rationale for doing them. This then raised question II: How do the actors first acquire these beliefs? The answer was, by being socialised into them. Complementary to this was question III: Why do these beliefs go on being held? The answer was to point to certain attitudinal and structural blocks to their falsification. Finally, Stage IV posed the remaining question: How did these beliefs originate in the first place? The answer was, out of a need to understand and control the natural environment – a function which they still fulfil.

Some general features of intellectualism

I have spelt out the structure of intellectualism at what may have seemed tedious length. Only when this is done does its plausibility become clear: it is easy enough, for example, by conflating stages II and IV of its programme, to make it look like a ludicrously rationalistic form of extreme cognitive individualism. But the main reason for mapping out the logic of the intellectualist's approach with some care is that I shall be interested in determining at what points other approaches (sketched out in a preliminary way in the rest of this chapter) diverge from it, in the character of these divergences and, finally, in the degree to which intellectualism can assimilate the more detailed material, concerning 'ritual', to be analysed in Part II.

Some points about intellectualism are already clear. Notice first that it is logically complete. Of course it is not *substantially* complete. On the contrary, all the interesting descriptive and theoretical sociological detail remains to be filled in: what form magical and religious beliefs do take, how they are held (with what attitudes, under what sanctions and so on) and how these things vary from culture to culture; why beliefs of *these* rather than other particular forms should emerge in *these* conditions out of the 'explanatory quest'. This is to say that the programme I have outlined is no more than that. But *as* a research programme aimed at explaining, in psycho-sociological terms, a cross-cultural pattern of action and belief, it is exhaustive, in the sense that if one grants the sequence in which its questions are raised, one must also grant that they are all the questions at this level of enquiry: further questions that could be asked either fall within the four stages or take one off the level of psycho-sociological explanation altogether. *Given* the sequence of enquiry, all the questions have been listed, and for each question the form of an answer has been blocked out. One thing to be asked of any alternative to the intellectualist programme, therefore, is whether its set of questions and answers is also in this sense complete. Of course the questions may not be the same ones, since the intellectualist's are dictated by his sequence of enquiry, which is in turn determined for him by the first step he takes from his starting point – in the observation of religious and magical practices. The correctness of this first step has been questioned, as we shall see in a moment. But the question then focusses on whether or not the objector can give us a programme of questions and sketches towards answers which is equally coherent in its structure.

One question in particular which I shall often come back to when considering quite different accounts of the nature of magico-religious beliefs, actions and institutions in a culture, and their synchronic relations, is whether these alternative accounts can be supplemented by any plausible diachronic story. The synchronic part of the intellectualist's account, as given in stages I–III, is not just consistent with its diachronic part as given in Stage IV, but seems to build up a definite momentum towards it. If one accepts the general approach of I–III there is an obvious economy and elegance in going on along the lines of IV. This rounding-off is not *entailed*, however, by I–III; it is indeed the last step, IV, which constitutes the distinctive intellectualist thesis. Writers like Evans-Pritchard, who could not be called intellectualists, follow the general lines of the first three stages I have described. More generally, one can perfectly well accept (*a*) that traditional religious beliefs are to be interpreted at face value as beliefs about the *natural* world and its underlying dynamic principles, (b) that they are deployed for the purposes of explaining, and providing a rationale for attempts to control, the natural environment; and yet still believe that these goals are not the only ones to be grasped if traditional religious thought is to be understood – that there are important needs and pre-occupations, significantly different from the activist, this-worldly ones of explanation and control, which from the first shape and form the content of religious thought.

Literalism and the symbolist approach

I shall call the broader consensus which leaves open this last question *literalism.*[9] The objections to intellectualism which have been made within social anthropology have shown a certain concentration of fire on specific features of the intellectualist position, and a certain agreement about the 'paradigm' concepts which must replace those of the intellectualist; this justifies one in treating them – subject to the qualifications of chapter 2 – as a comparatively unified alternative approach. Now this other approach with which I shall be concerned differs not merely from intellectualism in particular, but also from the literalist method-ological approach in general. The difference appears already over the form of question asked, and the answer given at Stage I. Whereas the literalist emphasis is unambiguously on explaining magico-religious *actions* in terms of the beliefs which give them their point, and then on going on to a further and independent explanation of the beliefs, our alternative theorist is likely to suggest that it is the 'rite' which needs to be seen as 'prior' to 'the belief'. A more sophisticated way of putting a similar kind of point might be to recognise that the unit of significance is the *action* – that is, a piece of behaviour whose meaning needs to be understood by grasping the purposes and ideas expressed in it – but to insist that further explanation would take the institu-tional form of behaviour as the autonomous factor in this com-plex, and would not run via the backing of beliefs; these might even be explained as rationalisations of that independently de-termined mode of behaviour.

The methodological principle (vaguely) expressed here is incompatible not just with intellectualism but with the more general literalist position; and so are the fundamental interpretative concepts which go along with it. They require a denial, at some level at least (complexities are involved, as will be shown in chapter 2) of point (a) in the literalist position. Hence they also cast doubt on something suggested by (b): namely, that it might be illuminating to treat traditional religious cosmologies comparatively with modern scientific theories as being in the same business of explanation and control. This suggestion is taken up by intellectualism and developed into a complete pattern of explanation, a pattern whose key concept could fairly be identified as 'theory' – where a theory is a system of beliefs elaborated to characterise and explain experience, but whose domain of reference goes beyond what is given in experience. Intellectualism is the idea that traditional systems of thought originate and persist as just such 'transcendental hypotheses', to use Kneale's convenient term.[10]

If the key concept of intellectualism is 'theory', then the key concept of the alternative approach is 'symbol'; and the understanding of magic and religion which is sought is not causal but hermeneutic. The literalist takes magical and religious rites to be, by and large, 'instrumental' acts: actions which the actors perform because of the aimed-at consequences which they believe their actions will have. This already commits him to a certain view of the actors' underlying beliefs – namely, that they are beliefs about the world which can be used to explain it and which underpin attempts to control it. The intellectualist seizes on this role which magico-religious beliefs do play and takes it to be the role which they were called forth to play. The alternative approach prevents this momentum towards intellectualism, built into a literalist account, from ever getting going, by denying the literalist assumptions. Whether or not it grants that there is a level at which rituals (magical or religious actions) are instrumental it claims that at the level at which understanding of them is to be sought they are not instrumental at all: they must be grasped as symbolic, expressive, as 'showing' and 'saying' rather than 'doing'. This in turn implies that if the beliefs which form the background of ritual in a culture are to be seen as more than mere rationalisations – if, that is, their link with ritual actions is to be preserved at the deeper level of ritual significance – then they too must be understood as symbolically or metaphorically expressed.

What these claims amount to, in the various ways in which they can be spelt out, will be considered in subsequent chapters. The point I want to make for the moment is that a metaphorically or symbolically expressed thought is a thought expressed in a form which normally *does* have a literal meaning: what makes it symbolic or metaphorical is just that (i) the literal meaning (if any) of the sentence is not the meaning to be understood, and (ii) the literal meaning of the words must be grasped if one is to 'decode' the meaning which *is* to be understood. Hence a theorist who claims that ritual beliefs are symbolically expressed can grant that the form in which they are expressed does have a literal meaning; and literalism is fairly so called against an approach which claims not that the literalist gives a mistaken literal translation of ritual statements, but that he is mistaken in thinking that the literal level is either the only level at which they can be, or the level at which they should be, understood.

The Wittgensteinian interpretation of ritual

It is this kind of approach, familiar in social anthropology, and acknowledging the influence of Durkheim, with which I shall be mainly concerned in Part I and indirectly in Part II. But there is another approach to the same range of issues, more familiar in philosophy, and acknowledging the influence of Wittgenstein; and in the context of this approach, 'literalism' looks like a question-begging term. The position is represented, for example, in Peter Winch's 'Understanding a primitive society' (1972). There are a number of distinguishable themes in this paper (some of which will be touched on in chapter 4); the account it ultimately gives of the meaning of traditional Zande magic is not at all like the literalist's (and, *a fortiori*, the intellectualist's), and not at all *unlike* that which some symbolist writers in social anthropology might give. But it gets to this similar endpoint by a very different route. The point I have made in terms of the notion of 'translating' a traditional ritualist's 'language' is that the literalist and the symbolist are agreed on what the *translation* of ritual statements is – the difference between them is that the symbolist insists on the need for further hermeneutic understanding of this translated corpus of statements, while the literalist takes it at face value. One strand of the Wittgensteinian position would be to question whether these statements do have the literal meaning which *both* the literalist and the symbolist are agreed upon, and to suggest that the 'translation' which gives them this meaning misunderstands the 'language-game' in which magical and religious beliefs are expressed. Naturally someone who held this position would question literalism's right to its name.

This line of thought has one obvious advantage, which accrues from its preparedness to be much more radical with translation than is the symbolist: the Wittgensteinian has no need to distinguish between levels of meaning, symbolic and literal, and hence avoids the grave difficulties to which this distinction leads. (These will be discussed in chapter 3.) But talk of 'translation' here needs to be qualified. The need for translation, or rather correct understanding, arises for the Wittgensteinian as much with the modern English speaker's religious language as, say, with the traditional Yoruba speaker's. Moreover, translation normally involves the notion of identical meanings expressed in different linguistic forms. In this sense, the Wittgensteinian might well deny that the meaning expressed in a use of religious language is any more translatable or even paraphrasable than the meaning expressed in a poem or play may be.

But this remark in itself does not express the full force of the Wittgensteinian position. The analogy with the unparaphrasable meaning which may be expressed in a poem or play (taken as a whole) could be accepted by a philosopher who was more willing to talk of religious uses of language than of uses of religious language: that is to say, someone who believed in the possibility of giving a completely unified account of strict meaning and truth for sentences in natural language, invariant in respect of their subject matter. The Wittgensteinian certainly rejects this possibility; he denies that one and the same account can be given of how meaning and truth are determined, say, for sentences which convey factual reports, the sentences of a scientific theory, sentences in mathematical discourse – and, in particular, sentences in the religious 'language-game'. Each of these language-games involves *sui generis* forms of understanding.

But the Wittgensteinian notion of a language-game cannot be correctly represented as the idea simply of a set of sentences of whose strict meaning a unified semantic account can be given. Such a notion would be a purely semantic one, relying on a distinction between the 'semantic' level concerning what a sentence 'strictly means', and the 'pragmatic' level which concerns what its use might in typical contexts express, convey, show and so forth. The Wittgensteinian is committed not so much to rejecting the idea of a unified semantic treatment, independent of subject matter, for a language, in favour of giving separate types of semantic account for different areas of discourse, as to rejecting *any* fundamental distinction between what is 'strictly meant' by a sentence and what a speaker conveys by its use on a given occasion. Just this is part of the force of the injunction to look to the use of an expression for a grasp of its meaning; there is ultimately no distinction to be drawn between the strict (paraphraseable) meaning of the sentences which constitute a poem, and the unparaphraseable meaning which taken together as a poem they may express. They have the meaning they do in that context. And so in general, what is said in a language-game has the meaning it has in that context; and to understand its meaning, one has to grasp the use of an utterance in the language-game of which it is a part. It is in some such sense that the Wittgensteinian might question the 'translateability' of the language-game of 'ritual': the language-game is as it is – an understanding of ritual statements is achieved not by anything non-trivially called 'translation', but by grasping their use in its context.[11]

Contrasted conceptions of meaning

Though there is obvious artificiality in imputing philosophical theories of meaning to approaches in social anthropology, the symbolist (to give him a convenient label) may usefully be seen as sharing with the literalist as an implicit assumption the classical view that a unified semantic account can be given of all sentences in the traditional religious believer's language. This account would take the form of outlining how the meaning of a sentence is determined by the meaning of its constituent expressions. Hence the meaning of sentences spoken in religious discourse can be ascertained when the meaning of their constituent expressions is known, and, given the assumption of unity, this knowledge can be acquired by determining their semantic function in translated sentences from another, more amenable, area of discourse; or, in the case of expressions specific to the religious context, by direct questioning which elicits an answer in terms of expressions already understood. Given this approach the symbolist finds himself in agreement with the literalist as to the *manifest* meaning of magico-religious statements – his next step is to insist on a hermeneutic understanding of what is latently conveyed or expressed in their use.

The Wittgensteinian's criticism of this should now be clear. He approves the symbolist's stress on looking to the emotional and social context in which ritual utterances are made, and ritual actions performed, for a grasp of what is conveyed in them; but on his view this approach should be extended to include the very meaning of what is said in such contexts: the symbolist goes wrong in recovering the ('literal') meaning of ritual statements by projecting the meaning of their constituent expressions from the function which these have in other areas of discourse. For their role in sentences in the language-game of ritual cannot be deduced indirectly from their role in other contexts (of factual reportage, for example) – it must be established directly, *in* the ritual context. The idea that these sentences have a literal, cosmological level of meaning *at all* is therefore an illusion engendered by a bad theory of meaning. If the symbolist followed his approach right through he would be freed from his residual literalist shackles and, with that, from the false dialectic of 'literalism' and 'symbolism'.

So much for the benefits of the Wittgensteinian approach; it also has costs, to do with obscuring or rejecting distinctions ('semantic' versus 'pragmatic' ingredients in the total communicative force of a given speech act) and giving up ambitions (a unified semantic treatment of natural language) which seem to me to be of central importance in the theory of meaning. This claim will have to be left here as mere assertion – the argument belongs to the philosophy of language and cannot usefully be summarised; and my main concern is with theories of religion and magic in social anthropology. In one sense, however, this book as a whole is directly relevant to Wittgensteinian accounts of 'ritual',[12] and the conception of language and meaning on which they partly rest – even though they are discussed in what follows only obliquely. For let us suppose that this conception of language and meaning can be fashioned into a workable account. As between such theories of meaning, the final test must lie in the degree to which they make sense of what people say. This is not merely a matter of whether and to what degree the 'translation' they produce of people's utterances in a culture is compatible with some principle of interpretative charity. Rather it raises a subtler question: Can what people turn out to mean, on the given theory of meaning, by what they say, be linked with a plausible psycho-sociological theory which tells us why they should be *given* to saying what – so understood – they do say?

As in the natural sciences the choice of geometry is not independent of the choice of physics, so in the sciences of man the choice of theory of meaning is not independent of the psychology and sociology of thought. Hence, if the literalist account can make good sense of traditional magical or religious beliefs and practices, and if the intellectualism which combines naturally with it can be plausibly worked out, then that will be a considerable vindication of the classical conception of meaning which underpins it. It will then be up to the Wittgensteinian to detail a better, more integrated account.

On the other hand, for someone who is convinced, on independent grounds, that the Wittgensteinian conception of language and meaning is inferior to the classical conception, but who is inclined toward the anti-literalist interpretation of religion and magic which both Wittgensteinian and symbolist seek to develop, the question of whether or not the symbolist account can be convincingly carried through will take on an added interest. I turn to this question in the remaining chapters of Part I.

2

The Durkheimian thesis

The symbolist approach: salient features

The symbolist approach differs from intellectualism in three important respects. It sees a difference between science and religion or magic as forms of life – a difference in the concerns, even the logic, of the two kinds of activity beside which the contrast among religions between tradition and modernity is insignificant. It considers religion and magic to be distinctive in that beliefs and rituals taken together constitute a symbolic system which describes the pattern of social relations in the society in which they exist; and consequently it distinguishes in some way between the literal meaning of religious and magical discourse and the perhaps overtly intended meaning of religious or magical actions on the one hand, and their symbolic meaning on the other. The sociologist, on this view, is not a theologian, and is not primarily concerned with the literal (or apparent) meaning of religious doctrines. Explaining the system of ritual and ritual beliefs in a society – 'ritual' will for the moment mean 'magical or religious action', and ritual beliefs will be those beliefs which inform or give point to ritual actions – is a matter of coming to understand what is conveyed, in the performance of such rituals, of the system of social relationships, actual and ideal, in that society. It consists of 'decoding ritual messages' by seeing them as a systematic whole and relating them to social structures; it has little to do with searching for the causes which produced the overt, surface form of ritual beliefs.

What is involved, then, is a sharp distinction between science and religion, a thesis about the nature of religion to fill out the distinction, and, as an apparent methodological consequence of that thesis, a new view about what kind of explanation is appropriate, at least at the sociological level, in the study of religion. Thus Leach writes (1954: 14) that

ritual action and belief are alike to be understood as forms of symbolic statement about the social order. Although I do not claim that anthropologists are always in a position to interpret such symbolism, I hold nevertheless that the main task of social anthropology is to attempt such interpretation.

Parsons asserts (1968: 431):

Ritual actions are not...simply irrational, or pseudo-rational, based on pre-scientific erroneous knowledge, but are of a different character altogether and as such not to be measured by the standards of intrinsic rationality at all.

And Beattie writes (1964: 210)

It is a function of ritual to enhance the social importance of something which is held to be of value in the society which has the ritual. If ritual is a kind of language, a way of saying things, then Trobriand canoe magic stresses the importance of canoe building for the Trobrianders; blood pact ritual emphasises the need for mutual support between the parties to it; and avoidance ritual asserts the need to maintain good relations between affinally linked groups.

Divergences within the symbolist approach

But to use these quotations (or the many others which can be found in the literature) as documentation of a single 'symbolist approach' is potentially misleading. These three authors all agree that ritual is a kind of language; but they do not agree what ritual is, nor as to what it is a language about. Parsons would reject the view that ritual concepts are symbolic representations of the social order; Beattie, I think, would accept it only in a partial or qualified way. Leach does not equate ritual with magical or religious action, preferring to see it as that "aspect of almost any kind of action" which "says something" (1954: 12–13) – though in his examples of it, on the other hand, magical or religious rites loom large. It is impossible to set out a research programme which a range of symbolist writers would accept, as I have done for intellectualism. The most that could be offered by way of generalisation is that many social anthropologists (and some sociologists) take it that the notion of symbolism is peculiarly valuable in the analysis of 'ritual'; that 'ritual' and religion and magic are more or less closely associated topics; and that what is in some fashion symbolised in 'ritual' has something to do with society – social groupings, social relationships, social norms.

Nevertheless, an explicit analysis of the symbolist approach as I have described it is by no means a pointless enterprise. Divergences from and elaborations on it can usefully be seen as attempts to cope with various objections. And, even for writers who make no theoretical claim to work out its implications, it acts as a pole which sets up a powerful counter-attraction to intellectualism. Indeed the power is partly due precisely to its status as vaguely formulated and unanalysed conventional wisdom. Influenced by it, one sees religion and magic in a distinctive light, even while accepting that there are still difficulties to be sorted out, and that the whole approach has yet to be systematically thought through. It is perhaps for this reason that explicit rejections of the intellectualist programme have been generally based on such offhand and in themselves unconvincing arguments. Notice that I am speaking here of the programme rather than of the specific views, within it, of Tylor or Frazer – such as Tylor's ideas about the emergence of concepts of soul or spirit, Frazer's evolutionary theories, the associationist psychology of both, and so on. These have all been well criticised (though of course analagous criticisms could be made of Durkheim's very specific speculations about the origins of ritual symbols) but I know of no equally cogent objections to the programme itself. This is a claim which can only be illustrated; consider, for examples, two criticisms by Leach.

In 'Virgin birth' he writes (1966; 45):

Tylor, Frazer and the latter day neo-Tylorians assume that statements of dogma start out as mistaken attempts to explain cause and effect in the world of nature...I repudiate such speculation about causes which are inaccessible to observation or verification. It may seem surprising that men persist in expressing formal beliefs which are palpably untrue but you won't get anywhere by applying canons of rationality to principles of faith.

But though detailed speculations of the kind in which Frazer and Tylor indulged may be unverifiable, it is a mistake to think that the *general* thesis, that magico-religious beliefs emerge and persist

as attempts to understand and control nature, is equally a supposition on which no evidence can in the nature of the case be
brought to bear. Again, in 'Ritual', Leach describes 'neo-
Tylorianism' thus (1968; 525):

> Ritual acts are to be interpreted in the context of belief; they mean what
> the actors say they mean. This common sense approach clearly has its
> attractions. Yet it may be argued that if culturally-defined behaviour can
> only be interpreted by the actors, all cross-cultural generalisation is
> impossible, and all attempts to make a rational analysis of the irrational
> must necessarily be fallacious. In contrast, I, along with other Dur-
> kheimians, continue to insist that religious behaviour cannot be based
> upon an illusion.

The inference involved here is a familiar one, but is given a new
twist. The familiar argument concludes that cross-cultural comparison is impossible, from the premise that social action is necessarily understood in terms of the meaning given to it by the
agents; Leach regards the conclusion as a sufficient refutation of
the premise.[13] In reality the conclusion does not follow from the
premise at all; there is no general reason why it should be
impossible to compare the *accounts* which people offer of their
actions in one culture with the accounts offered in another. (Here
we are concerned with the possibility of a descriptive comparative
approach, and not with the problems involved in an evaluative
comparison of the cognitive adequacy of different systems of
action and thought – these are discussed in the appendix.)

To take Leach's other point, if a 'rational analysis' of what
are in fact irrational beliefs or actions is to be an *elucidation* of
them which seeks to present them as rational, then it is of course
necessarily fallacious. But there is no reason why it should be
impossible to *explain* irrational beliefs rationally.[14] And in any
case, the intellectualist position, rightly or wrongly, is that when
they are seen in the light of the agent's world-view and his
reasoning within it, magical and religious actions turn out to be
perfectly reasonable, though the beliefs on which they are based
are false. The assumption of irrationality is not the neo-Tylorean's
but Leach's.

The Durkheimian thesis contrasted with some other theses of Durkheim and with functionalism

Although symbolist forms of approach are commonly linked with the name of Durkheim, they often, as we have noted, incorporate two features, neither of which plays a particularly prominent role in Durkheim's writings on religion. The first of these is the claim that magic and religion have a rationale quite different from that of science, and are not commensurable with it. The second is the rejection of an essential intellectualist assumption: namely, that in the explanation of religion and magic, beliefs have explanatory priority over actions and emotions, which are to be explained in terms of them. Here it is argued that ritual actions are remarkably invariant from culture to culture, whereas the actors' interpretations of them are in comparison highly variable – the latter therefore cannot be used to explain the former.

Now when this second point is pushed, it can lead to a bifurcation in the interpretation of ritual action and ritual belief. Ritual action may be seen as in some sense symbolically expressive of the social order; but, if ritual beliefs are simply variable rationalisations of this invariant substratum, they need not be seen as having a symbolic character at all. On the other hand, if the link between ritual belief and action is to be preserved at the deeper, symbolic, level of ritual significance, then ritual beliefs must themselves be seen as belonging, together with ritual actions, in a system of symbolic expression. In Durkheim's *Elementary Forms of the Religious Life* one finds, it is true, the idea that ritual actions express social relationships in a sense which carries no necessary implication for the interpretation of their context of religious and magical belief. (The notion of varying 'instrumental' rationalisations of a core of expressive actions is, however, rather more reminiscent of Pareto than of Durkheim.) In at least one of the ways in which this can be understood, it need not be true only, or particularly, of religious or magical actions, as will be seen in Part II. But Durkheim's work does also contain a very much stronger thesis, concerned specifically with the *meaning* of ritual beliefs: religion's "primary object", he says (1915: 225),

is not to give men a representation of the physical world; for if that were its essential task, we could not understand how it has been able to survive, for, on this side, it is scarcely more than a fabric of errors. Before all, it is a *system of ideas* with which the individuals represent to themselves the society of which they are members, and the obscure but intimate relations which they have with it. This is its primary function; and though metaphorical and symbolic, this representation is not unfaithful. Quite on the contrary, it translates everything essential in the relations which are to be explained; for it is an eternal truth that outside of us there exists something greater than us, with which we enter into communion [my italics].

Thus, as Lukes points out, there is some ambiguity in the conception of religion as a 'representation' of the social order: "On the one hand, religion could be seen as 'representing' society and social relationships in a cognitive sense, to the mind or intellect. In this sense religion afforded a means of comprehending or rendering intelligible social realities. On the other hand, it could be seen as 'representing' them in the sense of expressing, symbolising or dramatising social relationships" (Lukes 1973*b*: 465). What I am in this chapter calling the 'Durkheimian' thesis is the *cognitive* interpretation of the claim that the domain symbolically represented in ritual practice and belief is social reality. On the subject of religion, there are a number of Durkheims, not all of whose views are obviously compatible with the Durkheimian thesis. The newy rediscovered Durkheim who saw 'scientific' notions of causal relationship as developing out of religious categories of thought about the world may be a case in point. Nevertheless, the thesis has become associated with Durkheim's *Elementary Forms of the Religious Life*, and is in fact one important strand in the complex and sometimes disparate structure of that book.

As I have presented it, this thesis concerns the meaning of religious discourse as distinct from the social function of religious practice. This again is an idealisation, which sharpens the discontinuities between shades of opinion in social anthropology over the last fifty or sixty years. For though Malinowski, for example, was clearly a functionalist and clearly not a symbolist, while Leach is a symbolist and certainly not a functionalist, in the work of Radcliffe-Brown the concepts of meaning and function are impenetrably fused. Again, Gluckman, whose writings on ritual are squarely in the functionalist tradition, is very prone to talk of the meaning of ritual, while Beattie, who has devoted a number of articles to the elaboration and defence of a version of the symbolist approach, moves easily from talk of ritual language, and ritual meaning, to talk of the functions of ritual. This is not surprising, since functionalist accounts of religion and magic failed notoriously to distinguish clearly between the purpose, point or goal of institutions and institutional actions, and their social effects. Anthropologists writing from a functionalist perspective have given painstaking accounts of how religious beliefs can support and legitimate social positions – for example of the way in which ancestor-worship can bolster the authority of village elders, or of how these beliefs and the duties and rights they imply can figure in local political manoeuverings, or of how magical procedures can serve to give order and form to canoe-building or gardening. In doing this they have often brought vividly to life some of the ways in which magic and religion can enter into everyday life in a traditional society. But no one has ever explained how any of these acutely observed effects of magico-religious beliefs are relevant to explaining the origins or persistence of magic and religion in society. At best one might fall back on the familiar observation that beliefs which justify attitudes, opinions or a way of life which one wants to retain are harder to reject and easier to accept than others. In this sense, functionalism does not propose a theory of magic or religion; since this fact is now generally recognised,[15] and since my interest is specifically in such theories, I have sharpened the distinction between accounts of the social functions of ritual and the symbolist approach as such.

To summarise, three related but logically distinguishable thoughts are often brought together under the symbolist umbrella. Crudely, they are (1) that ritual *actions* in some sense express the social order, though ritual beliefs are posterior rationalisations, not necessarily themselves symbolic; (2) that ritual (action and belief) has distinctive functions in the *maintenance* of the social order; and (3) the Durkheimian thesis, that ritual actions and beliefs belong to a system of symbolic discourse, the true *referents* of which are to be found in the social order. The Durkheimian thesis itself is neither an explanation of the phenomenon of 'ritual' nor an analysis of its social functions, but an elucidation of its character. Hence the methods and arguments by which the philosophical analysis of an area of discourse is assessed are appropriate to it as well. Furthermore I think one can discern a broadly philosophical framework lying behind it.

Cosmocentric and anthropocentric aspects of religion

Consider, as starting point, the relationship between modern science and Christianity. A common claim is that the advance of science has been in some way inimical to religious faith. And yet many people would also say that scientific theory and religious teaching do not, at least in the strict logical sense, conflict. How can these two points be fitted together? In Western culture (and not only in it, of course) a distinction is made with varying degrees of emphasis between the world of nature – that is to say of objects and events in space and time – and the world of man. Men and their activities are a part of nature, but they are also thought to stand apart from it in some sense, in a moral community whose characteristic is that the lives and relationships which constitute it have meaning. (The distinction stated as baldly as this naturally lacks content; I am concerned only with the fact that contrasts of this general shape constantly reappear.) The Christian conception of God has two major invariant elements. One is the notion that God is the author, or ground, of nature, and the other is that He is the source from which the life of the moral community springs. I shall call religious teaching which concerns itself with the relation between God (or gods) and the world of nature (including man considered as a part of nature) *cosmocentric* religion, and that which concerns itself with the relation between God (or gods) and the world of man *anthropocentric* religion – it is of course 'anthropocentric' only in as much as it excludes nature from consideration, not in the fact that it excludes God, or treats Him as in some sense dependent on the existence of men.

As the belief that experimental science is capable of providing a unified and comprehensive framework within which nature can be understood has gained ground among Christians, so emphasis has been placed on conceptions of the relation between God and nature which will be consistent with this belief. One of these, for example, pictures the universe as a self-regulating mechanism made by God. The picture allows for occasional direct interventions on His part in its course, but the natural development is the idea of a *laissez-faire* rather than an interventionist divinity. Building a machine, however, or initiating an economic organisation presupposes the existence of laws, not in any sense themselves a 'part' of these systems, in accordance with which the systems are built and which determine their operation. Did God make the universe in accordance with laws which He did not himself create? The tendency is to answer that the laws of the universe are themselves God's creation. What does it mean to speak of creating such laws? Obviously they are not themselves an artefact which functions in accordance with pre-existing laws – to say that God creates natural laws is to say that He ensures that when the causal antecedents specified in a given law obtain, so also does the specified consequent. Here God plays a sustaining role with respect to each causal connexion, but in any case both these conceptions of the relation between God and nature, taken in themselves, in practice accord to religion a marginal position in the cosmological outlook of a society which accepts them.

If on the other hand one takes the cosmocentric teaching of traditional religions at its face value, whether it be, say, the 'primitive religions' of sub-Saharan Africa, or pre-seventeenth-century religious beliefs (in a broad Tylorean sense) in England,[16] one finds the reality of gods and spirits woven with many strands of belief into everyday experience. Their doings make a more or less direct impact on a wide array of events in the world. And so it seems that such a culture's explanation and description of the world must make repeated reference to their actions, and to the consequences of these. But for Christians who accept the explanatory claims of modern science, and who anticipate its greater success, explanation and description of the course of nature need make no reference to the reality of God at any level below the utmost generality of such cosmocentric conceptions as I have described. The cosmocentric side of Christianity can perhaps reach a *modus vivendi* with the idea of nature as having its own dynamic, but it certainly gains no support from it. The overall effect is that which MacIntyre has described in the particular case of the move from Aristotelian to Newtonian physics: "the replacement of a physics which requires a Prime Mover by a physics which does not secularises a whole area of enquiry. It weakens the hold of the concept of God on our intellectual life by showing that in this area we can dispense with descriptions which have any connexion with the concept" (MacIntyre 1970: 74).

Consider now the anthropocentric side of Christianity. The conception here is of a moral or spiritual community. God is in this community not merely in that He is one member, but also in the sense that He 'sacralises' every personal relationship: no personal bond should exclude him. In fact the roles which God is thought to play, and the patterns as well as the nature of the relationships between God and man which they respectively imply, vary greatly. He is the legitimating foundation on which the authority for all men of moral law rests; He is also the final judge of human conduct within those laws; He is at the same time a limitlessly understanding friend, a confidant with a distinguishing interest in each human being's affairs. But perhaps for many contemporary Christians it is simply the sense of a personal presence, conscious of one's fortunes, and from which one is never isolated, which constitutes the primary form of God's relationship to man.

Anthropocentric conceptions of God are by no means independent of beliefs about His cosmological role. That God is the creator of man is a part of the broader view that He is the creator of the universe. This latter belief is an extremely important underpinning for the moral and emotional roles He plays in believers' lives. To the degree that the broader view loses its conviction the meaning of its particular application to man also becomes problematic. So if successful science does 'weaken the hold' of cosmocentric conceptions of God by giving us fruitful conceptions of the world which do not require them, it can in doing so also undermine other, apparently independent, areas of faith. This chain reaction depends on the traditionally central links between the God of cosmological reality and the God whose presence vitalises the spiritual society. But it is characteristic of much modern Christian thought to shift, reinterpret or gloss over these links. The anthropocentric aspect of Christian teaching occupies the centre of the stage. That has an effect on the meaning of Christian belief. Traditionally what it means to say "God exists" was expounded not merely in terms of His effect in the spiritual lives of men, but more importantly in terms of His active relations with nature, conceived of as part of the larger cosmos. God was firmly rooted in the traditional Christian's conception of the reality around him: heaven, hell, the order of spiritual beings, the fall and so on.[17] A highly articulated conception of the spiritual society, and of the respective roles of God and man within it, rested securely on this cosmological base. For the modern Christian the cosmological side of Christianity is not, and cannot be, completely broken off (it includes the idea of God as creator but also the historicity and divinity of Christ),[18] but the weight of God's reality is not placed on it. God's existence is now most typically given in terms of His felt presence in the lives of men; and apparently cosmological teaching which links God to the world must derive its meaning from this. Within anthropocentric religious thought, too, elaborately structured conceptions of God's role in the spiritual community recede to give way to it.[19] At the same time the methods and results of science increasingly constitute our conceptions of reality: what is 'out there' is what the scientific net can drag up. Hence modern Christianity, in ensuring that nothing that might be dragged up can conflict with its teaching, ensures also that the religious reality with which it is concerned comes to seem more obscure. This does no more, it can be argued, than to bring into prominence a feature which has always been there: Christan thought has always accepted the mysteriousness of God's reality. Yet all these developments, even when they are changes of emphasis, amount to an overall shift in the intellectual and emotional claims that Christianity makes.

For some people this shift seems to be a scaling down of ambitions, perhaps to the point of vacuousness. To others it represents a shedding of inessentials, an emergence of religion into its true meaning; for them science is in no way in conflict with religious faith. The divergence between these two views must necessarily bear on theories in the empirical study of religion (and vice versa), since it ultimately concerns religion's nature and function. It cannot, to use a distinction popular among sociologists of religion, be placed as a subject of exclusive interest to the 'theologian' rather than the 'sociologist'. For a person who takes the second view, and in that light bases his understanding of what religion is on the example of contemporary Christianity may well emphasise two distinguishing characteristics. The first of these is that whereas science concerns itself with nature and with men in so far as they are a part of nature, religion concerns itself with men in so far as they form a spiritual community given meaning by belief in and experience of God; and the second is that religious discourse concerns itself in a dark or mysterious manner with a reality which is not commensurable with that of science.

Positivism and its influence

To follow through the effect this kind of view can have on the study of traditional religious thought we need first to take up another influence, that of positivism; I here take this to comprise the general empiricist position that knowledge of truths which are not necessary by virtue of being purely analytic is based on observation, together with the sharper doctrine that the real is the observable. There is in addition the thesis distinctive of *logical* positivism – that the meaning of a statement lies in the methods by which it may be verified.[20]

With respect to scientific theory the positivist method is to distinguish sharply between the theoretical language and the observational language. Sentences in the former are typically treated as, for example, analysable into sentences about experimental observations and observable states of affairs, or alternatively as instruments, expressing no statements, but designed to provide rules for inferring observational conclusions from observational premises. Where scientific theory seemed to tell of a universe of which the observable world was merely a part, discriminated in a fairly local area at a fairly low level of fine-grainedness, it turns out, on this approach, that the observable world was always its entire subject.

The point deserves more attention. A rough-and-ready methodological contrast could be drawn up among philosophers of science – between those who seek a descriptive analysis of how fundamental concepts of science are actually used and what criteria arguments in science are actually assessed by, and those who attempt to draw up logical and philosophical standards which a proper science would ideally attempt to satisfy, and look for 'rational reconstructions' of scientific theory to meet these standards. Worked out in detail, this contrast is far less clear-cut than when it is stated baldly, but it is still true to say that positivist accounts of science have been given from both perspectives. Thus a rational reconstruction, in positivist spirit, of a scientific theory would be an interpretation which sought to sacrifice nothing of the theory's empirical cognitive content while it hygienically avoided the conceptual difficulties and illegitimate commitments which the untreated version admittedly involved. But because the distinctive feature of *logical* positivism is its verificationist theory of meaning, it typically gravitates towards what is claimed to be a descriptive analysis of the semantics of the 'theoretical language', which seeks to show that theoretical statements seen in context, and properly understood, do *not* carry the illegitimate existential commitment which on the face of it they seem to. The illusion that they do results from an incorrect conception of meaning applied to scientific discourse.

For an empirical study of religious thought there can of course be no such choice of methodology – the first step is necessarily one of descriptive analysis, designed to show how the system of beliefs studied is actually understood and accepted by its believers. This follows simply from the fact that it is the system of beliefs as actually understood which constitutes the *explanandum*.

Consider now positivist attitudes to religion. Those varieties of positivism which preceded the more ambitious programme of descriptive analysis implied by the addition of the verificationist theory of meaning were not obliged to take any attitude to religious thought at all. My formulation of positivism, to apply to these forms, would have to be amended by writing 'scientific knowledge' for 'knowledge', and 'real for the purposes of science' for 'real'. Positivism could then be thought of as a scientific philosophy in the specific sense of being an explication of what scientific methodology should be; it need not touch religion. This would leave open the possibility of a legitimately realist account of religious discourse – a combination of views, which like Berkeley's philosophy, has the advantage (if it can be convincingly worked out) of reconciling the all too easily felt conflict of religious and scientific reality to the satisfaction of the religious believer.

Logical positivism, however, because it bases itself on a *general* theory of meaning, does have to give some account of the meaning of religious discourse, or else explain how it lacks meaning. There are various possibilities (apart from the purely dismissive one). One is to allow that there are ultimately important truths which can be seen, or apprehended, but not significantly expressed: another is to handle religious along with moral discourse in terms of the distinction between cognitive and emotive meaning. Each of these is to some degree reflected in social anthropology.[21]

Another possibility is to approach religion in the same way as scientific theory, and thus, given the anthropocentric emphasis, to treat religious statements as reducible to statements about empirical social relationships between people. Just as positivism projects the extended universe apparently described by science into its observable part, so this treatment of religion projects the extended spiritual community which seemed to be the subject of religion, in which God (or gods) appeared as an ultimate and independent presence, back into its observable part – a society of human beings.

The Durkheimian thesis results from combining positivism with an anthropocentric conception of religion

This is not a commonly adopted option among theologians or philosophers of religion, however influenced by broadly positivist considerations (though there are some similar sounding ones). But in sociology and in social anthropology it is more familiar; it amounts to the Durkheimian thesis, which only differs in that the reduction is effected by 'symbols' rather than the 'logical constructions', or 'heuristic instruments' of the logical positivists.

But it may be objected that to propose this philosophical background for the Durkheimian thesis is to assume it to be false from the start. One of the two pillars on which it rests, I am suggesting, is an anthropocentric conception of religion. This conception, I have said, is implicitly modelled on the characteristics of Western Christianity, which are in turn the result of a process in which cosmocentric teachings have been loosened, reinterpreted or shed partly in response to the progress of experimental science. The response was presumably triggered because scientific cosmologies replaced or cast doubt on religious cosmocentric teachings. The grounds of this incompatibility are not simple; but from the point of view of the Durkheimian thesis there is simply no place for any incompatibility at all. If religious conceptions symbolically represent social reality, how could they have come into conflict with scientific cosmology? But this does in fact draw attention to a real difficulty for the thesis. If it is to be a starting point for *explanation* it must be presented as descriptive analysis, not as rational reconstruction. Either, then, it has to give a plausible account of the historical character of Western religious thought in which the connexion between emerging scientific ideas and changing religious thought is no longer made, or, if the connexion is to be accepted, it must exclude those admittedly cosmocentric ideas of traditional Christianity which have been affected by science, from the domain of symbolically expressed representations of society. In that case, however, the relationships between the cosmocentric and the anthropocentric aspects of traditional Christianity remain to be elucidated. Of course the thesis has usually been applied to 'primitive' religions in other societies. But analogous difficulties arise there. In the rest of this chapter and the next I shall consider these in more detail.

Durkheim and Feuerbach compared

A clearer view of the problem emerges if we compare Durkheim's views with those of an earlier writer on religion which are at first sight very similar. Durkheim's study of religion, in so far as it does advance the claim that religious conceptions represent the social order from which they emerge, seems to differ from Feuerbach's account only in speaking of *society* rather than of *man*. Feuerbach wrote (1967: 12–13) that

consciousness of God is self-consciousness, knowledge of God is self-knowledge...But when religion – consciousness of God – is designated as the self-consciousness of man, this is not to be understood as affirming that the religious man is aware of this identity, for on the contrary ignorance of it is fundamental to the peculiar nature of religion...Man first of all sees his nature as if *out of* himself, before he finds it in himself...what was at first religion becomes at a later period idolatry; man is seen to have adored his own nature.

Now Marx (in his 'Theses on Feuerbach') criticises Feuerbach precisely in respect of the point in which Durkheim also differs: in effect, he replaces 'man' by 'society' in Feuerbach's analysis. What then is the remaining difference between Marx and

Durkheim? The relevant one for present purposes is this. Durkheim argues from the claim that "there are no religions which are false. All are true in their own fashion" (1915: 3), to the conclusion that religion symbolises society:

> When we commence the study of primitive religions, it is with the assurance that they hold to reality and express it... When only the letter of the formulae is considered, then religious beliefs and practices seem undoubtedly disconcerting at times, and one is tempted to attribute them to some sort of a deep-rooted error. But one must know how to go under the symbol to the reality which it represents and which gives it meaning ...Our entire study rests upon the postulate that the unanimous sentiment of believers at all times cannot be illusory.[22]

His line of thought here is analogous to that of the positivist who wants to acknowledge the legitimacy of an area of discourse which on the face of it refers to a domain of objects whose existence he cannot on his principles accept, and who thus needs an analysis of the meaning of statements within this area which eliminates the apparent reference. Religion does contain a truth, but it cannot do so if religious statements are really about unobservable beings presumed to exist independently of human experience; so they must in reality be about 'the ensemble of human relations'. Why about social relations, rather than about other observable features of the world? Because religious thought is seen as essentially anthropocentric in its character. So here the two tendencies of thought which have been discussed – the anthropocentric conception of religious meaning and the positivist constraints on an elucidation of it – combine; the Durkheimian thesis results from the intersection of the two tendencies.

With the view that religious beliefs have the ensemble of human relations as their 'real' object Marx and Feuerbach would in a certain sense agree, but they are concerned to emphasise the falsity of religion, not its truth – the fact that it is 'based upon an illusion'. Drawing their conception of it from Hegel's account of 'transcendental religion' in the *Phenomenology of Mind* (BIVB3; 1931: 200–19) they see it as a form of false consciousness or alienation. Thus Feuerbach states that when man recognises that it is his own nature which he has worshipped, religion breaks down. In essence the reason for this is analogous to my reason for ceasing to be frightened of something in the dark corner of a room when I realise that it is not a ghost but an old broom. In one sense it can be said what I feared was an old broom in a dark corner, and it is in that sense that, on the Marx/Feuerbach account, the believer worships society or man. While it is true that the object of my fear is *in fact* nothing more than a broom, it is not *as* as a broom that it frightens me – my fear depends internally on my mistaking it for a ghost. Equally it is not *as* man that man worships himself; the attitude of worship is only possible because its intentional – as opposed to its 'real' – object is something other and greater than man. If religious emotions depend internally on false beliefs they cannot properly survive the discovery that those beliefs are false.

For Durkheim, however, the religious faith which believers accept and practise is true: it amounts to a true statement, symbolically expressed, about society.[23] Yet he grants that acceptance of theories such as his own will undermine religious life and he considers other forms of social activity which might replace it in its social functions. This gives rise to two puzzling questions. Why should explicit recognition that religious symbols *are* simply symbols weaken the grip of religious belief? And why should there be a need for expressing truths about society in this surprisingly invariant symbolic form in any case (cp. Parsons 1968: 429)?

Take the first of these. Religious emotions – such as love, worship or fear – are not undirected effusions. On the face of it they depend internally on the belief that there are gods and spirits which, to adapt Durkheim's phrase, 'do not hold their right of existence from the believer'. If the symbolist account of religious discourse is the right one, however, then to talk of gods and spirits is to make symbolic reference to social groups, aspects of the social order and so on. When a man says "The crown is mighty in the land, I fear it", he is making, not a literal reference to the crown, but a symbolically expressed reference to the monarchy and its powers, and the object of his fear is not the crown, but the powers of the institution of monarchy and its incumbent. The Durkheimian thesis invites us to assimilate religious discourse to such examples as this, so that religious emotions and attitudes are emotions and attitudes towards gods and spirits *only* in the sense in which the fear is fear of the crown. If it is right in this, then pointing that fact out should make no fundamental difference to the beliefs and feelings of the religious.

But Durkheim is clearly correct in thinking that acceptance of his account by religious believers could not, to put it minimally, fail to affect religious life. It follows from this that religious life rests at least in part on *failure* to recognise that religious ideas are symbolic representations of social reality. When anthropologists, studying various cultures from widely differing theoretical perspectives, have given a descriptive analysis of how magico-religious beliefs are actually understood by people within those cultures, the account that invariably emerges is 'literalist' and has a strong cosmocentric emphasis. Within this framework there is usually a great deal of explicit symbolism and allegory (as there is in the Christian case – ash placed on the forehead on Ash Wednesday, the lamb of God, the cruciform shape and East–West orientation of churches and so on) but the symbolism is religious – that is to say it is given its meaning by the framework of literally accepted transcendental belief – and not sociological. Hence if the Durkheimian thesis is to be retained it becomes necessary to distinguish between an explicit, literal level of religious belief and practice and a symbolic level of which the actors are not (at least at the same level of consciousness) aware. In the next chapter we must examine the possible ways in which this distinction of levels might be made out.

3

Variations on the symbolist theme

Levels of belief and of interpretation

Anthropologists influenced by the symbolist approach have, I think, been less puzzled than they should be by the notion that a belief or practice can have a symbolic meaning which those who share it do not know it to have. (Discussions of such claims have been concerned with how they might be verified. But the more fundamental – though not unrelated – question is what *sense* they can be given.) One reason for this might be that the general formula 'Their beliefs are F, though they do not know that they are' has plenty of perfectly unperplexing instances: for example, when 'F' is replaced by 'false', 'typical of lower-middle class shoe-shiners in Chile' and so forth. Such instances of un-awareness, however, do not concern the *meaning* of the beliefs involved.

Be that as it may, one can try to make this distinction between the explicitly literal and the symbolic level in four ways. Religious discourse and action (*a*) may be unconsciously symbolic, (*b*) may turn out to be symbolic when its logic is properly surveyed and construed, (*c*) may have been originally symbolic and then become literalised, or (*d*) may be symbolic in the interpretation of the observer, but not in that of the actor. One can find these four types of approach in the work of various writers, and in practice they flow into each other. (*a*) involves the claim that the actors concerned do understand their statements and actions as symbolic (though only at an unconscious or unreflective level), whereas in (*c*) and (*d*) it is not claimed that the symbolic interpretation can be ascribed to the actors in any sense at all. (*c*) however still asserts that ritual beliefs have in the past been explicitly seen as having a symbolic character, where in (*d*) it is no longer claimed that awareness of the symbolic interpretation as given by the observer can be imputed at any level to people in the culture studied, either in the present or in the past. (b) is related to both (a) and (c); it implies that the actors themselves would grasp the symbolic character of religious discourse if they subjected it to philosophical reflection.

If any of these interpretations is to be accepted, it must meet two minimal criteria. The first is that it must be possible to see how the symbolist interpretation could have an explanatory bearing on the facts to be explained – if only as the first link in an explanatory chain. The second is that the symbolist interpretation and the explanatory direction it implies must, to put it broadly, make better sense of the facts than rival accounts can do. The rival account I am concerned with is of course the intellectualist thesis. These seem mild conditions, but we shall see that they have a cutting edge.

There are two very general features of traditional religion and magic on which anthropologists would agree. It is agreed in the first place that at one level at least ritual beliefs support attempted explanations of natural phenomena, and that ritual actions are frequently performed with the intention of bringing them under control (though the degree of prominence which is given to this point varies). It is also agreed that while the attitude of believers towards some spirits or gods may be one of emotional or moral indifference – whether it be because the beings involved are too unimportant, too unconcerned with human affairs or too distant – gods are characteristically the objects of emotions such as hope, fear, piety, worship, dutifulness or love. The various versions of the symbolist approach must cope with these two facts.

The unconsciously and the historically symbolic

Take the first option, (a), that religious discourse and action may be unconsciously symbolic. It is obvious in this case that the cognitive level at which religious or magical ideas are used to serve in explanation, or to underpin attempts at control of the natural environment, is not the symbolic level: at the level of awareness at which the gods and spirits, or magical forces, are simply symbols, functioning to replace literal descriptions of the social order and social relations, they cannot *also* be invoked as causes of natural events. To the extent that ritual actions are instrumental, informed by the objectives of control, they can be, indeed *must* be, explained by reference to the literal, cosmological level of religious belief. Religious emotions, on the other hand, are seen in this account as a function of the *symbolic* level of religious awareness: not the symbol, with its real or supposed properties, but the reality symbolised is their object. And it is their object in the sense that the emotion felt depends not on a *failure* to recognise the reality represented by the symbol, but on a recognition of it, at some level of awareness. This link is an important one for the theory; for, since the instrumental character of ritual actions is connected with the literal level of religious belief, it provides the only line by which the postulated symbolic level is moored to the data of ritual behaviour.

The point is pithily placed in Durkheim's mouth by Parsons (1968: 428):

put in positivistic terms the argument is as follows: the attitude of respect implies a source of respect. We cannot respect symbols as such because of their intrinsic properties. Therefore there must be a 'something' they symbolise which is its source. Now 'society' is the only empirical entity which exercises moral authority, hence it is the only possible source of the attitude.

The emotion aroused by a flag is aroused because it is consciously seen to be a symbol of the nation. Religious emotion, on the other hand, is interpreted as affect displaced from the 'referent' to what is only unconsciously a symbol. The theme is familiar from psychoanalysis, which specifically postulates the 'displacement of affect' from the referent to what is subconsciously used to represent it. There the criteria for diagnosis concern the inappropriateness of the patient's emotion to the symbol, and its appropriateness to the diagnosed real object. (But in psychoanalysis the displacement is caused by a repression of awareness of the real object of the emotion, and recognition and abreaction are expected when the object is diagnosed.) As Parsons makes clear, a similar argument is invoked in the present form of the symbolist account. The premise is that religious emotions cannot be adequately explained by the 'intrinsic' properties of their apparent objects. Now this is plausible enough when the 'sacred objects' concerned are totemic creatures and plants. These need not be of great practical importance in the life of the tribe – as anthropologists who work in societies which have such totemic objects are often informed, they are respected by the tribesman because they are the totems of his clan. So the totem is consciously associated with the clan, just as the flag is with the nation, and respect is in each case unproblematically felt in virtue of this conscious association. But even in the totemic case the situation is not always as straightforward as this. Consider, for example, the totemic spirits (as Evans-Pritchard calls them) of the Nuer. Whether one interprets a Nuer's statement "Crocodile is Spirit" as a straightforward statement of identity, or as meaning "Crocodile symbolises Spirit to my lineage", the respect is felt in each case towards Spirit. Here, if Spirit is *itself* to be a symbol of some aspect of social reality, it must be an unconscious symbol. But is it any longer plausible to argue that respect is in this case not justifiable in terms of the 'intrinsic' features of the (alleged) symbol? The extraordinary powers and protean character of *kwoth*, the interest in and authority over human affairs ascribed to it, surely explain the respect, hopes or piety which Nuer feel towards it in its various personae very well. A literalist approach can make perfectly good sense of such religious emotions – and the point applies also in the case of very different ones, such as the fears inspired by malevolent, extra-social spirits. In this case, too, the properties ascribed to them, taken literally, are sufficient to explain the emotional reactions they inspire.

Thus, the feelings which in thesis (a) are tied to a postulated unconscious level of symbolic awareness are explained perfectly well in terms of consciously held, literally expressed beliefs – and the thesis ascribes the traditional religious thinker's preoccupation with explanation and control of natural events to them in any case. What further explanatory role is left, then, to give life to the theory that there is an unconsciously symbolic element in the traditional thinker's conceptions of spirits or gods?

Moreover, the approach creates problems of its own making. Why should there be two levels of belief, symbolic and literal? What is the relationship between the two? Then, to add two which I have already mentioned: Why should there be a need to express judgements about society in symbolic form in the first place? And why should the symbolism used be so invariant?

An answer to the first two of these questions is more available in (*c*), the historical variation of the symbolist theme. Thus, what began as metaphorical utterances and enactments, more or less clearly recognised as such, came to be taken in an increasingly literal-minded way. The literalised interpretation then served as a base for further cosmological elaboration, answering the questions to which it gave rise. Doctrines of the real Presence in the Eucharist, proceeding from a literalised understanding of Christ's (on this view, symbolic) statements at the Last Supper, would serve as an example – the difference being, of course, that the present approach is applied to the whole cognitive framework of religious life, and not merely to certain teachings within it. Such a connexion between the cosmological and the symbolically social content of religion is impossible in (*a*): it would make the question of why the religious believer is *unconsciously* aware of the symbolic content a completely mysterious one. So the religious emotions of contemporary believers can no longer be explained as being directed, at an unconscious level, towards the social objects symbolically presented in religious discourse – there is no such unconscious level. As far as present-day religious life in a traditional culture goes, the theory would be no less literalist than intellectualism.

It is worth isolating it, however, not because it has been seriously and explicitly advanced (it is too much like just another of the 'just-so' stories which Evans-Pritchard castigated), but because it is one among the disparate lines of thought which severally colour the accounts of magic and religion which symbolist writers offer. Various writers do, on the other hand, propose an explicit explanation of why the social meaning of ritual should have to take a symbolic form. Beattie writes (1964: 70):

Sociologically this is the most important thing about symbols; they provide people with a means of representing abstract ideas, often ideas of great practical importance to themselves, indirectly, ideas which it would be difficult or even impossible for them to represent to themselves directly. We sometimes forget that the capacity for systematic analytical thinking about concepts is a product of several millenia of education and constant philosophising.

That religion is a way of saying metaphorically, or of pointing at, what cannot be said literally is, as I remarked earlier, a possible resolution of the predicament which faces anyone who is both influenced by broadly positivist considerations and inclined to see some form of truth in religious thought. For Parsons, religious notions symbolise a 'non-empirical reality' whose literal inexpressibility is a consequence of its nature. Beattie's remark makes the difficulty not one of principle – of truths which it is necessarily impossible to express literally – but an intellectual one which differentiates some cultures from others: some have 'systematic and analytical' concepts of nature and society, others do not.[24]

Perhaps the most obvious objection to this idea is that any attempted elucidation by an anthropologist of what is symbolically expressed by the primitive ritualist, be it a statement about social relationships, a commitment to social values, an affirmation of the social value of certain activities or whatever, usually turns out to be something which the ritualist has more than enough literal linguistic resources to cope with himself. (Although it must be admitted that as put by the anthropologist it normally involves the use of shiny 'systematic and analytical' concepts which have taken several millennia of education to evolve). Thus, for example, the Trobrianders could perfectly well express literally what – according to Leach – they are expressing symbolically (when they make the various statements which have lead some writers to the tendentiously expressed conclusion that they are 'ignorant of physiological paternity'): namely, that "the relationship between the woman's child and the clansmen of the woman's husband stems from the public recognition of the bonds of marriage."[25]

But suppose we accept Leach's interpretation. If it were consciously intended by informants, it would be easy enough for the enthnographer to elicit that fact. On the other hand we cannot, consistently with the explanation of the need for symbolism which is on offer, suppose it to be unconscious. It strains credulity to suppose that the Trobriander is unconsciously coping with his lack of analytical concepts while at the conscious level he thinks himself to be talking about the causal antecedents of procreation. So the explanation seems to lead back to the historical theory, which most anthropologists who see the symbolist approach as an alternative to supposedly unconfirmable historical speculations would want to avoid.

The symbolist interpretation as resulting from a correct construal of religious thought

Neither (*a*) nor (*c*) offers an attractive development of the symbolist theme – perhaps (*b*) can afford a more promising line. A proper analysis of the logic of ritual and ritual discourse, on this view, would show ritual to be an activity in which statements about society are expressed. Religious practitioners may themselves be unaware of this, perhaps in something like the way (and for the same sorts of reason) that – according to the philosophical behaviourist – one can fail to recognise the real relationships between mentalistic and behavioural statements. Let us see how this can be spelt out.

It is obvious in the first place that the analyst of ritual will have to distinguish between the *exemplary* aspects of ritual actions and agents' accounts of them, from which he will draw for his analysis, and the *symptomatic* aspects, which stem from the users' own failure to construe their discourse and their actions properly. So again there will be two levels, and the actors' characterisation of their rituals will belong to the symptomatic, and not the exemplary, level. The relationship between the two levels will presumably be along the lines of the historical precedence approach, (*c*), except that there need not be a clear-cut historical precedence of the exemplary over the symptomatic. There must however be an *explanatory* precedence: the symptomatic beliefs and actions are seen as resulting from a misconstruction of the first-level, exemplary class, which must logically therefore be prior to it.

A serious treatment of this thesis would have to explain what ritual actions and statements fall into the exemplary class, and would have to show how the Durkheimian interpretation could make good sense of their logic. By hypothesis, ritual actions in the exemplary class are misconstrued, which is to say that the descriptions which the actors would sincerely give of their rationale are not the correct ones. So, for example, the native believes that there are ancestor-spirits, and in tending what he regards as the shrine of the ancestors, he believes himself to be showing respect to them (whether because he really feels it or because he wants to make sure that they will not spoil his luck in hunting); whereas, according to the observer, the right descrip-

42

tion may be that the native is expressing his respect for the lineage, and affirming his vision of it as a social unit persisting continuously through time: so that the spirit is a symbol of the lineage, and the shrine a physical 'objectification' of it. And again, if he believes his own guiding spirit, the spirit of the lineage and that of the village to be each in turn personae or aspects of the high god, he accepts in this symbolically the organic ties which link him and the respective sub-groups of which he is a member to the wider society. (Note that to say all this is to say something considerably stronger than to say simply that the fact that he conceives of ancestor-spirits and pays considerable attention to their shrines *testifies* to the salience of descent groups in his society. The latter point could be accepted by any intellectualist.) To the extent, then, that the native's behaviour is a symbolic performance which enacts a social relationship, it belongs to the exemplary level, To the extent that it implies a reified conception of the 'ancestor-spirit' symbol – as in the idea that the spirit is an agency which has real power over the huntsman's game (though this idea too may, of course, have a symbolic meaning) – it is symptomatic. The action must be grasped under its correct description before the actor's own literalising rationalisation of it can be explained.

Variant beliefs, invariant rites

Put to use in this way – that is, when the exemplary class includes ritual actions and low-level descriptions of them, and the symptomatic class includes the agent's more general or 'superstructural' interpretation – the distinction between the exemplary and the symptomatic aspects of ritual dovetails neatly with the anti-intellectualist argument mentioned in the last chapter, which seeks to establish the explanatory priority of ritual action over the rationalising beliefs which accompany it. It is accepted (on this argument) that genuinely instrumental actions are straightforwardly explicable in terms of the agent's avowed reasons, and hence in terms of the beliefs in accordance with which they were performed. Within this field of apparently reasoned actions, however, there are regular forms of behaviour, such that they, but not the reasons given for them, are invariant across societies and time. Where forms of action are constant, but 'rationalisa-tions', 'ideologies' or 'derivations' vary, so it is argued, we should conclude that explanation goes from action to the beliefs which apparently inform it, and not vice versa. The most detailed and explicit exposition of this argument is Pareto's:

forms change more readily than substance... Banquets in honour of the dead become banquets in honour of the gods, and then again banquets in honour of the saints; and then finally they go back and become merely commemorative banquets again. Forms can be changed but it is much more difficult to suppress the banquets.[26]

Another example he cites in the same place is that of ritual cleansing. The liquid or substance used may vary – it may be water, blood, sulphur; the method used may differ – pouring on, immersion etc.; and the religious context (say, of Christian bap-tism and pagan lustration) may be quite different. But the ele-ment of ritual cleansing is constant.

The same kind of argument is used by Leach (1968: 523):

With minor variations the ritual of the Christian Mass is the same throughout Christendom, but each individual Christian will explain the performance by reference to his own sectarian doctrine. Such doctrines may vary quite widely; the social scientist who seeks to understand why a particular ritual sequence possesses the content and form that he observes can expect little help from the rationalisations of the devout.

The approach is consistent with an explanation of some (sym-ptomatic) rituals as being themselves the product of beliefs which are in turn rationalisations of actions in the exemplary class. Thus the fact that magical and religious techniques of healing, say, are to some degree responsive to the impact of Western medicine would be readily acceptable to Pareto; for, he says (1935, II: 607, para. 1008),

a religious custom or a custom of that general character offers the less resistance to change, the further removed it stands from its residues in simple associations of ideas and acts, and the larger the proportion it contains of theological, metaphysical or logical concepts.

The argument is not as strong as it may appear at first sight. A great deal depends on the respective levels of generality at which the action and its background of belief are described. If the supposedly 'residual' action is characterised very broadly (the 'Christian Mass' which 'with minor variations' is the same 'throughout Christendom'), while the actors' 'derivations' are stated in minute detail, it is to be expected that, in terms of these categories of classification, the one will vary more than the other. The generality of descriptions of action and belief should be matched. So if we speak merely of communal eating, then we would look for reasons at a very basic level, involving instinct and economic and environmental convenience, for the fact that men living in groups frequently eat together. If we restrict attention to celebratory, ceremonial feasts we should consider not merely the invariant action, but the invariant idea: namely, that communal eating is a proper method of celebration. It is the whole complex of action and idea which is invariant, and within it the action is explained in terms of the idea: banquets are arranged *in order* to celebrate something. If we now ask what, on a given occasion, is being celebrated, the answer will evidently vary widely from context to context – but this in no way shows that the object of the celebration is not operative as a reason for having the banquet. There are general reasons for having banquets when celebration is in order; and there are specific reasons for celebrating in the particular case.

Or take ritual cleansing. Again, if we give as general a description of the backing-up beliefs as of the action, we find an invariant complex of action and belief in which the action follows from the belief. On one possible theory (which Pareto himself suggests), the idea involved is that, just as cleansing the body can rid it of accumulated dirt, so ritual cleansing of the body can rid a person of accumulated stains of character. If some such idea underlies the widespread belief in the efficacy of ritual cleansing, it will no doubt be situated in any particular instance in a context of theory, myths etc., which will vary from culture to culture. But then one could equally well point to a whole corpus of experimental and technical procedures, together with low-level laws used to justify them, which remained invariant though theoretically redescribed, across the higher-level change from Ptolemaic to Copernican cosmology, or the supersession of phogiston theories of burning.

As for the differing interpretations given by Christians to, say, the ritual of Communion, the fact that these exist also points a moral rather different from the anti-literalist one drawn from it by Leach. It illustrates the interaction (in institutions whose legitimacy is largely derived from their claims to continuous links with real or supposed origins) between the procedures of ritual and interpretations of the *point* of these procedures – of why the founders should have laid them down in just this way. The interpretations vary with the changing intellectual frameworks of different social groups. But performance of the ritual is no less based on doctrinal and historical beliefs because its point varies with a changing amalgam of original instructions and varying interpretations of their purpose. What the persistence of rites and low-level doctrines through changing interpretations of them does bring out is the fidelity of committed believers to the letter of the original word, even when its spirit becomes dissonant with other beliefs they acquire. This is a phenomenon not restricted to religious belief, as the history of Marxism, for example, shows.

The arguments which have just been discussed are not pointless. But they do not show the primacy of action over belief. What they do show is that general or low-level grounds for a form of action can remain unchanged from culture to culture, or across time, even when the higher-level reasons by which they in turn are backed vary; and there are various reasons for this. Let us, however, consider more closely the claim that ritual has explanatory priority over ritual beliefs. If this is so, then ritual actions evidently remain in need of explanation. What form will this explanation take? It must be an explanation which will account for the performance of the ritual along lines independent of the reasons the actors themselves give for performing it. Thus, to return to our original example, the tribesman considers himself to be paying respect to an ancestor-spirit in order to safeguard his luck in hunting, whereas the observer describes the action as a symbolic affirmation, in which the spirit is only a symbol of the lineage, so that the shrine to the spirit is in reality a shrine to the lineage. If the observer's description of the action is correct, it implies a general pattern of explanation which must diverge from that which the tribesman himself would give. But what could it mean to say that the observer's description of the action's point is the *correct* one? For the sociologist, the correct characterisation of the ritual must be the one in terms of which it can be explained – which, as it were, lines it up in its *explanandum* form, properly prepared for contact with the *explanans* – and to explain a ritual is to explain why it is performed, or at least why it is performed in this way rather than that. It follows – unless the action is not a voluntarily controlled or intentional one at all (and this is certainly not true of ritual action) – that the right description of the ritual action is the one under which, at some level of awareness, it was done: that is to say, the one which identifies it in terms of the more or less conscious reasons *which made* the actor perform it. If this is so, then the observer's description can be correct only if it does identify those reasons – which must imply, where actor's and observer's descriptions diverge, that the reasons on which the actor himself *believes* he acted were at least not his *only* reasons for acting.

This line of thought leads back to (*a*) – to the notion of an unconscious level of symbolic meaning. If the observer's description is regarded as exhaustive the actor's avowed reasons must be a completely inoperative 'derivation'. That implies not that his reasons for acting (that is, the reasons which *made* him act) were mere rationalisations, but that they were not the reasons he consciously thought they were: the action has explanatory priority over his sincerely self-ascribed reasons, but is itself still explained in terms of (unconscious) reasons which made him act. Thus the claimed priority of ritual actions over 'the agent's reasons for acting' loses its paradoxical air.

But even if the tribesman acted straightforwardly for the reasons he gives (i.e. to induce the ancestor-spirit to exercise its power over game in his favour) there is another sense in which the observer's description of the action's point might be the right one. The ritual action may have a conventionally or institutionally recognised significance which the particular actor in question may have misunderstood, just as I might write a cheque or shake hands under a total misapprehension about the point of what I was doing. The observer's description of the action (as an affirmation of respect for the lineage and its continuity) might correctly identify its socially *recognised* point. There must then be people in the culture studied for whom the ritual has its standard meaning – but perhaps this connexion can be loosened. Can the observer's description be correct even if it gives the ritual a meaning which none of the ritual practitioners would recognise? (I am now excluding the resort to unconscious levels of symbolic awareness). People may perform a ceremony or rite without seeing any particular meaning in the performance, or their interpretations may differ widely. They may act simply in the knowledge that this is what someone in their position is traditionally expected to do. But the claim that the ritual has a social meaning, unless it collapses into a form of functionalism, now seems to imply that there *have been* individuals who performed the ritual, at some level of awareness, in the meaning which the observer ascribes to it.

Meaning and what is meant; symbolic meaning as a structural property

We seem again to be led back to the notions of unconsciousness and history which approach (*c*) was meant to eschew. On the underlying question, however, of how and to what degree the observer's and the actor's characterisations of an action can legitimately diverge, there is more to be said. A fairly detailed case to consider will be helpful – and I shall return to the issue in chapter 7. But the general point involved is that the links between *the meaning* of a shared form of action, and its meaning to the actors taken as a group – what they mean by performing it – cannot be completely severed; and it is for this reason that the notions of unconscious or historical meaning tend to come into play when the two draw apart. The sociology of thought is often cast in the role of a Hegelian observer, able to understand and penetrate the dialectic of consciousness from a standpoint unavailable to its owners. There is a sense in which at its best it can have that kind of role. But if what is implied is that meanings can be detected in a cultural form of thought and action which are neither known nor given to it by anyone, at any level of consciousness or reflectiveness, present or past, *in* the culture concerned, then the enterprise is confused. Symbolic meaning presupposes a symbolising intelligence, and 'consciousness', 'mind', 'conscience' or whatever cannot be personified independently of those whose consciousness it is, in order to play this part.

The point applies to symbolic interpretations of ritual at any level, and not merely to attempts to interpret the whole cognitive framework of ritual action in (socially) symbolic terms. One might grant, for example, that salt-spilling is a magical action intended to bring luck to the spiller. The belief itself is not treated as having a symbolic meaning, but the use of salt rather than of some other substance may have one. If salt symbolises wealth, throwing it away is a symbolic discarding of riches. But for this interpretation to have any explanatory bearing on the institutionalised action of salt-spilling, it must capture the meaning which the action at some level has for the people who perform it, or which it had for those who institutionalised it.

Note that my point is *not* that we can never legitimately ascribe non-conscious knowledge of meaning to people: a theoretical claim of that kind is justified if it brings with it sufficient explanatory benefit. What is ruled out – simply by dint of the logic of 'symbolic meaning' – is that a mode of action could have a symbolic meaning of 'its own' which no actor *in any way* knew it to have.

In particular, the idea that a structural approach to ritual symbolism can produce interpretations of the *meaning* of ritual actions which are quite independent of what they have ever meant to the people who perform them must be mistaken. Leach says (1972: 342):

I have been writing as if it were already an established fact that collective 'rituals' of the kind that are usually described by anthropologists always build their messages from repetitive sequences of symbols, rather than by free composition, in response to generative and transformational rules – as happens in the case of a spoken utterance.

Rites of passage, and eventually rituals in general, can be shown to have a form which is (p. 340)

'logical' in its nature...The view usually adopted by anthropologists is that this logical coherence is sufficient in itself to 'explain' the pattern of symbolism that is adopted. This does not preclude the possibility that other kinds of 'explanation' are appropriate for other levels of analysis.

The 'messages' decoded by the anthropologist need not be available to the ritual practitioners. Their extraction "depends upon the anthropologist's ability to make a syntactic analysis of the overall structure of the proceedings" (p. 321).

There seem to be three confusions involved here. The first is between syntax and semantics. We are able to distinguish grammatical from ungrammatical utterances, and we can recognise into which class new utterances fall. Linguists seek syntactic rules which will replicate this competence by 'generating' all and only the well-formed sentences. Now the notion of well-formedness can be applied to ritual sequences to the extent that these have a prescribed order and form. (In fact, of the actions which anthropologists call ritual, some do and some do not.) To that extent the anthropologist might hope to produce a 'ritual grammar' underlying 'ritual competence' for a culture, and perhaps even a universal 'ritual grammar' for all cultures. (Though it is worth noting that if the analogy between 'ritual grammar' and linguistic grammar is pushed it should imply that the practitioners could recognise *new* sequences of ritual action as well or ill formed.)[27] But this analogy with the syntax of language would in itself tell us nothing of the symbolic meaning of rituals or, indeed, whether they had a 'semantics' in any useful sense at all.

The second confusion is between knowing the syntax or semantics of a language in the sense that one can tell, with respect to any particular utterance, whether or not it is grammatical, whether or not it has meaning, and *what meaning it has*; and knowing it in the sense of being able to state rules of grammar and definitions, semantic rules, truth-theoretic axioms or whatever. The grammarian must base his syntactic rules on the verdicts of well-formedness which language-speakers deliver on particular utterances. General semantic accounts of a language – or of behavioural 'codes' such as clothing styles – must be based on the users' understanding of the meaning of particular utterances or bits of behaviour. Similarly, general principles for the symbolic meaning of objects and actions which feature in rituals must be extracted from an understanding of particular ritual sequences. The ritualists may not know, in the sense that they may be unable to state, these *general* principles of symbolism. But the position Leach wants to take is that they may also not know the symbolic meaning of the particular rituals they perform. The notions of unconscious and historical meaning suggest ways in which some or all of the people in a culture might be unconscious of the particular meanings which the rituals they performed had, or originally had. But the analogy with our ignorance of the general rules of syntax does not.

There is, finally, a confusion in thinking that an elucidation of the logic or meaning of ritual symbols is in itself an explanation of why they are adopted, or of why rituals are performed. The elucidation of such symbolism, where it exists, must of course be a first step, in the way that elucidating the meaning of what someone said must be a first step in explaining how what was said might have come to have the meaning it does, and why the person involved should have said it. But it does not provide an *alternative* to explaining the performance of rituals in terms of the reasons the actors have for performing them.

Symbolist interpretations as contemporary 'readings' of traditional world-views

The criteria of validity for observers' interpretations of ritual seem to lead back invariably to the meaning it has for ritual performers. Our last attempt, (*d*), makes the most decisive break in this link. The correctness of the observer's interpretation, on this view, does not entail the erroneousness of the face-value interpretation offered by the actors, even when the two are different and, in terms of any single framework of interpretation, incompatible. The anthropologist's task is to find a 'translation' of primitive thought-systems which will make them fully transparent to *us*.

Lienhardt's account of Dinka religion in *Divinity and Experience* might sometimes be interpreted as coming close to this approach. He writes:

I have tried to describe the contexts of experience within which Dinka assertions about the Powers may be understood and harmonized, as they cannot be understood by us if they are regarded as referring to theoretical 'beings' whose existence is posited as it were, before the human experience to which they correspond.[28]

But he is careful to avoid the suggestion that *our* understanding of Dinka religion entails that 'the subject matter of Dinka theology' is radically misconceived.

In a sense, of course, it is ridiculous to suggest that Dinka might themselves have an alternative conception, to the sociologist's, of what the sociologist of their religion is trying to explain, for it is precisely their conceptions which he *is* trying to explain. So long as the symbolist level of ritual and belief could be thought of as standing in some empirical relationship to the actions and expressed beliefs of the people studied, whether historically, unconsciously, or as an unreflectively misconstrued level of meaning, it was possible in principle to see what kind of relevance the symbolist approach had to the project of explaining *why it is* that people have magical or religious beliefs and institutions. But it is also possible to offer it not as a determining or constitutive element *within* the phenomenon of religious life, but as a 'reading', like a 'reading' of a literary text, of the kind whose validity for us is decided (without reference to the intentions behind the text considered, or its recognised meaning in the culture of its production, except in so far as these may themselves form a part of the 'text' which requires to be understood) solely by the sense and the place it accords to it within our own cultural mould. In that case it is clearly no longer a matter of explaining the existence of religion and magic in other cultures, but rather of expanding our own culture by incorporating into its imaginative world a freely reconstructed and metamorphosed interpretation of the thought-systems of others – that is, as possible thought-worlds for *us*. Lienhardt's symbolist 'harmonisation' of the Dinka Powers, as 'images' or 'emblems' of experience, hovers between these two motives, and the differing criteria of acceptability which they imply.

Each of the variations on the symbolist theme which have been discussed seems subject to its own stresses and strains. In each case these derive from a fundamental tension that exists between two propositions: (1) that ritual language and action, at the literal level of meaning, is largely cosmocentric, and (2) that at a more fundamental level its reference is entirely anthropocentric. The tension is created when these two are combined with a third proposition: (3) that ritualists are at least consciously and unreflectively aware only of the former. The tension is between the claimed real meaning of a language and the meaning which its users are consciously disposed to see in it; and the symbolist approach as we have studied it so far does not have enough distinctive explanatory successes to call its own for this tension to be genuinely overcome.

4

Symbol and theory

Difficulties in a purely anthropocentric conception of traditional thought

The problems of reconciling symbolic and literal levels of ritual, discussed in the last chapter, arise for the symbolist only if he accepts that magic and religion in traditional cultures have, as explicitly understood by the traditional thinker, a distinctively cosmological character, and consequently that, in at least one of their functions, they are invoked to cope with the intellectual tasks of explanation and control. That they do have this function has been recognised to varying degrees by various writers; nevertheless, no one has seriously questioned it.[29]

To free our conceptions of traditional magico-religious thought of this cosmocentric dimension, and to make it intelligible in purely anthropocentric terms, would require a major retranslation of the categories of primitive culture. But *could* we make sense of religious and magical rites if we were to suppose that they constitute *no more* than say, "a form of expression in which [the] possibilities and dangers [of life, social relations, moral agency]...may be contemplated and reflected on – and perhaps also thereby transformed and deepened"?[30]

Among the 'primitive modes of life' which would have to be understood in this way, one of the most common involves a link between affliction, divination and ritual. Someone is afflicted by illness, childlessness, or failure in hunting, fishing or farming. He goes to a diviner or oracle, or divines for himself the profounder nature of his trouble. In this light he performs the rituals which then seem appropriate. For an intellectualist the links are to be explained thus. The sufferer supposes that there is some cause for his affliction; divination is meant to diagnose the cause, which, once identified, the sufferer can try to eliminate.

53

Diagnostic divination may trace the affliction to witchcraft, an evil spirit, sorcery or a displeased ancestor or god. The appropriate remedial action may accordingly be accusation, counter-magic or sacrifice.

Reflexion on social relations, moral obligation and so on is certainly embedded in this pattern, since the root of the trouble is very commonly identified, through the afflicting agency, as the reaction to a moral or religious fault of the person afflicted or his kin. (Similarly, the dietary and sexual prohibitions which often accompany craft activities in traditional cultures imply a consideration for the craftsman's inner state, and for the effects of a man's spiritual state on his projects in the world. Yet there are also many magical actions which make no such connexions with moral conditions or social relationships). But the native's response to his affliction is *not* expressive of contemplation or of resignation: it is a practical (and, as many anthropologists have remarked, often a brisk and down-to-earth) attempt to get something done about it. It is up to anyone who wants to argue that the link between affliction, divination and ritual is not that of identifying and eliminating a cause, to show how the connexion between them could sensibly be elucidated.

Another aspect of the same point comes out when we consider the impact of Western medicine on traditional magico-religious curing. The two are seen by traditional practitioners as competitors in the same field. Why should this be, if traditional ritual is *simply* a way of taking stock of the contingencies of life? It might be argued that the contemplative, accepting attitude which takes life in its wholeness, whether good or evil, and which – Winch seems to suggest – is affirmed in magical rites, is incompatible with the expectations and interventionism which an acceptance of the potential of Western medicine fosters. But it is not *this* incompatibility which is involved in the conflict as the native healer sees it. For him it emerges as a question of reconciling the continued usefulness of the old ways, and the truth of the cosmology they imply, with the recognised effectiveness of the new ones. In traditional cultures which are at the moment increasingly affected by Western technology and medicine, there is a spread of positions along virtually every point of the spectrum from exclusive acceptance of traditional healing to aggressive rejection of it.

The symbolic representation of nature: symbolic control and control by symbols

We have been considering, in the previous chapter, the difficulties of reconciling the fact that religion and magic in traditional societies exhibit a notable preoccupation with explanation and control, with the thesis that their real domain of (symbolically stated) interest is exclusively that of the social and the moral. The first of these claims is generally accepted, but many anthropologists who broadly follow the symbolist theme would reject the second. What they would reject in it is the exclusively anthropocentric emphasis – ritual symbolism, for them, can serve as a symbolic representation of the natural as well as the social environment: "...much ritual and religious behaviour translates uncontrollable natural forces into symbolic entities, which through the performance of ritual, can be manipulated and dealt with" (Beattie 1964: 239). Behind this way of putting the point is, I think, an idea which comes from Malinowski: namely, that people in a traditional culture need to subdue the anxiety produced by their inability to control nature, and so retreat to a 'ritual' dramatisation of natural forces in a make-believe of control. "There exists no adequate body of empirical knowledge which might enable men to cope with these hazards, or even to hope to cope with them, by means of practical scientifically proven or provable techniques. So they must cope with them symbolically and expressively instead' (Beattie 1964: 227).

The symbolic-expressive drama of control is a response to its real absence. Now this response can occur only through the ritualists' own awareness, at some level, of their helplessness. But it is we who believe ritual procedures to be ineffective. Their practitioners believe that they can have a real effect – as they show when they perform religious rites – in as much as these constitute an appeal to gods or spirits from which, they believe, natural forces flow.[31] If the literal character of the framework which informs these rituals is granted, then the reply must be that one should distinguish between a level at which the rituals are believed to make control possible and a more fundamental level at which it is known to be lacking. It is certainly true that such levels of suppressed or unformulated awareness can exist: shades of consciousness, unreflectiveness, self-deception. Yet, when it comes to a body of socially shared and regularly practiced magical or religious rites, can the story be filled out with any real conviction?

What is methodologically more fundamental is that a story of this kind is in any case unnecessary. Someone who threatens a screw which refuses to come out is just venting frustration: he does not believe that screws can understand English. But ritual really is not like this at all. Nature rites *are* believed to be encounters with spirits, gods or powers, which are persuaded, cajoled, pleaded with or harnessed. Just as religious emotions can be explained at the literal level, so can the fact that such rituals help to reduce anxiety: if people *believe* that they work, their anxiety will naturally be reduced. In short there is nothing in the observed actions and statements of beliefs which requires postulaton of a level of awareness at which the rite is 'expressive' rather than instrumental.

But there is also a quite distinct line of thought which Beattie also follows, about ritual symbolism: namely, that for ritual practitioners *themselves* "ritual's effectiveness is thought to lie in its very expressiveness" (Beattie 1966: 69). The 'symbolic-expressive' and the 'practical-instrumental' are then no longer exclusive categories. On this view, what lies at the heart of magic is the belief that the symbolic enactment of an event or state of affairs can in itself bring such an event or state about. Clearly this thesis is best fitted to such paradigmatically magical activities as running pins through a wax effigy, or untying knots during childbirth, and not to religious rites such as sacrifice or prayer to a god. Magic is practised, then (to concentrate for a moment on this narrower field), not as a metaphor of control, but out of a belief in the controlling power of metaphor.[32] In that case, we can explain magical action as an attempt to bring about desired ends, and we can try to elucidate more closely the belief in the efficacy of symbols which underlies it. The approach is a perfectly literalist one.

This thesis apart, however, talk of the 'efficacy of symbols' seems to be a nodal point of liberal confusion in the study of religion and magic. Douglas, for example, writes (1970a: 86–7, 89):

What kind of effectiveness is generated by confidence in the power of [ritual] symbols?...There are two possible views: either the power of magic is sheer illusion, or it is not. If it is not illusion, then symbols have power to work changes. Miracles apart, such a power could only work at two levels, that of individual psychology and that of social life...Has the confrontation with the subconscious anything to do with primitive spell-binding and loosing?...Not the absurd Ali Baba, but the magisterial figure of Freud is the model for appreciating the primitive ritualist.

If we assume that traditional belief in the efficacy of symbols is not an 'illusion', then it cannot be a belief in the *cosmological* power of symbolic action (as Beattie and others before him have suggested it is). The point is obscured if we consider only magical curing. (Douglas cites two descriptions of shamanistic cures.) That is a case in which psychological suggestion, perhaps involving a 'confrontation with the subconscious', can have just the effect which the traditional curer expects his procedures to have. Yet even here, one can plausibly see in him the 'magisterial figure of Freud' only on the basis of a confusion between action whose effectiveness can be putatively explained *in terms of* Freud's theories, and action *based on* them, or on *significantly* similar ones. Where ritual is concerned with bringing rain, multiplying game and so on, the non-illusory power of symbols takes a necessarily foggier form, and shows a tendency to shift, from the level of the practitioners' beliefs as to the efficacy of ritual, to the anthropologist's theories as to what its effects might be. As for the absurd Ali Baba, it is Douglas' view, and not necessarily that of anyone who believes magic to be 'illusion', that *he* is the only alternative model to the 'magisterial figure of Freud'.

The symbolic representation of nature: symbols for thinking with

So long as ritual 'symbols' were thought to represent only the social order, their symbolic character and their role in explanation and control could not be placed on the same cognitive level in the mind of the ritual actor. When they are allowed a wider reference, however, their two characteristics can be placed together. One way of doing this, as we have just seen, is by hypothesising a belief in the intrinsic efficacy of symbols: a belief that symbolic enactments of a desired state of affairs may bring it about. The theory can be made to look quite plausible for a good many magical actions (see Chapter 8), but not for all of them, and certainly not for all ritual – that is, magical and religious – actions. And as noted above, it could be accepted, for those rites which suit it, within a literalist analysis of traditional magico-religious thought.

But there is another, more ambitious, way which would be more in line with the generally anti-realist tenor of the symbolist approach. Instrumentalism in the philosophy of science sees scientific theories as truth-valueless tools by which observable effects can be linked to equally observable events – for example, experiments. Scientific analogies are metaphors, not in the sense that they ascribe metaphorically expressed properties to theoretical objects, but in the radical sense that the objects themselves are a part of the theoretical metaphor. May not the spiritual agencies and magical forces of traditional thought also be seen in this way – as a radical metaphor? It is more appropriate on this approach to speak of models, or stories, which are 'good for thinking', in that they fill out the connexions between rituals and their effects, than of symbols: but the general spirit of the symbolist theme is retained.

Such a conception is very distant from the Malinowskian 'anxiety-reduction' thesis. The concern of traditional religion and magic with explanation and control is now given a full place and the specifically anthropocentric emphasis is eliminated, while the other pillar of the Durkheimian thesis, that of reductionism, is retained. Consequently the disagreement which remains between the intellectualist and what I shall call the 'cosmocentric symbolist' as regards the descriptive analysis of traditional thought is now in part analogous to that between scientific realism and anti-realism in the philosophy of science. There is, however, one other ingredient: the intellectualist considers traditional thought to be essentially similar to scientific theory in its functions and structure, and distinguished from science only at the level of attitudes and institutions, whereas the cosmocentric symbolist – so far as he has been presented at the moment – inherits the original emphasis on the incommensurability of science and religion. On this view the 'key' difference, in Beattie's words, between the 'magico-religious' and the 'scientific attitude', "if it is to be discovered at all...must be found in the nature and grounds of the beliefs themselves" (Beattie 1970: 265).

But this position is an inherently unstable one for the cosmo-centric symbolist. As Beattie implies, the disagreement about the structure and function of magico-religious beliefs is also a disagreement about their fundamental source. The anthropocentric symbolist sees religion and magic as ultimately a reflection on and an expression of the 'ensemble of social relationships', though he thinks they may acquire a relative autonomy which, at the literalist level, gives them a role of explanation and control with respect to *natural* events. To make convincing sense of the position is, as we have seen, difficult; but it is easy to see how someone influenced by it might emphasise the incommensurability of magic and religion with science: the first two are responsive not only or even mainly to explanatory imperatives, but also to the requirements of social symbolism. As for the 'anthropocentric realist' – to give a label to the fourth box in our table of possible views – he considers religion to be fundamentally concerned with the meaning of human life, and its relationship with divinity (realistically conceived); and he sees the preoccupation with explanation and control as a possibly misconceived offshoot of this.

But on the cosmocentric symbolist's view the notion of imperceptible cosmological agencies is a metaphor tailored to fit the bare bones of empirical correlation which the traditional thinker believes he sees in the world around him. The account which is then given of anthropocentric religion must be similar to the intellectualist's story: a cosmology modelled in personal agencies has a potential moral depth which an impersonalist one cannot have, and out of this potential the anthropocentric dimension grows. There are other possible views about the internal dependencies between these two aspects of religious thought, many of them more subtle; it is clear, however, that an unqualified cosmocentric symbolist is in no position to admit any fundamental opposition between modern science and traditional religious cosmology.

The logic of scientific and the logic of magical thought

The relationship between magic and primitive religion on the one hand and science on the other emerges, then, as it often has done, as a critical issue in the understanding of traditional thought. What contrast between the two can be found beyond the differences of attitude admitted by the intellectualist?

One "cannot apply criteria of logic to modes of social life as such. For instance, science is one such mode and religion is another; and each has criteria of intelligibility peculiar to itself" (Winch 1958: 100). I argue in the appendix that any set of factual beliefs which asserts some sort of system of empirical regularities in the world is thereby necessarily subject to the same overall requirements of rationality. There are no criteria of rationality which are bound to their theoretical contexts in such a way as to render these contexts themselves rationally incomparable. But Winch's emphasis on the fact that a system of thought is part of a mode of social life serves to remind us that understanding it requires an understanding of the *aims* of the overall pattern of activity to which it belongs. Of course, there are also rational dependencies *between* aims. If the Zande magician, the traditional spirit-healer or the Aladura who invokes God's anger and the force of prayer *are* concerned to explain illness and to do something about it, then to that extent they must also be concerned with broad empirical regularities, and this concern dictates the same criteria of intelligibility as for any other system of thought which shares the same aim.[33] On the other hand, as we have seen, there is a quite separate argument which has nothing to do with conceptual relativism, but rests quite simply on the claim that the aim of ritual is in no way 'instrumental', that as a mode of social life, it is not concerned with explanation and control of men's natural environment at all, so that the criteria of intelligibility which are appropriate to it are in no way those of science or of 'forms of life' which share the aims of science. But – in the absence of a radical reinterpretation of most of the relevant ethnography – this flies in the face of the facts. Is it possible then to accept that such explanation and control *is* a major concern of traditional religion, and yet *still* to mark off from that of science the logic of the thought and activity which flows from it?

In this context the word 'logic' has too much stretch for the question to be an unambiguous one. In so far as traditional religious thought is concerned to get a grasp on empirical relationships between events in the world, the tests of validity which are applicable to it are just those which are also applicable to scientific theories. But we can inquire into the structure and use of the concepts, and the logical relationships between the beliefs of a traditional system of religious or magical thought, and on this basis we can ask what degree of structural similarity and contrast there is between actual scientific theories and traditional cosmologies. If we are going to do this, however, we must be careful not to build too much into such terms as 'concept' and 'logical structure'. These points can be illustrated from Winch's discussion of Zande magic.

He argues that "Zande notions of witchcraft do not constitute a theoretical system in terms of which Azande try to gain a quasi-scientific understanding of the world', but adds: "I have *not* said that Azande conceptions of witchcraft have nothing to do with understanding the world at all. The point is that a different form of the concept of understanding is involved here" (Winch 1972: 48 n. 21). The crucial question is whether the understanding concerned is of how the world operates: that is, whether it in some form involves the notions of causality and uniformity. Winch suggests that the "Zande magical concept of 'A affecting B'" has a sense quite different from our own technical concept (p. 38). But if the Zande concept is a causal concept at all, then it includes the brute notion of one thing *bringing about* another, or *making it happen*; and, to take a further step, the notion of an association between *types* of occurrence. If these notions are present in Zande magic, they carry with them the appropriateness of certain general criteria of validity, and they also give a point to attempting to bring about a B-type event by making an A-type event happen. So Zande magical rites *are* "practical, 'technological' steps", misguided or otherwise (p. 38).

In fact, though Winch accepts that Zande magic does include a notion of 'A affecting B', the form of understanding the world which he at the same time thinks their magic embodies leaves no room for it. He wants to see in Zande magic not an attempt by Azande to control the practical contingencies of their way of life, but a way of freeing themselves from spiritual dependence on them. What Winch describes is a clearly recognisable form of religious experience, but just because it is it is clear that it is not the experience of, say, the Nigerian Aladura. Indeed, to understand Aladura it is necessary both to recognise the form of experience Winch describes and to recognise it as only *one possible form* of religious experience: for the movement of Aladura (*aladura* means 'one who prays') is precisely a reaction against the conception of prayer, which orthodox Christian churches have offered, as primarily a way of "freeing the believer from dependence on what he is supplicating for" (p. 39). It is the this-worldly efficacy of prayer which the Aladura place at the centre of the stage. When both of these attitudes are given a fair showing, it is difficult to doubt that the attitude expressed in Zande magic towards the contingencies of life is an activist one which seeks to bring them under control, similar to that of the Aladura although not religious in form, and not that of the stoic or of Job-like resignation to a greater will. (Each of these attitudes can be a reaction to the other, and both directions can be found in contemporary religions.)

Consideration of another point made by Winch brings this out even more clearly. He writes that "Evans-Pritchard's account shows [the Azande] do have a fairly clear working distinction between the technical and the magical. It is neither here nor there that individual Azande sometimes confuse these categories, for such confusions may take place in any culture" (p. 37). In fact, it shows nothing of the kind. What it does show is that Azande distinguish between 'observable', spatio-temporally 'contiguous' causal connexions (a stone breaking a window, for example) and those in which the connexion is 'hidden' (for example the relations between seed-planting and the growth of crops, or medicine-taking and cure) – magical connexions must obviously figure in the second class. As all who have read Hume know, this apparently obvious distinction is in reality not at all obvious. But we need to have it if we are to grasp, from the point of view of the traditional thinker, at what point magical or religious modes of action and explanation are brought into play. In the case of the Azande, occult connexions, be they 'mystical' or 'empirical', to use Evans-Pritchard's terms, are explained in terms of the actions of 'souls' (see e.g. Evans-Pritchard 1937: 36, 462, 492). Medicines work (where their efficacy is explained) through their souls – the soul of vengeance magic, for example, goes out to find the offender; crops grow by the action of the seed's soul. "The 'souls' of ... drugs go down into the body of a man and there seek out and destroy the 'soul' of the disease which is destroying the 'soul' of an organ" (Evans-Pritchard 1937: 492).

All of this is very much grist to the intellectualist's mill. Theoretical concepts are brought in, it seems, with respect to just those causal connexions which one might expect the traditional thinker to see as standing in need of explanation. (On the other hand, events of human importance, such as a man's death in a collapsed hut, are also often given an 'occult' cause, even when there is an 'observable' one. The integration of the two can cause problems.)

As I have said, we have to be careful, if we are comparing the Zande notion of causation with our 'technical' one, not to build too much of the particular theory in which it is exercised into the concept itself. Nor should the fact that we find no philosophical reflection on the notion of causality in Zande culture – no discussion of the relation between causation and uniformity, or of the nature of natural necessity – make us conclude that their core notion of one thing making another happen is any different from ours. What is relevant is that their actual practice and explanations show that they expect uniform procedures applied in uniform circumstances to produce uniform effects.

Discussions of the relation between magic and science have tended to be unproductive – Evans-Pritchard's often-cited criticisms of Frazer are an example (Evans-Pritchard 1933). Frazer asserts that magic is like science except that it lacks the experimental approach, and is not a consciously theoretical search for truth but a practical enterprise. Evans-Pritchard replies that magic cannot be compared with science, since it fails to adopt an experimental approach and is not a "conscious striving after knowledge". Frazer says that magical action involves an implicit assumption of uniform effects. Evans-Pritchard objects that the magician has no explicitly formulated conception of lawlikeness, and for good measure adds that "in any case the utilisation of magic to influence the course of nature is surely in direct opposition to the scientist's conception of the universe" (p. 13). There *is* a potentially substantive disagreement behind these terminological disputes, but it requires a closer and more rigorous consideration of the content and structure of traditional thought, and, equally, an approach to science which does not see in it merely a self-consciously critical "use of logic and experiment" but also tries to give an account of the systems of thought to which the logic and experimentation are applied. Here present-day intellectualism has made a step forward by focussing its attention on the deployment of theoretical concepts, the structure of theories and the use of models and analogies, and by attempting to compare science and traditional cosmology in these respects. This shift in the discussion can provide a much sharper picture of the contrasts and similarities between the two. (What emerges from it will be discussed in Part III).

Objections to an anti-realist conception of traditional thought

It also implies, however, abandoning the idea that there is a sharp discontinuity between science and traditional religious cosmology which makes comparison of them a futile error. Of course it may still turn out that the contrasts are more significant than the similarities as far as one's assessment of the specifically intellectualist approach goes. But once the thesis of incommensurability of aims or concepts is rejected, what remains to distinguish the cosmocentric symbolist from the literalist? The difference boils down to the fact that literalism has been presented as philosophically realist in its analysis of traditional religious discourse, whereas the cosmocentric symbolist's account is one form of anti-realism. Obviously then the principles involved in assessing their relative merits are broadly analogous to those involved in assessing realism and anti-realism in the philosophy of science.[34]

There for example, a central issue was the relation between the theoretical and the observational language. An anti-realist account of theory appears to require a clear-cut distinction between the two. Yet it is difficult to make a sharp break between observational and theoretical terms, and in any case, terms which are clearly observational are often theory-laden. These considerations lead to a more holistic conception of the relation between scientific and everyday discourse, and thus to an inte-

grated view of their respective domains of reference. The symbolist also needs to make an exclusive distinction between 'magico-
religious' and 'observational' concepts, but the same difficulties
apply. The Nuer, for example, believe that the lights they see
over marshland are nature-spirits (*bieli*) which have become visible
(see Evans-Pritchard 1956: 136ff.). That is an excellent example
of a theory-laden observational term, or alternatively of a term
which in its application may (but need not) have an observable
reference: theories affect beliefs about the nature of what is
observed – one cannot distinguish sharply between those concepts in Nuer discourse which refer straightforwardly to observable features of the environment, and 'ritual' concepts which
are simply symbols of social relations or even instruments for
making connexions between observable events.

A very common feature of traditional religious cosmologies is
the belief that there are procedures which, if followed, will give
a man the ability to see the spirits around him. Or people often
believe that there are certain places such as streams or glades in
which gods may be encountered – not simply in the sense that
their presence is felt but in the sense that one might get a glimpse
of them. This has a bearing on the cosmocentric symbolist's
account analogous to that of existence experiments (which are
seen by the scientist as attempts to detect a theoretically postulated entity) for the instrumentalist – though the argument
against the symbolist account is in fact stronger, in as much as
the sense in which the traditional thinker believes 'observation'
of spirits is possible is a fuller one than that which is given by
cloud chambers, electron microscopes etc. Admittedly this does
not amount to a knockdown case against the symbolist. He could
resort to the distinction (see p. 42) between the exemplary class
of religious statements and the symptomatic ones which result
from the traditional thinker's literalising misunderstanding of his
own radical metaphor. But if such moves are considered seriously
they begin to have very much the air of a progressive shift from
descriptive analysis to rational reconstruction.

In any case there are more decisive objections. One is that the
present version of the symbolist account fails to make sense of
the actual form which ritual procedures take. Consider a sacrifice.
It is normally accompanied by an invocation and some kind of
request to the god. But if we suppose that the god himself is seen

in the light of a theoretical metaphor, which merely provides a 'thinkable' link between an empirical procedure and an observable result, then what can we make of the point of these utterances? Finally, there is the difficulty with which this discussion of the symbolist approach began: that of accounting for religious feelings towards the gods. These emotions are internally dependent on a belief in the reality of their objects. But where the anthropocentric symbolist could at least offer a surrogate social object, symbolically represented by religious conceptions, the cosmocentric symbolist can only explain them by admitting that at least at one level, the traditional religious believer has a realist faith in the spiritual agencies with which his culture populates the world.

The philosophical framework

In the final form in which he has been presented the 'cosmocentric symbolist' is of course a construct – no known (to me) anthropologist approximates his position. Nevertheless, considered as a last stage in the gradual retreat from a full-blown symbolist approach his position is instructive. The first difficulty which we considered for the symbolist view lay in the way it coped with the admitted explanatory and instrumental aspects of traditional religion, by distinguishing between two levels of belief: symbolic and literal. This distinction could be avoided by dropping an important plank in the original platform – the anthropocentric conception of primitive religion, according to which its symbolically expressed subject was society – and accepting instead that what was symbolised in primitive religious notions were natural forces and natural phenomena. Given this change, the idea that some fundamental incommensurability existed between science and traditional religious thought was also weakened: the similarities or contrasts of structure and function between the two on this view would seem rather to be a matter of empirical investigation. This would be especially so if the anti-realism which residually distinguished the cosmocentric symbolist from the literalist were taken as stemming from a more general anti-realism with respect to apparently 'transcendental' hypotheses – and there seems no other reason for adopting it as against realism in the particular case of traditional religious thought. In fact, if we drop the particular semantic notion of 'symbol' as a tool for understanding the apparently transcendental element in traditional religious cosmology, we are left with the general form of what may be seen as an anti-realist form of literalism. In the last section we have found some grounds for doubting whether any account other than a realist one can describe traditional religious beliefs as they are *actually understood* by believers. But let us waive this for a moment. We then have two forms of literalism, distinguished on purely philosophical grounds. The classic form is realist, and, as we saw in chapter 1, builds up a natural momentum towards the full-blown intellectualist programme. Its possible alternative is anti-realist, but leaves open the possibility of an approach to traditional religion which would still be recognisably intellectualist in character.

In any case neither of these forms of literalism shows any trace of a distinctively *Durkheimian* symbolist analysis of the framework of ritual belief, according to which the real referent of ritual beliefs is the social order. But a practically minded anthropologist might feel impatient at these considerations. For him the major significance of the symbolist approach lies in the understanding it can afford of ritual action; whether or not it succeeds in providing a symbolic interpretation of ritual *beliefs* is of comparatively minor importance – still less important is the contrast between forms of literalism distinguished only on stratospherically philosophical grounds. Accordingly we must turn now to examine more critically the notion of 'ritual action', which has so far been taken for granted.

PART II

RITUAL ACTION

5

'Ritual'

In social anthropology the term 'ritual' has acquired a degree of rather uneasy autonomy from the context of magico-religious belief. This is in part the result of an emphasis on the study of ritual *behaviour*; for example, Beattie's stress on "the expressive and symbolic aspects of magic and religion" stems, he says, "from my interest in ritual as a way of acting as well as (or rather than) a way of thinking" (Beattie 1970: 267). As a result of this emphasis, social anthropologists have often sought to make a descriptive analysis of ritual actions without seriously working out what framework of beliefs must be imputed to the actors if the anthropologists' description is to have the explanatory significance which they intend. And so the formula that ritual has 'symbolic-expressive as well as instrumental' functions has seemed less puzzling than it should be.

This point provides a partial answer to anyone inclined to protest that the symbolist approach is to be understood as a tool for the analysis of ritual *action,* and not as an interpretation of the underlying meaning of religious ideas. There is no simple separation here. If symbolist writers have tended to concentrate on modes of action rather than on modes of thought, that is not to say that what they have said about the modes of action has no necessary implications for understanding the modes of thought, but only that these implications have been left as an exposed flank: towards which the critic will gratefully direct his attention. This I have done in the last few chapters.

However it would be quite misleading to leave the discussion there. Although thought and action, and thus their analysis, are linked, the idea that a degree of sensitivity to symbolism is especially necessary in the understanding of ritual behaviour *can* legitimately be separated from an ultimately philosophical concern with what basic categories – literalist or symbolist, realist or anti-realist – are appropriate for the understanding of traditional modes of thought. In various ways, rituals might turn out to have a dimension of symbolic meaning consistently with a realist and literalist approach to the framework of ideas which informs them.[35]

A second factor has tended to loosen the fit between the notion of ritual and the context of magico-religious belief. The term 'ritual' is associated with ceremony and ceremonious behaviour in general; and ceremonies, certainly in our own society, may be religious but may also be completely secular in character. In short 'ritual' floats free of its linkages with the study of magical and religious thought for two reasons on quite different levels – firstly, through a general tendency to disengage the study of 'ritual behaviour' from an investigation of its 'context of belief', and secondly, through the association of ritual with the broad concept of ceremony (cp. Goody 1961: 147). The resulting picture shows ritual as the genus, magical and religious actions as particular species, and magical or religious beliefs playing a somewhat shadowy background role, presumably as *differentiae*.

To understand this concentration on 'ritual' as the key category of which magical and religious actions are seen as a specialised form we again need to begin by going back to Durkheim. The "real characteristic of religious phenomena", for Durkheim (1915: 40–1),

is that they always suppose a bipartite division of the whole universe, known and unknowable, into two classes which embrace all that exists, but which radically exclude each other. Sacred things are those which the interdictions protect and isolate; profane things, those to which these interdictions are applied and which must remain at a distance from the first. Religious beliefs are the representations which express the nature of sacred things and the relations which they sustain, either with each other or with profane things. Finally, rites are the rules of conduct which prescribe how a man should comport himself in the presence of these sacred objects.

Sacred things, then, are distinguished through being set apart and marked off by prohibitions, the breaking of which incurs unseen dangers. As has often been pointed out, this is in itself an inadequate criterion. Electricity generators and atomic power stations fit it as well as any monumental shrine. The first stand isolated and set apart, surrounded by wire boundaries which carry inscriptions warning of unobservable dangers and designs – of lightning, skull and crossbones – depicting death-dealing powers. To enter certain inner parts of atomic power stations, a man must wear specially prescribed, all-enveloping clothes, and if by a mischance he neglects this prescription, he has to undergo an elaborate stereotyped process of cleansing in which particular attention is paid to such items of traditional ritual significance as fingernails and hair.

This general method of description is familiar from anthropologists' accounts of ritual – in itself it proves nothing about the *significance* of the interdictions involved. It is not enough to say that the interdictions Durkheim had in mind were *ritual* sanctions, incurring *mystical* dangers, since it is precisely such concepts as the 'ritual' and the 'mystical' that the distinction between sacred and profane things is meant to explain.

It was probably Radcliffe-Brown who popularised the now common practice of using 'ritual' as a term which can characterise attitudes, beliefs and things as well as actions. Where, for Durkheim, rites were defined in terms of the sacred, for Radcliffe-Brown the elucidating feature of sacred things is the fact that they are the objects of ritual attitudes.[36] "There exists", he says (Radcliffe-Brown 1952: 123),

a ritual relation whenever a society imposes upon its members a certain attitude towards an object, which attitude involves some measure of respect expressed in a traditional mode of behaviour to that object. Thus the relation between a Christian and the first day of the week is a typical example of a ritual relation.

Two characteristics of ritual behaviour are mentioned in this definition: it consists of a traditionally laid-down form of behaviour, and it expresses respect. The second of these is the more obviously inadequate, at least as a characterisation of how anthropologists, including Radcliffe-Brown himself, customarily use the term. There are, to begin with, plenty of magical actions which concern no sacred or respect-worthy object. But even if we restrict attention to ceremonial, which was perhaps principally in Radcliffe-Brown's mind, the attitude of respect is still not an indispensable ingredient. In our society, for example, a road-opening ceremony, or the ceremonious signing of a contract, need involve no expression of respect towards anybody or anything. What it does involve is a certain formality. It would be a mistake to treat this formality as being itself invariably an expression of respect. Formality may express respect towards a person, or towards such 'sacred objects' as a cross, the tomb of the unknown soldier or a saint's relic. But there are plenty of cases where it does not do so (e.g. a formal notice to quit, a formal rebuke), where no such person or object is involved; and it is pointless to dilute a useful concept and obscure an interesting distinction by treating all formality as equally expressive of respect towards an object. (Formality is a wider notion than ceremoniousness. Not all formal behaviour is ceremonial – for example, a formal caution. However, it is the formal element in ceremonial which lends plausibility to the idea that ceremonial is essentially expressive of respect.)

It also needs to be remembered that attitudes of respect are not always to be found where, from our own institutions, we would expect them. The peculiar respect which a Christian feels for God is by no means universally characteristic of the attitudes of the religious towards gods or spirits – they may emphasise instead the possibility of a mutually beneficial cooperation. Durkheim's dictum: "Les dieux, eux aussi, ont besoin de l'homme; sans les offrandes, ils mourraient" captures neatly the characteristic attitude towards the spirits found in a number of West African religions: out of mind, out of existence, or, at least, out of power.[37] Finally, as Radcliffe-Brown himself recognises, ritual attitudes are adopted not only towards the holy but also towards the unclean: spittle, excrement and menstruating women are no objects of respect (in the sense of deference and esteem, as opposed to cautious avoidance), but Radcliffe-Brown would certainly include the prohibitions which surround them in the category of ritual.

There is also, however, another side to Radcliffe-Brown's understanding of ritual: "ritual acts", he says, "differ from technical acts in having in all instances some expressive or symbolic element in them" (Radcliffe-Brown 1952: 143). The distinction which he here makes between 'ritual' and 'technical' actions, and the connexion which he sees, broadly following

Durkheim, between ritual and symbolism, have been fundamental to a good deal of modern sociological thinking about
religion. The essence of 'technical' or 'instrumental' actions is
that they are performed as means to some further end which
performance of the action is believed capable of producing.[38]
Ritual, or 'symbolic-expressive', actions are contrasted with
them.

The nature of the contrast, however, is obscure. Some writers,
associating the two categories with Durkheim's distinction between the sacred and the profane, treat them as mutually exclusive
in the sense that no action can belong to both. Others treat them
as marking out contrasted aspects, both of which an action may
nevertheless have – as would be the case if 'expressive' meant
'done for its own sake' (see e.g. Leach 1968). Beattie, as we have
seen, thinks that magical actions are believed to be instrumentally
effective *because* they are at some level recognised as being symbolic. Radcliffe-Brown himself recognises that many ritual actions
are 'instrumental' as far as the people who perform them are
concerned, but nevertheless declares that an approach which
seeks to explain them in terms of the purposes and beliefs of the
actors "is by far the least profitable, though the one that appeals
most to common sense" (Radcliffe-Brown 1952: 142). This way
of making the contrast one between different levels at which the
action may be, respectively, symbolic-expressive and instrumental – "The beliefs by which...rites themselves are justified
and given some sort of consistency are the rationalisations of
symbolic actions and the sentiments associated with them" (p.
152) – has been discussed in earlier chapters.

If the proper application of the contrast between ritual and
instrumental action is not clear, there has nevertheless been a
fairly broad degree of agreement about the connexion between
ritual and symbolic action.[39] But again, what ritual symbolises,
or in what sense it is symbolic, or indeed what symbolic action
is, remains obscure. Any or all of these actions might be said to
be symbolic acts: shrugging one's shoulders; throwing a tomato
at a bad performer; sending messages in semaphore: spitting on
the floor to show one's contempt for a person; planting a tree
as 'a symbolic attack on the asphalt jungle'; giving someone a
hug of gratitude, a flower from one's garden or a tweak on the
nose; breaking one's sword as a gesture of surrender. None of

these actions, except the tree-planting, and possibly the officer's sword-breaking, is in any normal sense a ritual or ceremony, though some of them might be said to express social relationships symbolically. (Incidentally, the tree-planting also shows that a ceremony need not be – though most of them are – a traditionally laid-down pattern of action. There is no traditionally prescribed method of protesting against 'asphalt jungles', nor is the protest itself traditional. Nor is it a question of *prescription*, traditional or otherwise). The list is a deliberately heterogeneous one: it is quite possible to explain a use for the notion of symbolic action which would cover some but not all of the items mentioned in it. We need to have some such account to know what is implied in the classing of rituals as symbolic actions, and we also need to know what marks them off from the category of symbolic actions in general.

To sum up: What seems to emerge from all this is the vaguely felt sense of some kind of connexion between ceremony, magico-religious action and the symbolically social. The connexion is made in terms of the idea of the sacred, or, where the emphasis is on action, of ritual; and ritual or sacredness are to be contrasted with the 'technical', 'practical' and 'instrumental', or profane. The criteria of what is *set apart* or what is *respected* cannot define these linked notions of sacredness and ritual – their meaning must lie in the relations between the three elements they bring together. What is needed, then, is a clear framework in terms of which the relationships between these various notions can be elucidated. To this end I propose to begin with the concept of ceremony: the next two chapters will be devoted to distinguishing two importantly different types of ceremony. I shall call them 'interaction ceremonies' and 'operative ceremonies'; the kernel actions ceremonialised in these respective types may in each case be said to 'say things' and 'do things', but in very different ways. In chapter 8 the definition of symbols and symbolic action will be considered, preparatory to a discussion of various theories of the logic of magical action in chapter 9.

The connecting thread in all this is the concept of ritual – but it will already be seen that the territory to be covered is hetero-geneous and far-flung. My discussion will tend to enforce this impression, for I shall be concerned mainly with separating out elements in the idea of ritual and symbolic-expressive action which are in their respective ways significant and important, but which seem to me to be profitlessly run together under the umbrella term 'ritual'. However, towards the end of the discussion of magic in chapter 9 I shall be in a position to broach the very difficult question of the relation between magic and ceremony, in particular between operative ceremonies and certain kinds of magial act; and finally in chapter 10 I shall try to bring the separate strands in the argument of Part II together and make some sort of knot.

6

Ceremony and interaction

Ceremonies in our own society; the interaction code

In our own society the occasions for ceremony are various. I shall discuss these domestic ceremonies first; whether – and, if so, how – the categories that emerge need to be expanded to accommodate ceremonies in other cultures will be considered later.

(a) Very many ceremonies come at the beginning and end of things. Thus: the opening of Parliament, academic ceremonies on graduation day, grace before and after meals, raising the flag in the morning and lowering it in the evening; ceremonies at inaugurations, appointments, investitures etc.; religious ceremonies – baptism, ordination, marriage, confirmation, funerals, ceremonies for the signing of contracts, treaties and suchlike – opening roads and buildings, naming ships, unveiling statues.

(b) They can have a backward-looking, frequently calendrical character: flags flown at half-mast, ceremonies at the Cenotaph or the tomb of the unknown soldier, flowers placed on a grave, commemorative ceremonies in the liturgical calendar.

(c) Often ceremony serves as an outward sign or formal mark of a social state or event. For example: wigs worn in court, gowns at lectures, evening dress on formal occasions; the flag flown at Buckingham Palace when the Queen is in residence, the light on Big Ben when Parliament is in session.

(d) Then there are interaction ceremonies: kneeling, bowing, taking one's hat off; greeting and sending off heads of state at airports and so forth; formal introductions and apologies; certain types of prayer.

These four categories can serve as an initial sorting out of the area to be considered, and should not be taken too seriously as either exhaustive or exclusive. 'Ceremony' is in any case not a word with a clearly established use; and so far as exhaustiveness goes, if we can find some general features or principles which fit the area I have outlined to a reasonable degree of approximation, the edges can be moved to make it fit exactly. As for exclusiveness it is again obvious that many ceremonies could be equally well classified under more than one of the four heads. The flag is raised in the morning and lowered in the evening, but it flies all day; ceremonious greetings or leave-takings are interaction ceremonies, but equally they come at the beginning and end of an interaction. The Cenotaph, or the tomb of the unknown soldier, are the 'sacred objects' of commemorative ceremonies; they can also be seen as permanent outward marks, or symbols, of an achievement or event of social importance.

Interaction ceremonies, to take the last of these rough groupings, are part of a more general form of social life which I shall call the 'interaction code'.[40] Saying "Sorry!" after I have jostled you, or raising my eyebrows as a sign of recognition when I pass you in the street, are two examples of it. The point of interaction-code behaviour is to establish or maintain (or destroy) an equilibrium, or mutual agreement, among the people involved in an interaction as to their relative standing or roles, and their reciprocal commitments and obligations. It consists of speech acts (such as greetings, thanks and apologies); specifically written formulae ('Dear sir", "Yours faithfully", etc.); gestures (waves, handshakes); facial expressions (smiles, looks of recognition etc.); posture and degrees of bodily proximity; voice quality, intonation, stress and so on; clothes (for example, suits to be worn at interviews); props (arms to be presented, hats to be raised, gifts to be exchanged, guns to be fired in salute); and supporting actors (bandsmen, household cavalry, butlers, hostesses to perform introductions.) From this variegated list it can be seen that while there are some actions – a handshake, for example – whose point is given purely in terms of it, the interaction code normally has a place simply as one significant strand in the overall pattern of a person's behaviour. In interaction ceremony, on the other hand, it is brought to the fore.

Evidently, interaction-code behaviour ('IC behaviour', for short) *is* in some sense 'expressive'. Normally it expresses the attitudes or feelings of the sender towards the recipient, such as gratitude, welcome, contempt, an interest in how he is getting on or in what he is saying; although it may also involve the expression of attitudes towards some commonly recognised third party, where the mutual acceptibility of the attitudes can establish the bond ("Heil Hitler", "God be praised", "Down with..."). One might perhaps also include here routine exchanges on a topic assumed to be of common interest (e.g. the weather).

The expression of inner states: grades of complexity in intention

It is necessary, however, to make some distinctions among the ways in which an attitude or emotion can be said to be expressed in behaviour. Suppose that, upon my seeing you in the street, my face lights up and I break into a smile; or that while I am talking to you at a party my gaze wanders restlessly around the other guests, and I smother a yawn. The smile and the yawn are natural, non-intentional expressions of feeling. Each of these two terms is worth considering.

An argument familiar from Wittgenstein's *Philosophical Investigations* shows that if we can be taught to communicate about an inner state then there must be forms of behaviour which are *natural* expressions of that state, in the sense that they are not taught. (Or, more precisely, they may themselves have been taught, but not taught *as* expressions of that inner state.) It is of course an empirical question whether or not smiles or yawns are in this sense natural expressions; I shall assume for the purpose of the argument that they are. If they are not, then whatever behaviour is natural would do as well. It is also plausible to suppose that at least some natural – untaught – forms of expressive behaviour are also natural in the sense that they can be naturally recognised, that is, that the understanding of them *as* expressions of an inner state by those who see them need not be taught. Thus there must be a minimum level of untaught expression of pleasure, say, for the full-blown 'language-game' of ascriptions and avowals of pleasure to be teachable; and it is also plausible to suppose that there is a minimum level of untaught recognition of these untaught expressions – as being expressions of *pleasure.*

When I recognise you in the street and smile at you, I express my pleasure at seeing you. This can work in more ways than one;

I may, as we say, smile *out of* pleasure at the sight of you, or *in order to show* my pleasure. The two cases are distinguished by the explanation which is appropriate to them. In the first case, the directly relevant explanatory fact is simply my pleasure at seeing you. In the second case, it is my desire to show my pleasure or the intention I had in showing it, and this introduces the question of what my reasons were for doing so. So, in the first case, I smile because I am pleased, and the action is a *non-intentional* one; in the second I smile because I want to show my pleasure, and I may want to show my pleasure because I am pleased – or for some other reason.[41] I show my pleasure by simulating the non-intentional expression of pleasure – and simulation also allows for dissimulation. With the intentional expression of feelings, the possibility of insincerity enters in.

Simulating the non-intentional expression of feelings is of course not the only way of making others think one has them. Consider the conditions which must broadly hold for it to work successfully: (1) The actors must be able to interpret each other's non-intentional expressions correctly. (2) They must know that others have this ability. (Simulating a spontaneous smile in order to make another person think that one is pleased presupposes the belief that he can read smiles as expressions of pleasure.) (3) They must be able to produce intentionally the behaviour which in the right context counts as non-intentional expression of the relevant feelings. And (4) they must be able to produce it as a simulation of them.

Now given this background of knowledge and ability on the part of the actors involved it is perfectly plausible to suppose that when the sender simulates a non-intentional smile of pleasure, intending the recipient to interpret it as a genuine one, the recipient may in fact interpret it correctly. That is, he may interpret it as a smile intended to make him think that the sender is pleased to see him by causing him to interpret it as a *non*-intentional expression of the sender's feelings. The recipient may well then infer, since the sender is in a very good position to know whether or not the sender is pleased to see him, and since he obviously wants the recipient to think he *is* pleased, that he probably is. Suppose in fact that there is general implicit acceptance that when someone who is in a position to know whether it is or is not the case that *p*, exhibits an intention of making one believe that *p*, then this gives one good reason, by and large and subject to obvious provisos, to believe it. In these conditions it will be possible for the smile to communicate feeling in a new way: the sender can smile, intending the recipient to think he is pleased, and *intending* him to think this on the basis of recognising the sender's communicative intention. (I shall call this case 3. Case 1 is the non-intentional smile of pleasure. Case 2 is the intentional simulation of case 1, intended to produce in the recipient the required belief by causing him to interpret it as case 1.) The smile is now beginning to assume the character of a *conventional* expression of pleasure, in as much as it is no longer essential – it could be replaced by another convenient piece of behaviour which would, by convention, be taken to convey pleasure (at a meeting, say): "Hi!" for example. (I shall call this case 4.)[42]

The distinctions between conventional and natural, and intentional and non-intentional, expressions of feeling are not equivalent, but they are related. Saying "Damn it!" is, like any linguistic behaviour, a convention-dependent way of expressing one's feelings; it is at the same time the kind of thing one says involuntarily when one hits one's finger with a hammer. And a man can behave intentionally to express feelings for which the self-same pattern of behaviour is a natural expression. Nevertheless, a form of behaviour which expresses a certain feeling in a *natural* – untaught – way is characteristically a form in which that feeling is *evinced* – expressed non-intentionally – whereas a taught, conventional form of expression for a feeling is characteristically *used*, intentionally, to express that feeling.

Communication: the interaction code is communicative; communicative openness v. social overtness

We can now return to the question of how IC behaviour expresses the feelings of the sender towards the recipient. A number of writers on non-verbal communication in effect lump all four of the cases I have distinguished together as 'communicative interaction'.[43] For my part, I exclude non-intentional expressions of feeling from the interaction code; although on the other hand I am concerned to stress the continuities between the *basic* level – at which feelings towards another person are non-intentionally and naturally evinced, and in which these natural modes of expression are equally naturally interpreted – and the more or less highly *derived* levels of expressive behaviour which belong to the interaction code. Code behaviour is communicative interaction in that it is not simply the evincing of an emotional response towards another; the sender *directs* it towards the recipient and intends him to recognise it as expressive. This still allows us to include behaviour of the case 2 type; but for present purposes I rule it out, too. I want to consider the place interaction ceremonies have in a broader cultural form of behaviour (the interaction code); yet it must not be too broad if it is to have the fully-fledged characteristics of communication. The broader cultural form can then be related to a more basic level logically prior to the cultural, but which has the same reciprocal feedback pattern of feelings inspired by another, expressed, recognised, responded to, the expressed response in turn responded to etc.

An example which shows the social importance of the differences between the four types of case may be helpful here. Suppose I am talking to you at a party and you suppress a yawn. I may interpret this as an involuntary expression of boredom. I will then react to it in a number of ways, for example by changing the subject or breaking the conversation off; but my only ground for offence is that you should have succeeded in hiding your reaction more effectively. Or I may interpret it as an exhibition of your boredom which is in fact intentional although presented as involuntary. In this case I may well be rather offended; but I have still not been given cause for offence, as I have been if I correctly interpret your yawn as being designed to let me know that you are bored, via securing my recognition of your *intention* to let me know. The yawn now belongs to the interaction code, and has the designed *openness* of intention characteristic of full-fledged communication.

In another sense, however, IC behaviour may be *more or less* open or (let us instead say) *overt*: the hint contained in the yawn can be a subtle one – you mean me to recognise it, I do, you know I do, I know you know and so on; but the mutual understanding can remain a tacit one. But the more overt the hint the greater the cause for offence; and case 4 must always be more overt than case 3 – even if you look me fixedly in the eye and casually suppress a rather obvious yawn, the situation is not quite as bad

81

as it would be had you explicitly said 'You bore me silly!" Some code-reaction, expressing resentment and the expectation of apology, is required if I am not to lose face – the more overt the hint the less I am able to carry off the pretence that I have not picked it up, and in the last case this option is completely closed. Such gradations of explicitness can be of great importance in the process of reciprocal adjustment by which people (and animals) find mutually equilibrated roles.

Norms of interaction; reference to them in some IC behaviour

An interaction code is regulated by norms of interaction. For example, good form suggests proper greetings when people meet, depending on their relationship. But often the directly important point is not so much whether good will is actually felt, but that it is expressed. Why? Because, in expressing good will in those circumstances where the interaction norms require that it *should* be expressed, the sender typically shows his awareness that he is in a situation where the norms apply, and his readiness to abide by them. In very many types of interaction (not all, of course) this is in itself enough to indicate to the other person that the appropriate kind of reciprocal relationship is possible.

What is intended as an expression of feeling ("I'm so pleased to see you") can, given its context, non-intentionally express the sender's responsiveness to interaction norms. Typically the other people involved are perfectly able to recognise this non-intentionally expressed responsiveness, and the sender is aware of the fact. These are just the conditions in which the smile developed from a non-intentional expression to a full-fledged communication of pleasure. So, to take the smile again, we have another three cases: the first is a species of case 3 – the smile communicates pleasure in the context of a greeting, and in this context non-intentionally expresses responsiveness to interaction norms; in the last (the 'conventional' smiles exchanged by a shop assistant and a customer, for example) the smile *communicates* responsiveness.

Greetings are forms of IC behaviour which norms of interaction prescribe as the proper way of initiating most kinds of interaction. Their basis in feeling is as the expression of good will; but often, overt acknowledgement of the norms of interaction will do as well, so that the reference to the basis of fellow-feeling can become, in this sense, increasingly derived or oblique. When speech acts like "I'm so pleased to see you", which have the function of greeting, are used to *communicate* responsiveness to norms of interaction, they can be replaced by an explicit performative formula – "I greet you" ("Greetings") – which has the same force as they do without having the sense which ties them directly to the basis of feeling.

The same general account holds also for apologies, for example. Apologies are prescribed where the equilibrium of an interaction has been disturbed through an imposition of some kind by one person on the other. Their basis in feeling is regret, concern for the harm caused etc., but again overt acknowledgement that one is in a situation in which the norms which prescribe apology apply, and that one accepts them, can often do just as well. An explicit performative ("I apologise") can directly communicate this acknowledgement, leaving only a derived or oblique allusion to the basis of feeling.[44] (In one way, this overt acknowledgement can have an even more effective role in the case of apology than in the case of greeting, for apology also involves the notion of reparation, of making up the injury; unless the injury caused is a great one, however, overtly expressed regret and, particularily, overt recognition that one is at fault and should apologise, since they put one in a certain sense at a disadvantage, can themselves serve as adequate reparation.)

Any society is made up of an enormous variety of relationships, permanent, occasional, momentary, each with their own normatively expected equilibrium: teacher – pupil, brother officers in an officers' mess, husband – wife, bank clerk – customer. Particular kinds of relationship inspire distinctive codes (e.g. clapping as a proper way of marking the end of a piano recital), and in a long and close relationship the people involved can evolve their own private code; beyond these is the overall code shared in a society, which can be used on appropriate occasions in any relationship. The general norm governing IC behaviour is that people should use the code to establish the relationship which ought – in accordance with other norms – to hold between them, to maintain it, to re-establish it if it is thrown out of equilibrium and to terminate it properly – *by respectively invoking in a more or less highly derived form the feelings which, if they were spontaneously felt and non-intentionally evinced and recognised, would establish an equilibrium, maintain it etc. naturally.* (A parallel with what animal ethologists call ritual, that is, the stereotyped simulation of e.g. attack and submission, is obvious).

I have made a distinction between non-intentional manifestations of feeling and codified, intentional expressions; it is obvious, especially where relationships are personal rather than impersonal, that a mutually acceptable balance is normally established predominantly at the level of feelings non-intentionally and naturally evinced and understood. What a person tells me, in the interaction code, of his attitudes towards me is a very small part of the knowledge of his feelings which I get from his behaviour. People's reciprocal responses are to a large extent naturally self-adjusting – to this extent nature plays a leading role, and culture, in the form of the interaction code, an auxiliary one. On the other hand, intentional, codified expression, although in one sense it allows as we have seen for gradations of overtness, necessarily has the open character of communication, and is therefore socially significant even when formally off the record in a way in which the natural level of mutual reponse need not be.

The more derived forms of code behaviour are not always adequate to the occasion. When people who have been very close are reunited after a long separation, inhibition can freeze the natural expression of mutual feelings. In this situation the interaction code comes to the rescue: but it certainly is not an adequate substitute. If I have caused you a great deal of trouble and inconvenience, it may not be enough simply to say "I apologise". Equilibrium may only be restored if I manifestly feel regret. Does this show that the greater the disequilibrium, the more underived must be the expression of feeling which re-establishes it? This depends on whether it is the acceptance of the relevant interaction norms or the mutually recognised existence of real feeling which is generally important in the relationship. When a husband and wife fall out, a recognition of the rules of apology might re-establish only a marriage of convenience; regret manifested and recognised as genuine might do more. But when footballers or lawyers fall out the situation is different; it is the fact of apology which is important, and the real feelings of the people involved are less so. A private, informal apology, however genuinely felt, may not be good enough – a formal apology clearly made and recognised as such can resolve the dispute by direct public acknowledgement of shared norms of interaction.

So much for a general description of interaction *codes* and *norms*. (A final reminder: one should not make the mistake of treating IC behaviour as invariably governed by norms of interaction.[45] The norms dictate that we should establish proper relations with the people we meet; though they may also tell us how we ought to react if someone gets too uppity, offensive or cheeky. But cocking a snook, snubbing someone or putting one's tongue out are as much code behaviour as raising one's hat, bowing, bidding someone welcome or thanking him.)

Interaction ceremony: elaboration and formality in the interaction code

Where now do interaction *ceremonies* fit in? They are among the more elaborate and formal parts of the code, and hence share its general characteristics. We must first consider the notions of elaboration and formality. Code behaviour – greetings, for example – can be more or less elaborate in terms of the *complexity* of the formula or script involved. In this sense, saying "How do you do? I'm delighted to have the honour of your acquaintance" is more elaborate than saying "Hi!" Again, saying "Watcher cock! How's tricks with you?", accompanied by a playful side-step, feint, punch on the biceps, etc., is more elaborate than saying "Hi!" and also more elaborate than saying "How!" in measured, solemn tones accompanied by a raised open right hand, palm facing forwards. Secondly, code behaviour can be more or less elaborate in terms of the *scale* of the production, or *mise en scène*, involved – roughly, in terms of the energy and resources expended in putting on the show. Thus, there are meetings in which people introduce themselves, smile and say "How do you do?", and there are meetings which are arranged in advance, in which a third party does the introductions, supporting actors parade, blow trumpets etc., and the leading figures smile and say "How do you do?" The distinction between scale and complexity is obviously a fairly rough-and-ready one, particularly where code behaviour is relatively stereotyped, but can easily be applied to ceremonies other than those which concern interaction. A road, for example, may be opened by someone's cutting a ribbon and saying "I declare this road open": the same formula may be performed by a minor official or by an important personage, with brass bands in attendance etc.

Formality, the third relevant feature, is more difficult to pin down, but goes closest to the heart of ceremony. The occasions for formality in IC behaviour occur (1) when the actors do not, at least as yet, know each other personally – have not made each other's acquaintance; (2) when their roles in a social event require that their personal acquaintance be ignored (the registrar presiding over the marriage of his next-door-neighbour's daughter, the military commandant awarding a medal on parade to his nephew); and (3) when their hierarchical roles are such as to preclude a personal relationship, on one side at least. If elaboration involves the scale and complexity of the drama, then formality implies an attention to its proper performance. But obviously the idea of a 'proper performance' in this sense applies only to certain kinds of IC behaviour. There is no proper or improper way of saying "How's things?" because it is in itself an informal mode of greeting – and thus in itself of course an inappropriate thing to say on formal occasions. (In another sense one might, as an outsider getting on terms of familiarity with an unfamiliar group, try to put in a good informal performance of the group's particular version of the interaction code.)

What is the point of formality? One view is that it serves to establish an order of shared expectations as to how one should behave, without which there would be an embarrassing or tension-producing chaos, in which uncertainty prevailed about how to interpret the intentions of other actors. But this at best ascribes a role to ceremoniousness which the interaction code and the norms which govern it play as a whole. Equilibrium in social life presupposes shared conventions about the expression of attitudes towards others; but there is no reason why the conventions should dictate formality. The essential requirement is a code. Whether the code behaviour is elaborate, stereotyped and consciously decorous, or lightly touched in and flexible is another question. Uncertainty about how much formality is expected for an occasion can induce tension, but certainty that none is does not (unless one is accustomed to it on occasions of the kind involved).

The prime significance of formality in interaction is that of marking out, emphasising, underlining the fact of code behaviour.[46] To make a formal apology is to underscore the fact, to 'put it on record', that an apology has been made. Interaction ceremony is at the fully explicit end of the continuum between overt and implicit forms of 'code communication'. The code behaviour underscored, however, must be in accordance with norms of interaction: thus in our present society there are no ceremonious insults. An insult can be fully overt and on the record, expressed with moderation and yet great elaborateness of scale – but it cannot have the punctilious regard for propriety which we include in the notion of ceremony; for there are no norms which prescribe insults. Of course there have been and are social milieux in which ceremonious insults could occur: precisely those in which norms of interaction prescribe that in certain circumstances one *should* insult a party.

As well as being fully overt, interaction ceremonies are highly derived. Ceremonious code behaviour is not merely governed by norms, but norm-regarding, in that it communicates acceptance of the norms which dictate proper feeling, rather than communicating the feeling itself. The interaction code in general is a neutral language – a person can use it equally to establish or to reject equilibrated relationships in which his own parts are those which the norms accepted in his society prescribe for someone in his position. Interaction ceremonies, on the other hand, always express reciprocal attitudes which, if naturally felt, would establish an equilibrium naturally, and where there are relevent norms of interaction the equilibrilum is in accordance with them. To this extent then, the commonly made claims that ceremony is *expressive*, and highly *conventionalised* or *culturally elaborated*, are borne out at least in the case of ceremonies of interaction. So also is the claim that ceremony is 'integrative', but only if this is taken as implying that interaction ceremony expresses on the part of the people involved an agreement or reciprocity of attitudes which is in accordance with canons of proper mutual feeling. But from this it does not follow that ceremony produces or reinforces that agreement (it may or may not have that effect) or that the attitudes expressed are sincerely felt by the actors.

In underscoring people's code behaviour towards each other and its derived, norm-regarding character, ceremonious formality also marks out the relationships between them, and the boundaries or social distance which separate them. In the ideal world of bygone books of etiquette, a man and a woman who have not been introduced are not personally acquainted. Without being 'stand-offish', they 'keep their distance', and the distance is marked out by formal behaviour. If they are then formally introduced by a third person, the gap is closed (or narrowed), the closure is expressed, say, in a handshake, and underscored by its formality. Thus formality is associated with *gravitas*, a sense of one's own worth and social autonomy, or of that of the other person. Aristotle's proud or 'great-souled' man, as described in *Nichomachean Ethics* (1125^a 11–16; 1954: 94),

is one who will possess beautiful and profitless things rather than profitable and useful ones; for this is more proper to a *character that suffices to itself*. Further, a slow step is thought proper to the proud man, a deep voice, and a level utterance; for the man who takes few things seriously is not likely to be hurried, nor the man who thinks nothing great to be excited, while a shrill voice and a rapid gait are the results of hurry and excitement [my italics].

Interaction ceremony is "beautiful and profitless" in the sense in which the great-souled man's things are; and to this extent again it fits talk of the 'aesthetic', and the 'expressive' as opposed to the 'instrumental', aspects of ritual.

Ceremonious formality is not itself, however, an extra item in the expressive repertoire of the interaction code. It does not enlarge the base of feelings towards another person expressible in it. It is not one of the keys on the piano keyboard – if anything, it is more like the pedals which alter the whole sonority of the instrument. (Of course the fact that a man's behaviour is formal – like virtually any other behavioural characteristic – testifies to the attitudes and feelings which lie behind it, and these will include the actor's sense of his own relative standing, or of the importance of the occasion.)

On ceremonious occasions which are not in themselves devoted to the aims of the interaction code – an inauguration, the opening of Parliament – code behaviour between the people involved becomes ceremonious, whatever its normal tone may be. Other ceremonious occasions, however, are specifically interaction ceremonies, in that the social event which they embellish with formality and elaborateness of scale is itself a piece of IC behaviour. We put on record our appreciation of Mr X's fifty years of service in the firm by means of a little ceremony in which he is given a gold watch. A visiting head of state is greeted at the airport by a representative of the government; the ceremony underscores a form of code behaviour which suits the officially aimed at harmonious relationship between states.

Commemorative acts

What has been said of interaction code and ceremony can to a large extent be extended to commemorative acts, such as putting flowers on a relative's grave or remembrance ceremonies at the tomb of the unknown soldier. Radcliffe-Brown tells of a Chinaman carrying a bowl of rice to put on an ancestor's grave, who was asked by a European whether he thought the dead man would sit up and eat it. "Do you believe", he inscrutably replied "that your ancestors will smell the flowers you surround them with?" Taking the point, one can still trace the continuities between IC behaviour and commemoration of the dead. A husband who gives his wife a bunch of her favourite flowers, and a husband who places flowers on his dead wife's grave "because they were her favourite ones", are concerned in the first case to communicate, in the second at least to affirm the same kind of feelings with the same kind of code behaviour. So if such commemoration of the dead is not itself IC behaviour, since it is not in the full sense intended as a *communication* of feeling, it at least exploits the same expressive resources as the code. And, where the commemoration is ceremonious, (1) feelings are expressed in derived, norm-regarding form; (2) the norms involved prescribe feelings which were they recognised and in due form reciprocated by the dead, would establish an equilibrium; and (3) the relationship in which the equilibrium would be established would be that which could properly hold given the respective social positions of the commemorator and the commemorated dead. (In societies in which the dead are believed to pass through to an after-life their social position there may not be the one they had while alive, but one which they acquire, by dying, in the extended spiritual community.)

Let me now review the discussion of this chapter. I have distinguished between *interaction code, interaction ceremony* and *norms* prescribing proper forms of IC behaviour on appropriate occasions. Consider first the interaction code:

(1) IC behaviour rests on a vast base in which the feelings and attitudes of interacting parties towards each other are expressed, recognised and reacted to at a purely natural and undesigned level.

(2) Thus both IC behaviour and this base on which it rests are in a straightforward sense *expressive behaviour:* expressive of feelings towards the other.

(3) But whereas the natural base on which the interaction code rests is naturally and non-intentionally expressive behaviour, IC behaviour does not merely evince feelings; it is the actor's way of *communicating* feeling. Hence it has the features of a full-fledged communicative act: in particular it relies on the characteristic designed openness of communicative intention which has been analysed by Grice. (There is also an intermediate case – case 2 – in which the natural expression of feeling is intentionally simulated but which does not involve communicative openness of intention.) To anticipate terminology which will be explained in chapter 8, IC behaviour has *non-natural* meaning, the base on which it rests has *natural* meaning.

(4) However, while IC behaviour necessarily has the openness of intention remarked on in (3), it can still be more or less *overt*, socially on or off the record.

(5) Where there is behaviour which has non-natural meaning, there is the possibility of stipulating that a certain action (e.g. an utterance) by convention has that non-natural meaning. Thus IC behaviour may be more or less derived (i) in the sense of being more or less *convention-dependent* communication. Since conventions are socially shared, the more conventionalised it is, the more it will be overt, socially on the record etc. (ii) It may also be more or less highly derived from its base in the natural expression of feeling in the sense that the allusion made to the original base of appropriate feeling may be increasingly indirect, increasingly

mediated by more direct allusion to norms of interaction which prescribe certain expressions of feeling as appropriate.

Turning now to these norms, the main points made were the following:

(6) That they presuppose other 'first-order' norms in that the first-order norms prescribe what relation (hierarchical etc.) is to hold between the parties, and the interaction norms then prescribe the expression of those feelings which, if the relation prescribed by the first-order norms were spontaneously acknowledged by both parties, would be naturally felt.

(7) The interaction code is in itself a neutral system of communication; it can be used in accordance with or against the norms.

Finally we come to interaction ceremony:

(8) Here the distinction of central importance was between ceremonial and the action ceremonialised. In the case of interaction ceremonies what is ceremonialised is by definition IC behaviour – it has non-natural meaning – but the ceremonialisation itself, if expressive, is not expressive in this non-natural way.

(9) The characteristics of ceremonial are (i) elaboration (of scale, complexity) and (ii) formality.

(10) Its point is, firstly, that it stands at the extreme of overtness. In fact formal actions in general have an explicit marking-it-out, putting-it-publicly-on-record character: this is what their formality consists in.

(11) Secondly, what is ceremonialised is marked out and elaborated as a *proper* way of doing things: the IC behaviour ceremonialised is always in accordance with the norms of interaction (or, rather, with what the organisers of the ceremony take those norms to be). It is also norm-regarding, in the sense of being derived and distant from the basis of feeling: what occupies the foreground is neither the feeling nor the expression of feeling, but the *propriety* of the expression of feeling.

Ceremony gives an image of how things should be, of order and harmony, rather like the snapshot of a Christmas family get-together, or the housewife's immaculate drawing-room. If there is a powerful human tendency to make such images of ideal harmony and order, and to set them against the actual messiness of human life and its tendency to crumble into grey or even threatening featurelessness, there is also a powerful urge to kick against them, particularly when the prevailing moral temper is one which stresses sincerity and a realistic warts-and-all acceptance of people as they actually are. It is interesting that we (and this is more than a fact about *our* particular culture) find amusement and temptation in the thought of such an image spoilt by profane intrusion: e.g. a muddy footprint on the housewife's carpet, a smelly hippy among the Tory ladies' flowered hats, a dirty old motorbike caught at the head of a royal procession. This is a debunking humour founded on the sense that what is being treated as 'sacred' is really nothing special; and that is also why, for example, excesses of municipal ceremony (e.g. the opening of a lavatory) are funny. Where there is thought to be real sacredness (e.g. the Eucharist), a profanation is not funny at all.[47]

7

Operative ceremonies

There is one division of nature where the formula of idealism is applicable almost to the letter: this is the social kingdom. Here more than anywhere else the idea is the reality...
> (Durkheim, *Elementary Forms of the Religious Life*, p. 228)

Operative acts; the relevant notion of the social

Many of the ceremonies in my first group (see p. 76) centre on operative acts – for example, the opening of Parliament, investitures, opening roads, naming ships. Other operative actions include: appointing someone to an office, making a mark in rugby, excommunicating someone, giving a verdict or passing a sentence (in a court of law), elevating someone to the peerage, dubbing him a knight, electing him to a club. The point of each of these actions is to bring about a consequence, which takes effect when the action is performed in due form by the right person(s). Thus a sentence is passed, a verdict delivered or a will made, and duly takes effect.

All the examples I have cited consist of a set procedure which the actor should follow. A list of the various kinds of behaviour which can be involved would be as variegated as in the case of the interaction code (see p. 77). (Consider, for example, launching a ship, dubbing a knight, conducting a marriage ceremony, topping off a building, unveiling a statue. Examples from other cultures would give a still greater variety of actions.) Considering for a moment only what is said, we find that operative acts often include verbal formulae which performatively declare something to be the case ("Mark!", "Out!", "Arise, Sir Knight!") or take the form of what Austin (1970: 239) calls 'explicit performatives' ("I declare this road open", "I sentence you to—" etc.).

In the case of interaction ceremonies I distinguished between the formula which may be used in code behaviour ("How do you do?", "I bid you welcome", "Sorry!" etc.) and which can be more or less complex, but still remains part of the interaction code, and the formality and elaborateness of scale which accompany it, and constitute the characteristic of ceremony proper. The distinction, although artificial and rather more simple than the facts (formality differentiates some formulae from others; it is not simply an optional extra which can be combined with any or all of them), is needed to bring out the general characteristic of ceremony – that of marking something out as proper and as socially on record – which is a common feature of all ceremonial and not restricted to the context of the interaction code. Operative actions, like IC behaviour, often (though not always) follow a customary pattern or formula. As in the interaction code, these patterns, by virtue of their stereotyped and customary character, tend to get included in the general notion of ceremonial or ritual; here again, however, the fact that operative actions typically take a customarily prescribed form can to some extent be separated from the fact that some of them are embedded in ceremonial. As before, the complexity and character of the script cannot be neatly separated from the formality and elaborateness of scale of the *mise en scène*; a rough distinction between the two, however, brings out what is often missed – that within the ceremony there can be an action which has a clear instrumental purpose going beyond that of the ceremonial which surrounds it. It allows us also to connect the *ceremoniousness* of an operative ceremony with that of other ceremonies which are not operative, and its *operative* character with other operative acts (such as licensing a car or writing a cheque) which involve an operative formula but no ceremony. On this approach three separate questions emerge: What is the logic of operative actions? Why do many of them tend to develop a stereotyped, customary form? Why do some among them become ceremonialised? It is to the first, purely conceptual, question that we must now turn.

Perhaps the most obvious characteristic of operative actions is that they can take effect only if performed by the right (or right kind of) person. Only an umpire can give a batsman out in cricket, only the king can elevate a man to the peerage, only the prime minister can appoint other ministers and so on. With respect to any possible operative action (as identified by the particular consequence it would have) there is a person, or persons, who have the power to perform it; others do not. And secondly, the ability of a person to perform a given operative act in given circumstances is a matter of his *social* characteristics: it is the social status of the performer which gives him his operative power, and not any psychological or physical characteristic (though of course he may acquire his social status by virtue of these). Equally, the consequences which he can operatively produce are social consequences.

The terms 'social status' and 'social consequence' need to be explained here, as I am using them in a rather specialised sense. There is a difference between having blonde hair, pigeon toes or a quick temper, and having two wives, two houses, or (owning) a ticket to the members' enclosure. These sets of examples might naturally be contrasted as comprising *natural* and *social* characteristics or properties. However the contrast between nature and society is complex and obscure: there are here many non-equivalent yet overlapping and mutually resonating distinctions, each of which would separate the particular two sets of examples I have given. To fix on one of them is therefore inevitably to some degree stipulative and artificial, and is subject to the danger of interference from others. But a proper account of the functions of ritual in traditional cultures, it seems to me, does require an explicit grasp of how the understanding of these notions which underlies it differs from our own. Some general stage-setting, then, however compressed, is desirable.

Being married, or owning a house, consist in nothing other than having certain rights and obligations with respect to particular persons or objects. Again, my dog is called 'Fido' because I have given it that name, thus establishing the convention that it should be so-called. In general, the conception I want to work towards here is that of a *social* characteristic, property or status as one whose possession is constituted purely or partly in terms of the existence of certain *rules*.

Here it will be necessary to distinguish between three types of rule.

(1) Some rules are hypothetical imperatives, or maxims for the guidance of practical reason. They are commonly expressed in the form: 'If you want to ϕ then you should ψ.' Such a sentence, when its antecedent states a factually described objective, and its

consequent a factually described means to it, is logically equivalent to a non-evaluative categorical sentence. For example, "If you want to get to the station as quickly as possible, then you should catch a taxi" is equivalent to "The quickest way to the station is by taxi." Rules of this kind are therefore also often stated in the form of some such categorical factual sentence. They are also often stated simply in terms of their consequent, the aim on which it is conditionalised being implicity understood: "Don't let the brake fluid sink below the minimum mark."

The other two types of rule on the other hand are not hypothetical imperatives, conditionalised to an objective.

(2) There are what I shall call *normative* rules, which permit, prescribe or forbid certain courses of action, and belong to morality or law.

(3) Finally there are *conventional* rules, which again regulate certain courses of action, but on the basis of received convention.

Henceforth I shall *ignore* rules of type (1), and use the term 'rule' to cover *only* cases (2) and (3). We shall shortly have to consider some important differences between these types of rule, but for the moment they will be taken together. A distinction may now be drawn between general rules (such as 'Everyone who is F may/must/must not ϕ in conditions C') and particular rules ('X may/must/must not ϕ in conditions C'). The latter may, but (at least if the idea of an instantiated general rule is taken non-trivially) need not be, instances of a general rule. A person's (or being's, since this definition is meant to cover the characteristics of non-human actors where these are believed to exist) given property, characteristic or status may now be said to be *social* if and only if it consists exclusively in his being subject to certain particular rules in his behaviour towards other people and things, and/or in other people's being subject to particular rules towards him. Thus for example being a judge or a managing director are social statuses. A social *fact* consists entirely in the existence of certain rules: it is for example a social fact that the Prince of Wales is heir to the throne or that the second entrance to the left is the members' entrance or that a piece of paper with such-and-such printing on it is a cheque.[48]

A great deal could be done by way of refining and extending this account, and making it more precise; but our concern with the notion of the social is primarily in connexion with the logic of operative acts. However I list here a number of points which may clarify some salient issues.

(1) A social fact, in the present sense, *consists* in the existence of certain rules; it should therefore be distinguished (i) from facts in virtue of which a particular person comes under a rule, and (ii) from facts in virtue of which there exists a rule.

As for (i), a general prescription (permission, prohibition) that anyone who is so-and-so should (may, should not) act in a certain way in such-and-such circumstances, will apply to a particular person in as much as he is so-and-so, and in such-and-such circumstances. These are the facts in virtue of which the rule applies to that particular person. As for (ii), a rule *may* exist in a particular social group because it has been specifically promulgated, instituted, agreed on etc. These facts of agreement, promulgation and so forth are the facts in virtue of which the rule exists. A subclass of this kind of fact would comprise facts to the effect that a person with proper authority has performed a certain operative act (made an appointment, declared a truce etc.). Of course, in this sense, there may *be* no facts *in virtue of which* a given rule exists.

(2) People's characteristics are often said to be 'social' in senses other than that in which the word is used here:
(i) A characteristic may be said to be social in as much as it is entirely or importantly the causal consequence of contact and interaction with other people (speaking a certain language, with a certain accent, or generally any characteristic acquired through socialisation).
(ii) It may be said to be social in as much as it consists of a regularity in or disposition to certain kinds of interaction with others – for example, being a grocer. Being a grocer is not in my sense a social status, since it does not *consist* in having certain rights and obligations. Of course a grocer will typically have characteristics which are in my sense social (*owning* certain goods, which are *for sale*); and he may acquire certain social statuses *qua* grocer (by appointment, sole supplier to the Queen.)
(iii) Characteristics may be said to be social in as much as it is in virtue of them that the person who has them comes under certain rules. For example, being the member of a certain clan is in the first place a matter of birth. But here one's birth to these

parents brings with it certain rights and obligations. Membership of a clan may be said to be a social as much as a biological fact: part of what is meant here is that a certain (in my sense) social fact, consisting in this person's having rights and obligations, is supervenient on a biological fact, that of his birth to these parents.

(3) Finally, some points about the rule-constituted nature of social characteristics or facts:

(i) Suppose that it has been decided by the commanders that all army units should attack at the moment when the moon appears over the horizon. The appearance of the moon is then the signal for a general attack. The moon's appearing has non-natural meaning – but is this a social fact? It is not a conventional rule that the moon's appearing should be the signal for attack; for the event has this non-natural meaning not regularly but only on this occasion. In contrast, a red traffic light *regularly* means that oncoming traffic should stop. I propose to extend the notion of a social fact in such a way that anything's having non-natural meaning, whether regularly or on a single occasion, will qualify as a social fact.

(ii) It may be noted that on the account I have given only persons (or rule-following beings) are said to have social characteristics. Here is an event, the moon's appearance over the horizon, which has a property – that of being a signal. That it has this property is a social fact, but the property is not itself a social property of the event. Again, Fido's being called 'Fido' is a social fact, but not a social property of Fido. It consists in rules for people wanting to refer to Fido but not in rules for Fido (though Fido may respond in regular, as opposed to rule-guided, ways to the sound 'Fido'). But nothing very much hangs on this: there would be no great difficulty in extending the notion of a social characteristic or property in such a way as to make these properties social.

(iii) The notion of the social as rule-constituted can also be naturally extended to cover the concepts 'role' and 'institution': a person's given role will then consist in his having a certain pattern of social characteristics, a given institution will consist in the existence of a certain system of rules.

Operative acts set up or cancel rules

Operative acts are performed to set up new patterns of rules. Hence we can also say that they can establish people in new statuses or rules, and can set up new institutions.

There are however many actions which are not operative acts but which can be said to be performed *in order* to set up an obligation or right, or to remove it. For example, I may give you hospitality, intending to put you under a reciprocal obligation (which I expect you to feel) in the hope that you will discharge it by inviting me to your Riviera villa. The distinction we need here is clearly that between *creating* or *cancelling* an obligation, in the sense of issuing or abolishing a rule, and *incurring* or *discharging* an obligation as under an existing rule. If I tear the prize stamp in your collection I at least put myself under an obligation to apologise, and possibly give you the right to demand reparation as well. If in a game of chess I place my knight in an empty diagonal in line with your bishop, I give you the right to take it. But when, on the other hand, I say "Feel free to take a walk in my grounds whenever you want to", I operatively create a right on your part.

On the basis of this distinction between acts which create or cancel an obligation, and acts which incur or discharge one, we can distinguish operative actions from what I shall call *obligative* acts – actions performed explicitly in their character of incurring or discharging an obligation. Suppose, for example, that any driver whose insurance did not cover passengers was legally obliged to announce to all prospective fellow-travellers: "I hereby warn you that my insurance company will accept no liability for injuries which you may suffer while in this car." A pronouncement of this kind implies a background of more or less official regulations in which the proper person has a duty to perform a certain action, and to make it clear that he is doing so, often by means of following a formal stereotyped procedure. The essence of such actions is that their obligative character is underscored – usually by formality, sometimes by full ceremonial (oaths of fealty, the ceremonious signing of contracts, treaties etc.). Nevertheless the formula involved (to take our present example) retains the function of warning essentially – it can only discharge the obligation to warn by *being* a warning. In general an obligative act can only discharge or incur an obligation by having, as an action, the characteristics which bring it under the relevant rule. In contrast an operative act consists in nothing more nor less than the creating or cancelling of a general or particular rule.

Ceremonies which initiate a new social status or condition often hover ambiguously between a genuinely operative and a purely confirmatory or formalising status. Thus a society may believe that when a king dies his eldest son automatically assumes the authority of kingship. The event of death itself, it would therefore seem, results in a new set of rights and obligations between the subjects and the new king. Yet there is also a coronation ceremony, in which the king is confirmed in office. In this kind of situation, people's views as to the degree of operative force in the ceremony can vary. Speaking more generally, a great many operative acts are context-bound in that (*a*) they are tied to producing a specific new rule-pattern applicable to effectively identified persons, and (*b*) they can be performed only when specific non-social preconditions obtain. Then the operative actors have a purely 'on/off' function. Given specified preconditions, they can, as it were, switch on the new rule-pattern or leave it off. This operative action may itself be optional or pre-scribed. So a coronation can take place only on the death of the previous king, only the eldest son can be crowned, and performance of the coronation is prescribed. (In reality, of course, various other contingencies have to be catered for.) A mark in rugby can be made only if the ball is caught on the full from an opponent's boot etc., in which conditions the player has the option of making the mark – if he does so, he has the right and obligation to take a certain kind of free kick. Now clearly where operative actions are context-bound in this way, and in particular when their performance is prescribed, the operative force can easily drop out, leaving the new rule-pattern directly hooked on to the preconditions of the operative action.

Another interesting case here, in a sense the converse of the preceding one, is that of verdicts, such as umpires' or juries' decisions. A verdict establishes rights or obligations, but does so by means of a decision as to what the facts are. The rights and obligations are in some sense consequent on, and in principle come into force in virtue of, these factual preconditions. The accused must be sentenced because he is guilty, not because the jury has found him guilty. In fact however, the verdicts cannot be seen as having a purely formalising character, precisely for the reasons which make it necessary to have specially appointed persons to deliver a verdict: they are required to give a verdict because the facts themselves are not sufficiently incapable of dispute for the rights and obligations to be hooked directly on to them. Thus the verdict does in reality create rights and obligations and its point is to do so, although it is a necessary feature of the institution that the verdict should aim at the facts. So verdicts too must be included as operative acts.

So much for the boundaries of the notion of operative action; we must now consider its logic in more general terms. Operative actions are performed in order to create or cancel a set of rights and obligations. Typically the action is performed by a person who has the operative authority to establish or abolish the rules in question. But this need not be the case. Where a rule is regarded as resting on the agreement of the people whose behaviour it governs, it is they collectively who can act to institute or cancel it. The operative action is performed collectively by all or by a representative whose business is simply to meet the requirements for the decision to take operative effect. (From this of course it is a small step to the election of a representative who is delegated with operative authority which he exercises on his own responsibility). But it would seem that there can also be operative procedures which when duly performed under the right conditions establish a rule-pattern, but where on the face of it *none* of the actors involved has the operative authority severally or collectively to create the rule-pattern which is established. *Are* these operative acts?

Consider for example the ceremony, which Evans-Pritchard describes (1962; 66–86), by which the divine king of the Shilluk is invested with kingly authority. The kings are believed to descend from Nyikang, a leader of the Shilluk in the heroic age. Furthermore Nyikang is not merely the medium between god and man, but is also thought in some sense to 'participate', as Evans-Pritchard puts it, in the identity of God. The investiture is a lengthy ritual process in which, among other things, a certain effigy of Nyikang at the head of its army defeats the army of the king-elect and takes him prisoner. In what seems the actual operative part of the drama, however, the effigy of Nyikang is placed on the royal stool, then taken off; and the king-elect sits down on it instead. There is here no human actor, as far as one can tell from Evans-Pritchard's account, who is thought of as having the operative power to establish the king-elect in his office. It is the ceremony of the stool itself which establishes the new pattern of rights and obligations. Nevertheless there is *someone*, it might be thought, from whom the authority for the assumption of office stems – it comes from Nyikang, and thus God. This must be so, if we are dealing with an operative act: there cannot be an operative act which does not gain its operative force from the authority of some person or group of persons; for an operative act creates a new pattern of rules, and there cannot be a created or instituted rule which is not created or instituted *by* someone, directly or indirectly. The notion of a rule's coming into existence on its own (in so far as this means something other than a convention springing up by tacit agreement), or simply from the existence of certain non-social facts, is indistinguishable from the notion of a non-instituted general rule brought into play by the instantiation of its factual conditions. Thus an operative procedure either must be carried out by persons who are re-garded as having the relevant authority, or it must be instituted or recognised by them as operative, when performed in given conditions. Otherwise there is nothing to mark the supposed operative action as being anything more than an event which meets the factual requirements for the applicability of a rule.

Operative and causal efficacy

Operative efficacy is evidently not causal efficacy. It should by now be clear, however, that a simple contrast between nature and convention is, here as elsewhere, treacherous. One cannot argue that, since operative effects such as the investiture of a king or the enactment of a law are not 'natural' effects, they must hold by convention. When we call a rule 'conventional' we imply that it could be altered simply and solely by people's agreeing on another arrangement. (This merely states a necessary condition of conventionality: it does not follow that every rule-constituted state which could be altered by general agreement is a conventional state. It is not *by convention* that a person – for example the President of the United States – holds an elective office.) Now if there are rules which can only be instituted or cancelled by those persons who have the operative power to do so, then they will hold, once instituted, whether those who are governed by them agree that they do so or not; and so even among instituted rules there will be those which cannot be said to be conventional. For, although the actual procedure by which the operative act is performed is a matter of convention, the operative authority to perform it, and the rights and obligations thus established, are not.

But let us consider further the conventional character of the operative formula. The *only* way in which a person who has the authority to do so can perform a particular operative act is by stating, or in some other way making it known, that he is performing it, or by making it known that its operative effects hold. There is nothing else which has to be or can be done for the operative act to take effect. (I ignore here the impure case of verdicts, where the statement deciding the facts of the case has an implicit operative force.) It is because an operative act consists purely in the creation or cancelling of rules, or rights and obligations, that its performance need require no more than an act of non-natural meaning which signals that it *is* performed. Moreover, publicity is the essence of operative actions – the consequences which are to take effect must be made clearly known. Hence the need for a codified formula in which the operative act can be couched. A set form is most likely to emerge where the need for clarity and publicity is greatest.

Operative acts are produced, then, by being *said* to be produced (the 'saying' need not be verbal, of course); to bring about natural effects, on the other hand, is more than a matter of laying down that they should hold. The fact that an operative action can be performed by certain persons and not others is of course one aspect of the non-causal character of operative efficacy. Causal effects can be brought about by anyone who has the technical knowledge which may be required and whatever equipment may be necessary. The only other qualifications that can discriminate between people with respect to a causal technique are the possession of skills and appropriate physical characteristics for the performance required; social status is irrelevant. With operative acts, on the other hand, knowledge of and the ability to perform the right procedures in the right circumstances is not enough. If the actor does not have the operative power to perform the act in question, the performance is null and void.

Now clearly, the contrast between the causal effects of an operative action and its non-causal efficacy rests on the distinction between the pattern of rules which obtain in a society, and people's beliefs about what pattern of rules obtains. It is evident that the connexion between being appointed a judge and being a judge, or between being raised to the peerage and being a peer, is not a causal one. Similarly, we need carry out no statistical investigations to discover whether all men who get married become husbands; not because there is here an obvious causal relationship, but because the relationship is not causal at all. Being a husband (judge, peer) is a social status in my sense of being a rule-constituted condition; and it is in *this* sense that operative actions can be said to take non-causal effect on social states of affairs. At the same time, of course, the marriage ceremony is itself an event which has a *causal* effect on people's beliefs about what persons are married, and thus on their beliefs about what new patterns of rights and obligations obtain – precisely by virtue of the fact that they perceive the ceremony as an action having operative force.

The special case of conventions

The distinction involved here is customarily elided in social science: when one speaks (as a sociologist) about who has authority in a society, for example, what is often meant is who is *believed* to have authority. There may be good space-saving reasons for this, but there is also, I think, another kind of consideration involved. The distinction between rules, on the one hand, and beliefs about and obedience to the rules, on the other, is clear enough in the case, say, of moral principles; but it is by no means clear when we consider conventions. What more is there to my dog's being called 'Fido' than that everyone thinks that to be his name and refers to him by it? Now a rule is one thing, a usage in accordance with a rule another. How then can a convention be both?

Deciding to call my dog 'Fido' is forming the general intention to refer to him by that name. If we take a group of people who together decide on a convention, the same point holds: the instituting of the convention consists in the general intention, which they collectively form, of acting in accordance with it. But what is it for a convention (which may be tacit, and never explicitly instituted) to *hold*? It is, in Lewis's words, (1969: 118), for there to be a "regularity in behaviour produced by a system of expectations", expectations in the case of each person about how most other people are mostly likely to behave, together with a conditional preference to behave in this way if most other people do. Some readers may prefer to think here in terms of a disposition to regular behaviour rather than a regularity in behaviour; the important point is that for a convention to hold in a group is no more than for the members of that group to have certain reciprocal beliefs, and based on them, certain conditional preferences.

Now sociologists tend to assimilate all rules to conventions. But if for a *conventional* rule to hold in a group is for people in that group to have certain beliefs and dispositions to behaviour based on those beliefs, there is, given the assimilation, no distinction to be drawn in the last analysis between the 'norms' and people's beliefs about what the 'norms' are. The assimilation, however, is mistaken. If we use the term 'morality' to cover instituted rules and obligations as well as moral principles, the contrast between morality and nature (including convention) would have more truth in it than the contrast between nature and convention (including morality) has. In other words, conventional 'rules' are included only with some strain among rules constitutive of the social. I have included them here because it seems to me that we have in mind a notion of the social as rule-constituted, we do so include them. It is, however, evident that a convention cannot be made to exist by a direct authoritative fiat, and cannot therefore be internally dependent on any act of that kind. Consisting as it does in a regularity of behaviour based on mutual expectations, it must always be the natural effect of causal antecedents.

These considerations make it clear that, since conventional 'rules' are not rules in the sense in which rules can be directly instituted or created, one cannot strictly speaking talk of conventions operatively created. (In a purely conventional set-up such as cricket the obligation to walk when given out by the umpire is in a sense 'conventional', but is at the same time operatively created by the umpire's verdict – more precisely, however, the overall framework is conventional, but the rule is not conventional relative to the framework.) What *can* be operatively created is a rule, acceptance of which would result in a pattern of dispositions to behaviour constituting a convention. Consider a society in which parents are taken to have the sole right of naming their children. Suppose a parent decides to call his son 'Clive'. Everyone then refers to him by that name. We can distinguish between the conventional fact that the son's name is 'Clive', which consists in the general usage of that name rather than another based on certain reciprocal expectations among the users, and the rule which the parents operatively issue, governing what the usage should be. It is not the rule issued by the parents, but the expectation-based usage it inspires, which constitutes the convention. If everyone were suddenly perverse enough to fly in the face of the parents' wishes by making it a general principle to call Clive 'Max', then the convention would change, but the obligation created by the parent's decision would not.[49] Clive's name would now be 'Max', although it ought still to be 'Clive'.

But so long as this procedure is clearly distinguished from the establishing of a convention in the sense simply of forming a general intention to act in a certain way, it would perhaps be pedantry to refuse to count it as an operative act directly creating the convention–constituted social state itself (so that the parent is counted as operatively conferring a name on his child).

Modern and traditional conceptions of the social

The foregoing discussion will serve as an outline of the logic of operative acts; we can turn now to see what application the notion has to the understanding of social behaviour and, in particular, of ritual. The account I have given of rules, rule-constituted social states and operative acts stands in sharp contrast to the way in which they are typically seen in traditional cultures.

There are three possible kinds of rule. (1) There are rules which no one can institute or issue (create), or cancel. (2) There are rules which can be established or cancelled by the agreement of those whose behaviour they regulate. (3) There are rules which can be established or cancelled only by persons who have a given social status with respect to those whose behaviour the rule governs (headmaster, parent, chairman) and who may or may not themselves be among those governed by the rule. One and the same rule may be classified differently by different people. For example, those who see it as an essential property of moral principles that they can neither be laid down nor abolished by any person or agreement of persons, would place the moral realm in the first category; Christians, on the other hand, have often been inclined to treat moral principles themselves as edicts issued by God. Human authority is similarly seen as delegated from Him. On the face of it, however, there is one rule which (as is often said) even they must place in the first class: namely, the rule that one ought to obey the rules issued by God. Others consider class (1) to be void for different reasons. They consider moral rules to be in some sense instituted or validated (and not merely recognised) by common agreement. They equally see all human authority as ultimately derived from agreement or consent. They too, however, must it seems place at least one rule in class (1): namely, the rule that one should be governed by rules which have been generally agreed upon. (It is only when agreement is taken in the sense of free unbargained acceptance that this rule becomes genuinely otiose).

Now one very general difference between modern and traditional conceptions here is that whereas our own tendency is to see the social framework of rules or norms in a conventionalist and/or contractarian light, the tendency characteristic of traditional culture is to see it as instituted and handed down by divine or heroic founders. (In Weberian terms, the contrast is between 'legal-rational' and 'traditional' modes of legitimation.) This difference poses no methodological problems of 'translation', for the traditional conception exploits one of the three concepts of rule, all three of which are familiar to us. But it may be suggested that there is *another*, crucial difference which does give rise to a methodological question. Whereas I have distinguished sharply between operative and causal efficacy, it may be thought to be precisely characteristic of traditional culture that this distinction is *not* made with respect to ceremonies which on the face of it have the character and function of operative action. Thus I mentioned earlier the investiture ceremony for the divine king of the Shilluk, and I interpreted it as a procedure instituted by Nyikang and deriving its operative force from his authority. What I did not mention, however, was that when the effigy of Nyikang is replaced on the stool by the king-elect, the spirit of Nyikang is believed by the Shilluk to pass from the effigy to the king. Thus for the actors the ceremony does not have the operative effect of investing the king with the delegated authority of Nyikang – the king *becomes* Nyikang and so comes to have Nyikang's inalienable rights. Since Nyikang is also in some way identified with God, the kingship is divine. The ceremony is thought to produce an ontological change, and not merely to confer rights and obligations on a person who did not previously have them.

In this respect the example is in no way untypical. It repeatedly turns out that ceremonies which could be interpreted as operative actions, conferring a new rule-constituted status on a person, are believed by the actors themselves to produce a natural change in his inner state, this change being characterised within the theoretical terms of the religious framework of the ceremony. Should we then say that the ceremonies are not operative acts – because they are taken to have the very different logic of causally effective actions which produce a *non*-social (in this case a supernatural or spiritual, as well as a physical) change in the person involved, *in virtue* of which he incurs new rights and obligations? Yet frequently such ceremonies have features which we associate with operative actions. For example, it may be thought that the procedures are only effective when performed by persons who have a certain social status. Again, very often the procedures which constitute the effective part of the ceremony serve to *declare* – either verbally or in a symbolic enactment, or both – what is being done, and in doing so (so the actors believe) to *do* it.

The Catholic sacraments

Here then is the puzzle. We have come back to the question of what legitimate divergences there can be between the actor's and the observer's descriptions of the point of a ritual. In chapter 3, the question was incompletely resolved. One approach discussed there started with the idea that a proper account of the logic of a ritual may show it to have a character and function which is misconstrued by the actors. There is no doubt, in the case of many apparently operative ceremonies in traditional cultures, that the actors themselves see them as naturally productive actions. Can these ceremonies nevertheless be correctly interpreted as operative acts? We need not in fact go beyond our own society to find a case-study which illustrates the methodological point perfectly well – for the sacraments of the Roman Catholic Church have the advantage of being familiar, well documented and much pondered by believers themselves.

Consider Baptism and Absolution. Both of these can certainly be interpreted as operative acts. They can be seen as serving to create a new pattern of rights and obligations: for the salvation of the soul and membership of the Church may be regarded as constituted by patterns of rights of which the major one is the right of eventual entry into heaven; and the remission of sins as the remission of an 'obligation' to eternal punishment. The sacraments are 'outward signs of inward grace'. If they are to be seen as operative acts, then the state of grace must be a rule-constituted status consisting of a newly acquired or re-acquired right to heaven. The Church's doctrine that sacraments produce their effect *ex opere operato* – that is, by their own efficacy rather than by the will or personal merits of the recipient or officiant – is consistent with this view. I can appoint you judge not simply because I want to, nor because of my own moral characteristics, but because I have the power to do so in virtue of the position I hold. Equally you become a judge not directly because of your personal virtues, but because the appointment has been made by a person with the power to make it. The same purely operative analysis could be made of *ex opere operato* efficacy: the sacraments must be performed by a priest, and a priest's authority is derived ultimately from God, who has vested in the Church the keys of the kingdom. The procedure of the sacraments, consisting as it does of 'matter' (i.e. action involving the use of sacramental 'instruments') and 'form' (words), is again strikingly reminiscent of the procedures of many other operative acts. The pouring of the water, for example, may be seen as a symbolic moral cleansing, just as the cutting of a ribbon to open a road is the symbolic breaking of a boundary.

Thus a perfectly coherent account can be given of these sacraments (and of marriage, ordination, confirmation) which, given the Catholic's acceptance of the moral authority of God, does full justice to their efficacy without incurring any accusation of magic. But the early Church, and the Catholic Church still, gives the power of the sacraments a quite different interpretation. Grace is conceived realistically as a spiritual force; the sacraments signify and contain grace in such a way as to produce it *ex opere operato* – "real, efficient causality is intended" (*Sacra. Mundi*, 1970, v: 380). In Baptism, the Council of Trent teaches, the physical act of washing with water together with pronouncement of the proper words is essential not as a "mere sign of faith", but for the efficacy of the sacrament. Although modern revisionist theologians seek to reinterpret these positions, the traditional view of the Church, still defended by orthodoxy, is clear (or rather obscurely realist, but clearly not 'symbolist'). The point is particularly obvious in the case of the Eucharist. No interpretation of it as an *operatively* efficacious symbolic act is consistent with doctrines of the Real Presence, in particular with Transubstantiation. It has the appearance of a magical binding or localisation of the god in a physical thing, of the kind which is familiar from other cultures.[50] Now an operative act cannot have ontological as opposed to prescriptive effects, and Puritan attacks on the 'hocus pocus' of the mass were not answered by an 'operative' interpretation. With this as with other sacraments the Catholic defence against accusations of magic was not that the power of sacraments was operative rather than causal: but that the causal power was God-given and hence could not be said to bind God.

The causal view of the sacraments, however, generates problems of its own. There can be no salvation without grace, the Church teaches – and grace is dispensed through the sacraments. In practice, however, for obvious reasons, the insistence on a formal sacramental act performed by a priest has to be relaxed. Thus the Church allows for Baptism by desire, and teaches that an act of perfect contrition can have the efficacy of absolution. But now is the sinner's act of perfect contrition productive of, or produced by, salvific grace? The orthodox idea of grace is of a divinely created healing medicine which cures the sin-caused ravages of the soul. The Church, as the accredited agent of God on earth, is the sole distributor, dispensing it through the sacraments. Thus: "The sacrament [of Penance], with dispositive causality, *completes* the process of repentance, *giving* the sinner grace and justification (my italics; *Cath. Dic. Theol.* 1967, II: 124). To fit in with this sequence, perfect contrition itself should produce the grace which cleanses the soul. But this gives a man greater power to save himself than has ever been acceptable to many believers. Outside the sacrament, the sinner must be *given* the grace to save himself through perfect contrition. Thus grace comes to be seen as a God-given force which boosts a man's spiritual strength in the face of temptation, giving him the power to repent. (Here it is obvious that grace is seen as a spiritual force rather than an acquired set of rights).

Furthermore, once a distinction is made between higher and lower forms of repentance, there is a natural religious tendency to suppose that it is the highest form which is required for salvation. But if perfect contrition is a *necessary* as well as a sufficient condition for reconciliation with God, the penitential sacrament is otiose. Considerations of this kind – the need for example to explain why there should be any particular urgency in absolving the dying – were advanced against the contritionism of the Jansenists. Even while admitting the *sufficiency* of perfect contrition, the Church ties it internally to the sacrament by means of the ingenious Trentine doctrine that repentance out of pure love of God must logically include a desire for the sacrament, given the fact that the latter was instituted by Christ as a means of reconciliation with God. But within the sacrament itself, the Church teaches, attrition is sufficient for the remission of sins. Given the view that *ex opere operato* efficacy causally produces an 'infusion of grace', this leaves Catholicism open to the accusation of purporting to provide a mechanical substitute for what can only be accomplished by a truly good will. Since attrition is repentance springing from a motive lower than the unselfish love of God, Luther castigated it as 'gallows remorse'. Catholics replied with the somewhat fine distinction between *timor serviliter servilis*, which is exclusively a fear of punishment, and *timor simpliciter servilis*, in which "while punishment is the actually operative motive, it is not considered as the greatest and only evil. It is seen as the loss of God and thus the sinner sees the ultimate evil of offending and losing God" (*Cath. Dic. Theol.* 1967, I: 207).

The believer's idea that the ultimate evil of sin lies in the offence

111

given to God may seem anti-human to the unbeliever, but points the way in which Penance can be interpreted with the notions of interaction code and operative action. If sin is an offence to God, equilibrium can be restored only by an apology. The feelings expressed in apology are good will towards the other, and regret for what one has done *because* it has injured or offended him. Thus the Church regards an unselfish love of God, and regret at causing Him offence, as a higher motive for repentance, higher not merely than the fear of hell, but also than the realisation of the 'intrinsic foulness of sin'. Now the expression of feeling in an apology can be more or less oblique, depending on whether acceptance of the interaction norms or the existence of real feeling is of importance in the relationship between the people concerned. The sacrament of Penance involves a derived, 'norm-regarding' form of apology, recorded and underscored by formality. Hence, within the sacrament, the precise feelings of the offender are not of primary importance (although there is, as it were, a bottom limit, at least in theory) – the sacrament is instituted by God as a shared procedure, common to all the faithful. In this we find reflected Catholicism's relatively 'social' view of the Church as a hierarchical, ordered community in which the relationship between a particular man and God is only one strand in the whole pattern and is mediated by 'secondary organisations'. An act of perfect contrition outside the sacraments will then have the nature of a special, personal plea which by-passes normal channels. As such the form of apology must be that which is appropriate to a personal relationship. This is a case, therefore, in which the basis of feeling is directly involved. For Protestantism, for movements like Jansenism within the Catholic Church, and typically (I think it can be argued) for modern Christianity in general, it is also the paradigm case. Apology to God is underived, spontaneous, private; it is not formal and follows no set procedure. In this it reflects Protestantism's relatively individual and 'privatised' or 'massified' view of the relationship between each man and God as personal, and set apart from others.

Again, an offence or injury creates an obligation to make amends, which can sometimes be discharged by the apology itself. In creating this obligation, it also creates an operative power on the part of the person offended to cancel it. On the side of the penitent, the sacrament of Penance is a formal apology to God, a piece of IC behaviour; on the side of the officiant, absolution is an operative act performed in the name of God, which cancels the obligation to make further reparation. Protestantism, rejecting mediated relationships with God, rejects in particular such a delegation of salvific power.

To sum up the results of this 'case-study': we can make good sense of absolution, and of what might be called its first-order level of meaning to Catholics, by interpreting it as an operative act. When it comes to a reflective interpretation of this first-order level of meaning, however, our description differs from that of the traditional Catholic. Here we have a case in which one can see how the observer's description of the action could legitimately diverge from that of the actor. The divergence entails an explanatory commitment: the rite, with its first-order level of significance must have explanatory priority over the actor's second-order interpretation. In other words, the belief that the sacrament has a causal power to generate the cleansing spiritual force of grace must be explained (if the observer's description of the action's rationale is the correct one) as a reifying *misinterpretation* of the sacrament. Of course the observer's own interpretation of the sacrament still makes sense of it only *within* its overall framework of religious belief. Only given the belief in God on the part of the actors can the sacrament be seen as a familiar mode of social life – an order issued and disobeyed, an apology made and accepted. It is this familiar form of social relationship which (on this view) is then reified by the religious into transcendental soul-cleansing machinery. Anyone who wants to take the further, Marxian or Feuerbachian, step of seeing the theistic framework itself as a reification must explain what it is a reification *of*. But the less ambitious approach which is suggested by our consideration of Penance would be in accordance with two guiding principles which apply more generally to traditional religious thought: (1) traditional religious rites are based on a belief in spiritual beings who are integrated into human society by the normal hierarchical ties familiar within the particular society itself; (2) a social status is seen not simply as constituted by a set of rights and obligations, but as consisting in an inward spiritual condition of those who hold it, and on which the rights and obligations rest. Operative actions which change a person's status or role cannot therefore be clearly distinguished from causal actions which change his psycho-physical condition, and will typically have a religious or sacramental character.

In the last two chapters we have been considering two very different modes of social action: the interaction code and operative action.[51] These modes of action nevertheless have a number of interesting points in common.

(1) Both, though in different ways, consist in 'outward' signs of states or changes which stand in need of a sign, being socially significant but not themselves directly and publicly observable. In the interaction code it is the feelings or attitudes of the actor which are signalled; in an operative action it is the change in the pattern of rules, or rights and obligations. An operative act does not merely signal, but in doing so *effects*, such a change. And, somewhat similarly, at the more derived end of the interaction code, where what is primarily in question is not the expression of feeling but the acknowledgement of norms which prescribe such expression, to say "I apologise" or "I welcome you" *is* to apologise or welcome.

(2) With both operative acts and IC behaviour there is a tendency for stereotyped, conventional formulae of speech and action to emerge.

(3) Each mode of action is often, though by no means invariably, ceremonialised (and the ceremonial may itself often follow conventionally stereotyped patterns). Extending the points made about ceremony in the last chapter to operative ceremonies, we can generally say that to ceremonialise an action is to put its occurrence formally on record and to present it as an ideal pattern of social life.

(4) IC behaviour and operative action are both fully *communicative* action: the actor non-naturally means something by his performance. The ceremonial which may surround it is not communicative in the same sense. Naturally it expresses (evinces, testifies to) the actors' sense of the importance of the occasion; but it is not a way in which *they* express (say) *that* they think it is important.

Ceremonial marks what is ceremonialised; and in the case of interaction ceremonies what is marked is itself a mark of something which stands in essential need of a mark. But it is the inner mark which is fully communicational, and which can properly be said to 'say something'. And in the case of operative action the performance 'says it does something and does something by saying that it does'. In this formula we are already very close to the kind of remark which often turns up in anthropology as a way of characterising magic.

The emerging possibility that there is some connexion here will be considered explicitly at the end of chapter 9. But some of the ground has been prepared in this chapter. To distinguish between operative and causal efficacy I introduced a notion of the 'social' as rule-constituted. A change which is in this sense social is a change in the pattern of rules, of rights and obligations, which is in force in a society. The relation between the operative act which brings about such a change and the change itself is not causal but internal. The social, thus conceived as rule-constituted, does not and cannot belong in the domain of causality. This is no idealism – the operative act does of course have causal effects on people's *beliefs* about what rules are in force. (As noted on pp. 104–6, these points are not strictly correct when purely conventional rules are included among those constituting the social. A convention cannot strictly speaking itself be an operative effect.)

Now the suggestion may be made that a distinction of this kind between the social and the non-social, and with it between operative and causal efficacy, is characteristically absent in a *traditional* system of thought. Of course in so far as the distinction is not made in a given culture, we should not say that operative acts are conceived in it as causally *rather than* operatively efficacious. The point just is that they are not distinguished in this way. But with this there arises the possibility that actions which, if efficacious, could only be causally so, might nevertheless be modelled on the paradigm of an operative act; and this idea may well appear to have considerable bearing on the analysis of certain kinds of magical action.

The point will, as I have said, be considered in chapter 9. But before turning to theories of magic we must first consider explicitly a pair of concepts on which many of them are based – the concepts of symbol and symbolic action.

8

Symbols and symbolic action

Symbolic character of some operative formulae

'Ritual', I have said, is (for social anthropologists) pre-eminently symbolic action. It also brings together things which apparently have little to do with each other: ceremony and magic. And yet, in the notion of symbolic or mimetic action, the two seem to have a common strand. The magician kills his enemy by pushing pins into his wax effigy. The priest cleanses a man's soul by washing his body. The local dignitary opens a road by cutting a ribbon. In each case the symbolic or mimetic quality of the action is obvious, and in each case an action, by being *symbolically* enacted, is actually performed (or so the actor believes).

When we consider our own society we find that the ceremonies which involve such mimetic representations are very commonly operative acts. A great many of these ceremonies involve a performative utterance ("I declare this road open", "I name this ship the S.S. *Fido*") and also a symbolic enactment (cutting a ribbon, breaking a bottle of champagne). I have drawn a rough distinction between ceremony and the operative act ceremonialised. There is on the one hand the operative formula or 'script', and on the other the formality and elaborateness of scale of ceremony. Formal behaviour serves to mark out what is being done, or the relations between the persons involved and so on. Thus a policeman's uniform marks out his status, and the formal caution, "I hereby warn you" etc., marks out the fact that a warning is being given. Neither the uniform nor the obligative warning, however, constitutes ceremonial – the specific feature of ceremonious formality and elaborateness of scale is not merely that it marks out the occasion but also that it heightens it, gives it aesthetic expression. Now it seems artificial to include the cutting of a ribbon to open a road as part of the operative act itself, and to separate it from the degree of ceremoniousness with which the act is carried out; for in this case the symbolic action clearly has the character of an embellishment, to be placed in the 'beautiful and profitless' rather than the utilitarian category.

But this is no longer the case when we turn to the sacraments: here matter and form are equally officially indispensable for the efficacy of the act. Baptismal washing is not a 'mere sign of faith', nor an embellishment to mark out the importance of the occasion, but an integral part of the efficacious formula. The same point would, I think, hold for most operative actions in traditional cultures which involve a similar kind of mimetic representation. (I use the word 'operative' here subject to the discussion at the end of the last chapter.) If we remember that an operative act is, necessarily, performed by being *declared* or in some other way *shown* to be done, then it becomes plausible to suppose that the kind of mimetic enactment which we are considering stems from the logic of operative action, rather than from the embellishing and heightening function of the ceremonial which may surround it.

Thus the connexion made by the notion of symbolic action (supposing for the moment that there *is* a connexion to be made) is not between magic and ceremony, but between magic and operative action. Here the value of distinguishing between the operative and the ceremonious aspect of operative ceremonies is evident. We must now consider a little more closely the concept of symbolism and symbolic action involved.

Definitions of 'symbol'

Anthropologists have often made much of the importance of ritual symbols.[52] And yet quite what is to be meant by the concept of symbolic action has remained remarkably unclear. "Whatever has meaning", says Radcliffe-Brown (1952: 143), "is a symbol and the meaning is whatever is expressed by the symbol." But this, though commendably straightforward, casts the net too wide to catch the specific concept required by symbolist writers, including Radcliffe-Brown himself (as Beattie remarks, 1964: 69). Parsons, in discussing Durkheim's theories about religion, aims for greater precision (1968: 416):

the essence of a symbol is first that its importance, value or meaning is not inherent in the intrinsic properties of the symbol itself, but in the thing symbolised, which is by definition something else; secondly, that insofar as it is a symbol it has no intrinsic causal connection with its meaning, the thing it symbolises, but looked at in such terms the relationship between them is arbitrary, conventional.

All cognition, according to Parsons, is couched in symbols; but whereas scientific thought involves only a "simple symbolic relation" – that is, the symbol refers directly to an observable object – a religious symbol has a "double symbolic reference". For science the word 'stone' simply refers to an observable object; for religion, the stone itself may symbolise a 'scientifically' undetectable religious reality. "That there is a need to...'visualize' and concretize the content of 'religious experience', must apparently be taken simply as a fact about human beings as we know them", Parsons says, though there is evidence "that on certain philosophical and mystical planes this intermediary symbolism tends to be altogether dispensed with" (p. 423). The intermediate symbol may be either an "actual object of empirical experience" (a stone) or an "imaginary object" (Zeus). Where no actual physical object is used as a symbol, then, something having perceptible qualities – although of course never perceived, since it does not exist – is 'imagined', and plays the necessary symbolic part.

Parsons does not explain why this should ever be necessary (why should one not restrict one's religious symbols to the perceived objects lying conveniently around in one's immediate environment?), nor why it is that, when the 'imagined' religious symbols *are* visualisable and concretised, they are invariably personified; and when they are not personified, they are conceived as *forces*, which are no more visualisable in religion than they are in science. The immediately relevant obscurity in Parsons' account, however, lies in the move he makes from the notion of a symbol to that of a symbolic action. Thus he writes: "Insofar as sacred things are involved in action, the means–end relationship is symbolic, not intrinsic" (p. 431). But although we have been told what it is for a thing to be a symbol, we have not been told what it is for an *action*, let alone a *means–end relationship*, to be symbolic. A similarly obscure move, from the concept of a symbol to that of a symbolic action, is made by Beattie in his *Other Cultures*.[53]

Beattie begins by distinguishing among *signs* – "things that have meanings and which stand for something other than themselves" – between *signals*, "which give information about some state of affairs", or "convey a specific message", and *symbols*. The latter are positively characterised in three ways. First, they are not "merely conventional": normally some underlying appropriateness links the symbol with the thing symbolised, as when a serpent biting its tail stands for eternity, an owl (large-headed, inscrutable) represents wisdom, or whiteness expresses purity. Secondly, symbols normally stand for an "abstract notion" (power, group solidarity, familial or political authority) and not for events or concrete entities. And thirdly, what is symbolised is affectively charged, and this affect tends to get transferred to the symbol (a national flag, for instance).

How then do symbols enter into symbolic action? The natural answer here is that in a symbolic performance an action with respect to something which serves as a symbol *represents* an analogous action with respect to the thing symbolised. Although this account does not on the face of it fit all the actions which Beattie wants to include in the 'symbolic' category, it is I think the account which he has in mind; and it is the account which I shall also adopt. Before considering it further, however, we need to decide on a reasonably precise use for the term 'symbol'.

Types of meaning; denotation and representation

Two distinctions are required to begin with. To take the first of these, an object or an event or state of affairs may be said to have a meaning because it *stands for* (denotes, designates, represents) something; or again, an event or state of affairs (but not an object as such) may be said to have meaning in so far as (1) its occurrence implies that something is the case, or (2) it is brought about by someone in order to state that something is the case (command that it should be, question whether it is etc.). Thus, for example, the word 'Fido' *denotes* Fido, such-and-such a numeral *designates* such-and-such an athlete or convict, the pepperpot *represents* a car and the table top *represents* the roadway in my reconstruction of an accident. On the other hand, a broken twig *indicates the fact that* something has passed by, a red traffic light indicates that one should stop, an arrow at the bottom of the page, that one should turn it over. Notice that it is the twig's being broken or the light's being red which conveys the message. Similarly, the position and direction of the arrow convey the instruction to turn over – the arrow in itself does not denote or represent anything at all. In short, it is the fact that the twig, traffic light or arrow has one rather than another of a number of possible characteristics which conveys the information; they do not, as objects, stand for or designate anything. Where, on the other hand, something has meaning in the sense of designating (representing, denoting, standing for) something, I shall call it a *designator*.

The distinction is obscured by Beattie, for he classifies *signals* (which 'convey a specific message') as a species of *signs* (which 'stand for something other than themselves') – he cites, for instance, a red traffic light as an example of a signal. Hence it remains unclear whether the distinguishing feature of symbols is that they do not convey a 'specific' message, or rather that they cannot be said to convey a 'message' at all, in the sense in which the pepperpot which represents a car, or the name 'Fido', does not in itself convey any information.

The second distinction which we need is between what Grice has called *natural* meaning – that is, the sense of meaning in which clouds mean rain, a blush means that the person blushing is embarrassed, a broken twig can mean that something has passed by; and *non-natural* meaning – the sense of meaning in which a red traffic light means that one should stop, in which the word 'Stop!' means that one should stop, in which my smile of greeting means that I am pleased to see you.[54] Given this distinction the apparent conflict between Parsons, who stresses the 'arbitrary, conventional' character of the relation between symbol and thing symbolised, and Beattie, who insists that a distinctive feature of the relation is that it is not 'merely conventional', is easily resolved. Parsons' point is that the meaning of symbols is non-natural meaning – a symbol has its meaning by convention, in that it has the meaning which people who share it agree it to have. Beattie on the other hand, when he remarks: "Signs can be merely conventional, as in a language;...This is not the case with symbols" (Beattie 1964: 69), is pointing, as we have seen, to the fact that symbols often have an underlying appropriateness or rationale. (The notion of underlying appropriateness has more than one sense here, however, as a comparison between that of whiteness as a symbol of purity and that of a snake biting its tail as a symbol of eternity shows.) So the meaning of the symbol is non-natural, but at the same time its connexion with the thing symbolised is not an arbitrary one.

The distinction between natural and non-natural meaning is again obscured by Beattie's category of 'signals', for he includes in it examples of both natural meaning (a footprint, which means that someone has passed by) and non-natural meaning (a traffic light). Often, however, it is just this distinction which the terms 'sign' and 'symbol' are used to mark – as, for example, by Price (1969, ch. 6, 'Signs and symbols'). Parsons, who adopts what Price calls the "Symbolistic theory of meaning", in effect uses the word 'symbol' in this way. Now as Price also points out, this gives the term a very wide sense; it is too wide, in fact, to be useful for present purposes, for it straddles both sides of our first distinction.

That distinction was between, on the one hand, what has meaning in that it designates or stands for something, but on its own conveys no message – so that it stands in need of completion before it can play a role in a communicative act – and, on the other hand, what has meaning in that it can stand on its own as conveying a message. Our second distinction, between natural and non-natural meaning, divides this latter category into two. (Not the former – there are no natural designators.) The first of these subdivisions is commonly covered, as I have said, by the term 'sign'. When 'sign' is used in this way, 'natural sign' is a pleonasm.[55] It is in the nature of signs in this sense that they are not *given* their meaning; hence they can only convey a fact (and not a command or a question, for example), and they can have no internal syntactic structure: that is, they cannot be broken down into parts which have a meaning, but which stand in need of completion, and do not in themselves constitute self-contained information-conveying signs. If a sign has parts, the relation is that between a part which conveys a part of the information and the whole which conveys the sum of the information. (That is why there are no natural designators.)

The second of the two subdivisions consists of self-contained communicative acts (the word 'act' being used here in the usual broad sense): they include sentences, written or uttered, but also for example traffic lights, demonstrative gestures, skull-and-crossbones designs on a wire fence etc. As the examples show, they may or may not have a syntactic structure. Communicative acts are covered by the wide sense of 'symbol' (as contrasted with 'sign'), but must be excluded for present purposes. Yet to use the word 'symbol' to signify anything which has meaning in that it stands for or designates something would also still cast the net too wide. The word 'chastity' is not on any reckoning a *symbol* of chastity. Hence we need to distinguish within the inclusive class of designators between those which are symbols and those which are not. One possible line of distinction is the Stebbing/Beattie type of contrast between 'natural' (i.e. in some sense 'non-arbitrary') and 'conventional' (i.e. 'arbitrary') designators. The distinction however is a difficult one to draw (see Price 1969: 173ff.), and is in any case not the one which is required – as will be seen in the next chapter – if our aim is to throw light on the symbolic character of magic.

For this purpose, the distinction we need is that between designators which can be said to *name* or *denote* a thing, and those which can be said to *represent* it. Thus 'Fido' names or denotes Fido – it does not represent him; on the other hand, a serpent biting its tail represents eternity – it does not name it or denote it; equally, the pepperpot represents – it does not name or denote – a car in my reconstruction of the accident. Symbols can now be characterised as designators which *represent* what they stand for.[56]

The discussion so far may be summarised in the two diagrams below. Notice that, on this usage, symbols can have any degree of arbitrariness. Selection of the pepperpot to represent one of the cars involved in an accident is completely arbitrary; the hull-shaped plastic counters which represent fleets and the shell-shaped ones which represent armies in the game of Diplomacy are presumably less arbitrary, as is the use of a wax effigy to represent an enemy. Again, the letters 'UN' *represent* (not arbitrarily) the name 'United Nations', but *denote* the organisation. Words themselves have been said by some philosophers to be arbitrary symbols of ideas. (Here incidentally the distinction between representing and denoting serves to bring out the fallacy involved in the common objection to such a view, that it interposes a 'veil of ideas' between language and reality, with im-

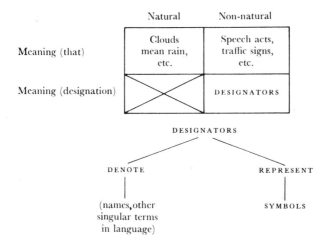

minent danger of idealism. For, right or wrong, the position is
not that words denote ideas, but that they represent them. What
they and the ideas they represent denote, *is* reality.)

Let us consider further this notion of representation. One
thing is often made to stand for another – the pepperpot for a
car, for example – by some such phrase as 'Let *x* be *y*', 'Suppose
x is *y*', 'Call this *x*, "*y*"' (not, be it noted, 'Let this *x* name *y*', 'Let
this pepperpot *name* Smith's car'). Thus the symbol substitutes for
the thing symbolised. We are sometimes said to think in words
– certainly we communicate with each other in words. *In* words,
about things. We do not, in contrast, think *in* symbols *about* the
thing symbolised: symbols are good for thinking 'with', not 'in'.
The symbol is itself made the object of thought. It stands for,
or *re-presents*, the thing symbolised. In other words it makes it
present to the senses, and is treated for the purposes of symbolic
action as being what is symbolised. On this picture the structure
of a symbolic action is clear: it represents or enacts an action,
event or state of affairs in which the thing represented by the
symbol plays a part analogous to that which the symbol plays in
the symbolic action itself. Thus the Nuer sacrifice a cucumber
which represents an ox; I move a plastic counter which represents
an army into a coloured sector of a Diplomacy board which
represents Silesia; an official cuts a ribbon which represents a
physical boundary to open a road; a magician pushes hot needles
into a wax effigy which represents an enemy and so on. The actor

may himself have a role in the symbolic enactment, as a symbol or *in propria persona*, or he may be a backstage manager (as in the Diplomacy case).

It is worth noting that a number of actions which one would normally call symbolic are not, at least on the face of it, symbolic or mimetic actions in the present sense. Take for example the gift of a gold watch to an employee of long standing. The gift expresses, testifies to or, as one might naturally say, symbolises appreciation. But it is not obvious that the gift is to be construed as enacting a gift or transfer of some other thing which is symbolically represented by the gold watch. Nor do we need any such construction to explain why the gift of a gold watch should express appreciation of service – the instrinsic value of the gold watch is the obvious factor involved. Of course the watch does in another sense have a certain symbolic appropriateness: it serves as a reminder of the *time* spent in service by the recipient. But, important as this kind of symbolic meaning often is in giving one a richer understanding of what people do and say, it needs to be firmly distinguished from the notion of a mimetic action in which 'symbols' play a role in the particular sense of representing 'something other than themselves'. Otherwise the important and specific insight which I think is contained in the idea of magic as symbolic (mimetic) action can all too easily get lost in sententious vagueness about the general place of symbolism in human life.

But if symbol is mere substitution, it is itself a convention, and cannot, ∴, be thought of as metaphor in Ricoeur's sense of providing a surplus of meaning by the combination of differing "semantic" fields.

Durkheim and Frazer

To this rule Durkheim's account of magic provides an apparent exception. For Durkheim (and, in a closely associated sense, for Mauss) magic is individualist, religion collectivist. Since he has defined both religion and magic in terms of the notion of sacredness, Durkheim tries to make this supposed contrast, rather than any distinctive pattern of belief, the defining characteristic of magic *within* the general domain of the sacred. The magician has a clientele, whereas religious rites unite their practitioners in a congregation or church (Durkheim 1915: 43ff.). Religion is shared in a social group as a common binding legacy, a constitutive element in the identity of the group. But magical beliefs, however widely shared, do not unite the believers into a moral community: to borrow phraseology from Weber, religious rites are communal actions; magical activity, even where it mobilises the co-operative effort of a large number of individuals, is only societal action. Again, according to Durkheim, failure to observe a stipulated religious practice is sin; but to ignore a beneficial or danger-averting magical rite is no more than imprudence.

There is real insight in these contrasts of Durkheim's, but they cannot be taken as providing *criteria* which distinguish the magical and the religious along the rough lines of demarcation which in practice he himself clearly had in mind. Magic, as pre-definitionally understood along these lines, is not invariably performed as a service, implying no communal bond, by specialists for laymen – it can itself be a non-specialised, lay activity. It is not always performed by people acting on their own – it can, essentially, involve the interaction of a group of practitioners, who may organise themselves into a communal association or club. Religious observance, on the other hand, can be individual and private – an objection Durkheim recognises but fails to avoid. Some religious rites are supererogatory, some are purely 'instrumental'; and some rites which would be called magical are hedged by prescriptions which it is not simply dangerous and therefore imprudent, but *wrong* and therefore dangerous, to break.

But the decisive objection is that many of the great integrative rituals which Durkheim had in mind contain a mixture of what would normally be called magical elements in a religious framework. The 'opposition' between the two 'institutions' of magic and religion does not exist as a general fact. As an example, consider the sacrifices which Kalabari make to water spirits, at shrines in the creeks of the Niger Delta.[57] A shrine contains a sculpture representing the water spirit in question. The spirit is called by drums which beat out its name, perhaps for an hour or more, while the sculpture is stripped, washed, repainted and purified. Eventually the spirit is localised in the sculpture. Facing the sculpture, the priest invokes the spirit and, by pointing the animal offering towards it, transfers its spirit to the god. The invocation complete, the animal's throat is slit, some of its blood is smeared on the sculpture itself or on the cloth in which its loins are draped, some parts of it are left to lie before the sculpture, while the rest is cooked and eaten by the congregation.

The sacrifice is clearly a religious rite; but should we not say that belief in the localising and confining power of the sculpture and the drummed-out name is a magical belief, and that the transfer of the animal victim's spirit by the act of pointing it towards the sculpture is a magical action? If so, then we have here magical procedures essentially involved in a ritual framework dictated by religious belief. An example closer to home is the cleansing of original sin by the application of water in Baptism. The power of the sacrament is, so the Church teaches, God-given, and cannot therefore bind God. But in as much as it is conceived to have an ontological effect on the soul rather than being thought to have a purely operative character, it still has the characteristics of what is commonly discussed under the heading of 'magical action'.[58]

Durkheim's proposed criterion does not tell us on what grounds we are inclined to discriminate 'religious' and 'magical' elements in such rites. Religions create moral communities in that they conceive of spiritual hierarchies in which particular groups of men share a common ultimate status. They are ruled, helped, judged, befriended by a common divinity, which may itself serve a higher divinity which rules over other divinities and thus over other men. In this way a religious community is unified and, within its unity, differentiated. This is the integrative force of religious belief which Durkheim saw, though he tried to present it as an integration effected directly by collective ritual actions.

But in distinguishing religion from magic in this respect he showed himself to be working with a conception of magic which he took from Frazer: the conception of a body of techniques – based on a belief in impersonal sympathetic powers – having an existence independent of the institutions of religion. Such an institutional framework of belief, if it existed, could not itself have the integrative force that shared religious beliefs can have, because it would not postulate an extended spiritual hierarchy in which people are bound together by the authority of spiritual beings beyond themselves. Thus Durkheim's notion that religion has this binding, integrative character, which magic cannot have, already rests on Frazer's contrast between a belief in personal agencies and a belief in impersonal powers, and hence on a distinction between the contrasted patterns of thought which provide a rationale for, respectively, religious and magical action.

Now it has often been pointed out how wide of the mark is the conception of religion and magic as distinct and autonomously comprehensive world-pictures, each giving rise to independent institutions and practices, and to specialists – priests and magicians – who feel a professional animosity towards each other. But the purely *analytical* distinction between religion and magic as belief in personal versus belief in impersonal powers, on which it is based, remains on the face of it a useful one. In itself, however, it is not adequate, as Frazer himself saw. "It is true", he says (1911, 1, 1: 225; 1957: 67–8),

> that magic often deals with spirits, which are personal agents of the kind assumed by religion; but whenever it does so in its proper form, it treats them exactly in the same fashion as it treats inanimate agents, that is, it constrains or coerces instead of conciliating or propitiating them as religion would do. Thus it assumes that all personal beings, whether human or divine, are in the last resort subject to those impersonal forces which control all things, but which nevertheless can be turned to account by anyone who knows how to manipulate them by the appropriate ceremonies and spells.

The distinction which is made here between magic and religion is that beliefs about the world on which magical procedures are based either make *no* reference to personal intermediaries between the rite and its effect at all or, where they *do* invoke a personal intermediary which is presumed to produce the required effect, they suppose it can be brought into action by the binding power of a *spell*, or some other magical rite, rather than the appeal of a *prayer*. What then distinguishes magic from 'practical' or 'scientific' techniques? Although Frazer calls it "a truism, almost a tautology, to say that all magic is necessarily false and barren; for were it ever to become true and fruitful, it would no longer be magic but science" (pp. 222; 65), he has no need to build the falsity of magical beliefs into his definition of magic. What he does in effect is to define it in terms of his account of its rationale: magic is that set of practices which get their point from a belief in the laws of similarity and contagion. So, from a logical point of view, 'science' and Frazerian 'magic' are not mutually exclusive terms.

Turning now to contemporary anthropology, we again find, as I have said, that the distinctive character of magic is in practice understood by reference to the beliefs which are thought to underlie it. On the question of what these beliefs are, there are three main lines of thought. (1) There is the conception of magic as an attempt to instruct or bind the actions of beings, more or less personified, which the magical practitioner supposes have the power of producing the effects he aims at. (2) There is a common underlying acceptance of the 'homoeopathic' and 'contagious' character of magical analogies, along more or less Frazerian lines.[59] (3) Perhaps most influential, and most diffuse, is the idea that magical action is in some way based on conceptions, or rather misconceptions, of the relationship between nature and culture, or 'convention' in general, and in particular between symbolism or language and the world. If Frazer is the major origin of the second line of thought, then one could point to Tylor, among anthropologists, as perhaps the earliest to have laid stress on belief in the power of symbols over what is symbolised as a central characteristic of the magical consciousness. But this thesis has evidently been in the air for some time quite apart from Tylor's writings. Ogden and Richards (1949, ch. 2) wrote of the 'denotative fallacy' and traced a belief in the power of words to it. Malinowski, in his supplement to their book and elsewhere (1935, 1949), concurred, writing of the 'mystical relation' between symbol and referent in magical language. More recently Beattie (1964, 1966) has proposed that magic is based on a belief in the efficacy of symbolic enactments; Horton (1967, 1970, 1973b) has revived Tylor's emphasis on the lack of a clear distinction between language and the world as a distinctive feature of traditional thought, and has suggested that magical objects serve as physically embodied and hence manipulable surrogates for words; and – still in the same area, though more marginally – Tambiah (1973) has attempted to explicate the notion of magic in terms of a distinction between the 'conventional-persuasive' as against the 'scientific-predictive' use of analogy.

The magic of commanding spells

There is, I think, *some* basis for each of these three lines of thought. Let us examine first of all the relation between magical action and concepts of intervening agency. The important distinction here was that epitomised by the contrast between *prayer* and *spell*. In fact, however, we need to distinguish three 'ideal-typical' patterns of thought.

Prayer can consist simply in a communion with the god: commonly, however, a prayer takes the form of a request – and this for present purposes is the relevant case. A man prays to a god, asking for the recovery of his son from illness, or a bountiful harvest, or for his own spiritual salvation. Such a request presupposes a belief that the god is able either to accede to it or to refuse it. The believer's conception of the god has written into it not merely an idea of the god's powers, but also of his interests and dispositions. The god has an interest in the fortunes of the religious practitioner and in his moral life, and can be prevailed upon, other things being equal, to help him in a worthy project. Prayer is thus effective, when it is, because it gives the god a *reason* to act. The same point applies to those religious actions which are conceived to be bargains or exchanges of gifts with a spirit or god. Again the action presupposes some conception of the interests and purposes of the god which dictates, for example, the suitability of the offering made; and it serves to give the god a reason for making a reciprocal gift.

'Magical' compulsion, on the other hand, can take two forms. In each the preferences, dispositions or interests of the compelled agency are irrelevant, for it is *not* by means of an appeal to them that the agency is made to act. The first of these two patterns of thought follows the logic of instruction or command. Here we have the notion of an agent's performing a required action because he has been instructed or ordered to – *whether or not* he wants to. The model is that of prescriptive compulsion: if I have the authority to give you an order then you are obliged to obey, whatever your preference in the matter. The preferences and dispositions of the magical agency are irrelevant, then. In fact it is often personalised only to the extent presupposed by the logic of command: it is ascribed simply the ability to understand and the power to fulfil orders within a given domain. From an intellectualist point of view, the comparison which springs to mind is with the scientist who ascribes to a theoretical entity only those properties which are required for the explanatory functions which it is invoked to fill. (This may suggest one reason why the religious conception of a god or spirit is usually much richer in content than the concept of an agency which plays a role only in such rites.)

Although an appeal to preferences and interests is relevant to the logic of a request in a way in which it is not relevant to the logic of a command, both contrast with the second pattern of magical compulsion, in that carrying out a command or acting out of one's own purposes are both forms of intentional action. The third of these ideal-typical patterns of thought, however, envisages, as Frazer says, a constraint or coercion on the magical agency such that the behaviour to which it is bound could not be called *intentional action* at all. The model for magical compulsion in this case is natural rather than prescriptive necessity; if the magic were to have the same effect on a human being, it would be beside the point to think of it as acting on his behaviour through his will.

Thus the first two patterns are concerned with a mediating agent in the strict sense of invoking it *as* an agent. The relationship which the practitioner sees himself as establishing with it is – although it may only be minimally so – a social one; in each case, that of request and that of command, the concept involved has its paradigms in human interaction. In the third case, on the other hand, it is really irrelevant to the *logic* of the magical action that the entity, real or imagined, which is bound by the rite is conceived as an agency rather than as an inanimate thing.

One of the best-documented and most often referred-to studies of what one might call the magic of commanding spells is

Evans-Pritchard's of the Azande.[60] A Zande spell typically consists of (1) an identification of the medicine or magical object used, and (2) an issued instruction to it (or occasionally to the person or thing at which the magic is aimed). For example: "You are *gbau* [medicine used to make a person invisible]. When I stalk the man who has brought my vengeance on him may he not see me" (Evans-Pritchard 1937: 407). From the logic of their spells one would infer that Azande conceive of their medicines as agencies with limited powers, understanding and a capacity for response: in rather the same way as they conceive of their oracles, in fact. Facts which bear this out are that, for example, a magical object or medicine "may lose its power unless its owner is happy at handing it over to another man, and it will not work unless it sees it has been paid for" (p. 430); and that, when vengeance magic is used against an unknown offender, it is able to seek out and punish the right person. As Evans-Pritchard says (p. 389): "Azande say of it that 'it decides cases' and that it 'settles cases as judiciously as princes'"; "Azande speak of the medicine as searching for the criminal and eventually, being unable to find him, for he does not exist, returning to slay the man who sent it forth." (It is thought that the soul of the medicine does this travelling.)

Zande medicines, then, are primitive agencies, capable of response to instructions from the right man; their actions, however, are not traced back to a personality – that is, to preferences or motives (of justice, for example, or of interest in the magician's welfare).

Spells couched in the form of commands can be found throughout the world, sometimes spoken in a special language, supposedly the one understood by the magical agent.[61] The agency thus addressed may be specially tailored, as in the Zande case, with no further characteristics written in than are necessitated by the logic of the spell, or by some other requirement, such as the possibility of ownership; or it may be a demon or a spirit of a more personified kind, perhaps with a variegated role beyond that of intermediary in a specialised branch of magic.

In the second form of magical compulsion, the beings on whom the magic is exercised are properly speaking the objects rather than the agents of magic. Hence the magical rites often involve no spell. Very often the magic is performed either to summon the agency or to keep it away. (The genie, it will be remembered, is summoned by a rub on the lamp, in order to be given its instructions.) Kalabari water spirits are summoned to the sculptural effigy by the drum; throughout the world, on the other hand, demons and witches are kept at bay by a variety of magical precautions.[62]

There is in fact no point in distinguishing between magic which in this way binds the agencies postulated by the believer, and magical rites designed to constrain the behaviour of human beings – such as love-magic and so forth. Frazer is right in claiming that in *this* pattern of magic, in which personal beings, human or otherwise, feature as objects rather than as agents of the magical process, they are no part of the logic of the magical action: its effectiveness, that is to say, is not to be understood in terms of the actions of an invoked intermediary, as is the effectiveness of action which follows the first two patterns.

In practice, of course, the ritualist's attitudes and behaviour towards the intervening agency he invokes may not be so readily analysable, for a number of distinct reasons. In the first place, the character of what he says and does may not be so sharply in focus as to admit of classification within the three patterns. Secondly, our own notions of what is a command and what is a request, of what is a free or intentional action and what is compelled behaviour outside the agent's voluntary control, are explained in terms of paradigms or central cases and do not have sharp lines of demarcation. Hence a set ritual pattern within a determinate framework of belief may still not be easily classifiable, because the story it implies falls within these peripheral areas. But these two points do not make the separating out of ideal patterns which can then serve as an orienting framework any less necessary.

A third point, of a rather different order, is that a unified sequence of rites, directed towards a single spirit or god, often can, as Firth among others has pointed out, mingle requests with commands, entreaty with admonition (see Firth 1971, ch. 7: 223ff.). Only if it is assumed that religion and magic must be separate institutions or systems of ritual action, however, can this be an *objection* to the drawing of a distinction between the two in terms of the respective notions of 'prayer' and 'spell'. So much the worse for the assumption: the fact that people can take up both religious and magical attitudes towards the spiritual agencies they conceive, and indeed mingle them in a single rite, is more usefully seen as a pre-theoretical datum for any analysis of the notions of magic and religion than as something to be ruled out by the anthropologist's definitional fiat.[63] Yet the Frazerian version of the proposed contrast is inadequate: in effect it takes into account only the first and third patterns – there is no room in Frazer's discussion, as Philsooph remarks, for spells, in particular for spells which take the form of a command. On closer inspection, Frazer's distinction involves two separable criteria: one distinguishes between rites which presuppose an intervening agency and rites which assume no such intermediary, the other distinguishes between 'propitiation' on the one hand and 'coercion' through a natural power which works equally well on beings and things on the other. The first of these is exhaustive but, as Frazer recognises, too crude; the second is still too crude, but no longer exhaustive.

This leaves open the question of where to draw the line, or indeed of whether it is worth drawing one; but before coming back to it we need to take account of those forms of 'magical' action which are not based on the logic of an intervening agency and a commanding spell. For the moment, then, I shall continue to use the term 'magical action' simply to cover the types of 'ritual behaviour' to which it has customarily become attached.

Contagious transfer and symbolic identification

I shall proceed by developing a classification of my own and then relating it to that of other writers. The first pattern to be considered follows what I shall call the logic of *contagious transfer*. For example, a man chews salmon-berry sprouts (a white flowering raspberry) and spits them out onto his child in order to make the child grow rapidly like the salmon-berry (see Benedict 1933). He aims to *transfer* the property of rapid growth from the berry to the child. The general pattern here is:

(I) A certain property, F, is transferred from the initial object, *a*, to the goal object, *g*, by some method of transfer such as surface contact, admixture, incorporation, inhalation etc.

To give another example, mussel shells are reduced to ashes and smeared on a child – the property to be transferred being the shell's long-lasting, enduring qualities (see Benedict 1933).

Four points are worth noting here: (1) The identity of the transferred property must of course be given in terms of the classifications of the culture studied. What is there regarded as a single property, instantiated in different objects, may not be counted as one and the same property by us. (2) The question of similarity or dissimilarity between the objects *a* and *g* is irrelevant to the logic of the magical act. (3) The question of whether *a* and *g* have been in contact, or associated in some other way *before* the magical action, is equally beside the point (except in so far as previous contact may already have effected the transfer). (4) There is nothing in the logic of the action which rules it out *a priori* as an effective technique. On the contrary, there are plenty of apparent causal interactions in every person's experience which can be presented as following just this pattern: a man eats hot food and becomes warmer, a flaming torch is applied to dried grass, which bursts into flame, a man comes into contact with a leper and catches leprosy, and so on.

A quite different pattern of magical action follows the logic of what I shall call *symbolic* or *mimetic identification*. It is here that the notions of symbol and symbolic action explained in the last chapter become relevant. The stock examples of damaging an enemy by damaging an image of him, a piece of his clothing etc. fit this pattern well. The image, or article of clothing, represents the enemy; it is therefore in my sense a symbol of him. But I also want to claim that the symbol for the magician is not, as we say, *merely* a symbol: it is taken in some sense as being, or manifesting, the enemy – 'mystically participating' in him, to use the Lévy-Bruhlian phrase. Thus, on my interpretation, the general pattern of thought involved is this:

> (II) Some form of change is produced in an object, *s*, which is taken as standing for, or 're-presenting', the goal object, *g*. So, *s* 'is' *g*. Therefore the same change is produced in *g*.

Thus, for example, pins are pushed into the chest of a wax effigy, and the enemy feels shooting pains in his chest and dies.

The points to be noticed here are: (1) The change produced in *s* and the change produced in *g* are one and the same change, for the magician; but here again the identity of the change has to be seen from the point of view of the practitioner. (2) A similarity or some form of previous association between a and g may well suggest s as an appropriate symbol for g, but it need not be present in every case. (3) On my account, the principle of the magical action is necessarily defective: it rests on an identification of symbol and thing symbolised – but the two are necessarily distinct.

These two 'elementary structures' of magical action can be combined into a third. For example, a man ties the navel string of his baby boy around his wrist while he is at work, in order to transfer his own technical proficiency to his child (see Benedict 1933). Thus the father's proficiency at work is fed, by contagious transfer, to the navel string and hence, by symbolic identification, to the child. The general pattern here is:

(III) A property, F, is transferred from a to s. $s = g$, hence F is transferred to g.

I shall return to the question of how comprehensive an account of magical actions this three-fold analysis gives, and what form elaborations on and divergences from it can take. First I want to compare it with some other theories: to begin with, with Frazer's. Frazer says (1911, 1, 1: 52; 1957: 14):

If we analyse the principles of thought on which magic is based they will probably be found to resolve themselves into two: first, that like produces like, or that an effect resembles its cause; and second, that things which have once been in contact with each other continue to act on each other at a distance after the contact has been severed.

On the first of these two principles 'homoeopathic magic' is based, on the second, 'contagious magic'. Frazer's theory is vaguely stated and further confused by the heterogeneity of the examples he gives. Does the dictum that 'like produces like' mean that a like change in one object produces a like change in another? Presumably not – for this applies equally to *contagious* magic. The similarity must be in the objects involved, and not merely in the changes produced. The point is obscured by the fact that the 'Law of Similarity' is stated in terms of the relationships between events, while the 'Law of Contagion' is stated in terms of substances and their powers.[64]

For the purposes of contrast it will be useful to consider a rather sharper version of Frazer's account than Frazer himself provides.

So let us take the 'Frazerian' or 'sympathetic' theory to be that magic is based on two principles:

A change produced in one object, *a*, may produce a like change in another object, *g*, if

(A) (Similarity) *a* and *g* are in some way similar;

(B) (Contagion) *a* and *g* have in some way been in 'contact'.

The first point to be noticed about this double-barrelled theory is that it fails to cover the magical actions which fall under my category (I). For in their case, (i) previous contact or similarity between *a* and *g* is irrelevant, and (ii) the magical procedure consists of bringing the two together in order to transfer the required property, and not of acting on *a* in order to produce a like change on *g*. The salmon-berry has not been in previous contact with the child, nor is it similar to it; and the desired effect on the child is not brought about by making the berry grow fast: it grows fast already. Frazer himself places such examples of contagious transfer in his category of contagious magic – despite the fact that they make nonsense of the 'Law of Contagion', which is supposed to have something to do with continuing action at a distance. In fact Frazer makes a point of the magician's presumed belief in such action, and of his supposed postulation of an invisible ether to explain it; but in our two patterns, at least, 'action at a distance' is precisely what magic eschews. In (I), the objects *a* and *g* are brought together, while in (II) the whole point of the magical object, on my interpretation, is to make *present* or *manifest*, under the form of the symbol, the object of the magician's rite.

And yet, although contagious transfer is not covered by the sympathetic theory, it does to some extent vindicate the more general Frazerian position, which sees magic as based on empirical beliefs which happen to be false but might have been true – unlike those views according to which magic stems, so to speak, from confused semantics: that is, from misconceptions of the relation between language or symbolism and the world. If the sympathetic theory could give a successful account of the more restricted field of magical actions which I have interpreted in terms of pattern (II), then the position would be fully vindicated. So the next question is: Are there grounds for preferring the symbolic to the sympathetic account of this more restricted domain?

As Beattie remarks, "Nobody in their senses could possibly believe that all things that share some common quality, and all things that have once been in contact, are continually affecting one another; in a world so conceived almost everything would all the time be affecting almost everything else, and all would be chaos" (Beattie 1964: 206). Admittedly, this is hardly a knock-down objection to the sympathetic theory. Frazer could perfectly well reply that his account purported to provide only necessary, and not sufficient, conditions on magical efficacy – whether because he was providing an incomplete version of the magician's comprehensive, if implicit, beliefs, or a comprehensive account of an incompletely worked out set of beliefs. But the reply would have to be assessed for its plausibility against the rival symbolic view: and it is in the context of this comparison that Beattie's point gets its force.

The magical image of the enemy – a seemingly standard item for magic-workers throughout the centuries and the world – is among the first of Frazer's huge collection of examples in his chapter on 'Sympathetic magic' (1911, 1, 1: 52–219; 1957: 14–62). He sees in it an example of homoeopathy. And yet here is a case in which it seems essential to the magic practised on the image that the image should *be an image* of the enemy: that is, that it should stand for or represent the person who is the object of the rite. It is the symbolic relation between the image and the person which is directly relevant, and the likeness only in so far as it contributes to the function of the symbol: that of making the goal object present and actable on. For if it is simply the likeness which is believed to underlie the efficacy of the rite, then why should the rite not have the same effect on many other persons to whom the effigy is equally similar? (Such magical images, it may be noted, typically have a highly schematised character.) The Frazerian has possible answers to this, but the answer provided by the symbolic theory is a much more satisfying one.

When we consider magical symbols of the enemy more generally, it becomes obvious that the symbolic thesis is more comprehensive and provides a simpler explanation of the variety of magical objects involved. Magical bundles which include things which have been in contact with the goal object (nail parings, hair, pieces of clothing etc.) are explained equally well by the Law of Contagion and by the symbolic theory – according to which they are tokens taken as *standing for* the goal object. But the magical object need be neither like, nor previously associated with, *g*. A case in point is Frazer's very first example: 'North American Indians' who, "we are told, believe that by drawing the figure of a person in sand, ashes, or clay or *by considering any object as his body*, and then pricking it with a sharp stick or doing it any other injury, they inflict a corresponding injury on the person *represented*" (my italics; 1911, 1, 1: 55; 1957: 16–17). In short, while there may be some underlying appropriateness which gives the magical object its connexion with the goal object, there need not be: the only essential is that it should be *taken as* representing it. It needs a very liberal stretching of the already elastic 'Laws of Sympathy' to account for this fact. On the other hand, the point fits neatly with our discussion of symbols in the previous chapter. There it was noted that while a symbol may often have some natural appropriateness which fits it to the object represented, this characteristic is not constitutive of its semantic status *as* a symbol: what is essential for this is simply that it is taken as standing for an object, as when the pepperpot is taken to represent a car involved in an accident. There are many bases on which an object might be selected as an appropriate symbol for another, and it would be strange if similarity and previous contact were not prominent among these, especially when liberally construed; but it is also true that there need be no basis of appropriateness to link the symbol and its object at all.

This logical point – namely, that a symbol means what it is taken to mean – brings out another divergence between the Frazerian and the symbolic theory. The Frazerian magician regards his rite and its effect as two distinct events between which there holds a causal connexion; and there is for him nothing which dictates that the magical cause must be a humanly produced event: "he tacitly assumes that the Laws of Similarity and Contact are of universal application and are not limited to human actions" (Frazer 1911, 1, 1: 53; 1957: 15). But symbols have a non-natural meaning; hence if the efficacy of type (II) magic rests on the symbolic meaning of the magical object, then it might be argued that there can be no magical efficacy without a magician who *gives* the object its symbolic meaning. Beattie remarks (1964: 206): "Magic is not thought to take place by itself, as Frazer's theory implies. It is only when men make magic, that is, when they perform rites, that results are to be expected." Now if this statement is interpreted narrowly as meaning that magical effects are believed to occur only from rites which are performed with the intention of producing them, then it is certainly false. It is easy to find observances dictated by a fear of unintentional magical consequences – witness for example the various avoidances observed in many cultures by the kin of hunters or warriors out on an expedition. But this fact is not inconsistent with the symbolic theory, for a piece of behaviour might be regarded as a symbolic enactment, and therefore magically efficacious, even if not intended to have that effect: the actor may have been unaware of the standard symbolic meaning attached to such-and-such an action in such-and-such a context in the culture concerned or, knowing it, he may nevertheless have acted unintentionally as under the description of his action provided by that cultural meaning.

What of natural events, not humanly produced – which for the Frazerian magician could be as magically productive as any others? I have not been able to find any beliefs which could plausibly be taken to be evidence for the acceptance of the possibility of events which are not humanly initiated (nor initiated by other agents) but which have magical consequences. Quite apart from this difficulty, however, the argument becomes at this point more than a little inconclusive. Suppose such beliefs are not to be found. What else could one expect, replies the Frazerian, given the occasion-bound, untheoretical nature of magical thought? Suppose on the other hand that they are to be found. In this case the symbolic theory has defences at the ready. In the first place, it must be shown that the magical events are believed to be not only independent of human action, but also independent of the actions of gods or spirits who might have conferred on them their symbolic character. In the second place, to say that magic is based on the logic of symbolic enactment is not necessarily to say that the magician himself has explicitly formulated the thought that it is *because* he treats the magical object as a *symbol* that he considers action on it to have magical power. If practitioners of magic were to generalise explicitly and consistently on the patterns of thought which underlie their behaviour, then, on the Frazerian theory, they would admit the possibility of an inanimate universe operating on magical principles. On the symbolic theory, they would think there could be no magic in a world which contained no symbolising intelligence. (Or, more probably, they would relinquish belief in magic.) But it is hardly worth speculating on what the speculations of magicians might be, were they to speculate. For if my argument is correct then a study of the forms of magical action and the effects aimed at by the performers is on its own sufficient to show that Frazer's theory is mistaken. It gives no account of contagious transfer, and it gives a far less plausible account of magical action of types (II) and (III) than does a combination of the logic of symbolic enactment and contagious transfer.

Leaving Frazer now, let us compare the present version of the symbolic theory with that of some other writers: I particularly have in mind here Beattie and Horton, and before them Tylor. The first point of difference is that they consider, or at least give the appearance of considering, that all magic is based on a belief in the efficacy of symbolic action. The present account on the other hand takes the logic of symbolic enactment as one of a *number* of patterns of thought which are involved in what would commonly be called magical behaviour. Secondly, Horton in particular assimilates symbolic magic to a belief in the magical power of language, whereas I consider the two to be separate. I shall return to this below, but for the moment I want to concentrate on a third point.

My account differs from Frazer's not merely (1) in arguing that a good deal of magic rests on symbolism, but also (2) in taking its ultimate logic to be that of identification, so that the ideal-typical magician takes himself to be really performing the action which he symbolically enacts. He does not, therefore, envisage two distinct events, the rite and its effect, with some kind of causal relationship between them. Now this identificationist version of the symbolic theory is not the only possible one: one could also adopt a causalist account, according to which the magician does see the symbolic action and the event enacted as two distinct events, and considers that the former has some kind of power to produce the latter. It is not clear which of these alternatives Beattie would be inclined to follow; I take Horton's view, on the other hand, to be a causalist one.[65] Yet there are, I think, a number of considerations which count in the identificationist's favour.

In the first place, although the image-impaling example fits both positions equally well, others fit more naturally into the identificationist than the causalist account. Consider, first, a Zande way of coping with ulcers, quoted by Evans-Pritchard (1937: 409):

If you want to rid yourself of...ulcers go to the centre of a path and take some grasses in each hand from either side of the path and tie them together. Then squeeze an ulcer and put some of its pus on the grass, saying 'You are ulcer. I place you on the grass. I tie you in the centre of the path...Ulcers, you leave me altogether and go after any man who breaks you in the path'.

An identificationist account catches the spirit of the description given by Evans-Pritchard's Zande informant more aptly than does the causalist view: the pus extracted from the ulcer and tied in the centre of the path is taken as concretely manifesting, as *being*, ulcer. The act epitomises one of the great themes of magic: that of the evil bound by the magician and set loose by the unwitting victim.

Notice in particular that the spell begins with an explicit identification of the pus as ulcer. Such explicit identifications of the magical symbol with the object it stands for are often associated with symbolic magic. A Malay spell, one of the comparatively few spells quoted by Frazer, is spoken over a wax figurine: "It is not wax that I am scorching. It is the liver, heart, and spleen of So-and-so that I scorch."[66] Again, compare the words of conse-cration spoken in the Roman Catholic mass ("This is my body... this is my blood...") which are taken as effecting the 'real change' of transubstantiation *ex opere operato*, or the beating out of the water spirit's name over its sculptural effigy in Kalabari ritual. Admittedly this consideration is not decisive. The causalist can always argue that such procedures are ways of identifying the magical object *as* a symbol, rather than of identifying it *with* what it symbolises. But this reply is strained (and in the case of the Eucharist, we know it to be incorrect).

There are, in any case, two other points to consider. It is, in the first place, not difficult to see the magic of contagious transfer as an uncritical extension of a familiar pattern of action which is often effective. But why should people believe in the *causal* efficacy of a purely *symbolic* enactment? For Horton, the belief is ultimately traceable to a view of the relation between language and the world which sees words as having power over things. But symbolic magic cannot thus be assimilated to verbal magic, for it presupposes a belief, not in the power of the symbol, but in the power of action *on* the symbol – as I shall argue in the next section. On the other hand, Beattie's account is, I suspect, the result of a kind of double exposure, superimposing two incompatible views of magical action. At one moment the magician is presented pushing pins into his wax effigy, a sophisticated figure working out his frustrations, and aware of the 'purely symbolic' (i.e. non-instrumental) character of his act. Our next view shows the same figure engaged in the same pursuit, but this time perfectly convinced of the instrumental efficacy of the rite. When the two are rapidly alternated we get the magician who believes that a purely symbolic enactment can be instrumental in bringing about the event dramatised.

The identificationist view does in contrast offer some understanding of why it is that a symbolic enactment might be thought to have magical power. To see this we must begin with the contrast, pointed out in the last chapter, between names, or generally words, and symbols. We think and speak in words about things; symbols in contrast *stand in* for their objects – they make them present to perception and action. The picture associated with the first of these two relationships is one of language as a medium which mirrors the world, but remains independent of it. Such pictures are notoriously misleading, but in this case it is precisely the misleading character of the picture which is suggestive. Words in language refer to objects in the world. But symbols *are* objects in the world – which stand in for other objects.[67] The relation between words and things is that of conventional reference, in which words somehow get hooked onto things, and the things are 'brought to mind'. The relation between symbols and things is that of conventional identification: symbols are *taken to be* their objects. The final piece of the jigsaw is an often noted point: namely, that traditional cultures are relatively insensitive to the distinction between the conventionally constituted and the naturally given – whereas it is characteristic of modern thought to devote much philosophical reflection to the question of what the exact character of the distinction is. So we must leave out the words 'purely conventional' from our description of the relations between words or symbols and things. The referential hook is then no longer seen as giving a word a purely conventional pull on things: language appears as having a powerful causal grip on the world. Malinowski tackled this point in his supplement to Ogden and Richards' *Meaning of Meaning*. But on the same principle, symbolic identification is no longer seen as a purely conventional identity: the symbol in some sense *is*, or participates in, the reality it represents.[68]

This brings us to the second point. It might be objected that the magician knows as well as anyone else equipped with a pair of eyes that the image and the enemy, his rite and the enemy's death (even supposing it occurs), are spatially and temporally distinct. Of course this is true – but it is not an objection to the identificationist account. The traditional Catholic can tell as well as anybody between the host he eats and that received by his fellow communicant. But he nevertheless believes that each is the living body of Christ. There is no sharp distinction made here between the symbol as mere representation, on the one hand, and as manifestation, or revelation, on the other. Thus the Council of Trent speaks of the Eucharist as the "symbol of a sacred reality", while enunciating the doctrine of the true and substantial presence of Christ.[69] Or, as Evans-Pritchard says in *Nuer Religion*: "Nuer know that what they see is a crocodile, but since it represents Spirit to some of them it is for those people, when thought of in that way, also what it stands for."[70] We cannot make such a pattern of thought fully clear, since it is intrinsically incoherent: to make it clear in this sense would be to defuse and falsify it. The clarity we can legitimately look for is clarity in the characterisation of what the obscurity is and where it lies. But of course the magical consciousness cannot itself represent *to* itself, clearly and synoptically, the obscurity which lies at the heart of its own thought, or it would resolve it, and with this resolution lose its magical character.

Magic and language

We must now turn briefly to the relation between magic and language. A comprehensive and systematic survey of verbal magic would be a monumental task for a scholar. Here I am concerned only with two questions. The first is: What is the relation between verbal and symbolic magic? And the second, which is much more difficult to get hold of, is: Is it anything more than coincidence that certain magical procedures follow a pattern very similar to that which is typical of conventionalised operative acts? Nevertheless, if we are to get our bearings, some general outlines, however schematic, are required.

Firstly, then, words can feature in magic in three ways: in utterances, in inscriptions (though obviously not in non-literate cultures) and finally as supposed entities logically if not causally independent of both utterance and inscription. Secondly, we shall need a cross-cutting distinction, between magic which draws on language in as much as it involves the casting of spells, and magical action which operates specifically on or with words – often names – without necessarily involving spells, or complete speech acts of any kind at all.

I begin with the magical use of words. Here we need to separate three ideas. (1) There is the idea of a 'natural' or 'world' language in which things, beings, qualities answer to their *real* names. This idea does not depend essentially on the objectification of words. (2) Words may be treated as magical symbols, standing for the object with which they are associated (by being its name or in some other way). In this case, the words are typically treated as invisible pseudo-material particulars. Of course words, as sounds, are objective particulars in that they can be misheard, and that one and the same sound can be heard by more than one person. But the magician also seeks to capture and confine them, and to act on them in ways appropriate to a material object. In literate cultures, an inscribed token of the word may also be used in this way, as a magical symbol to be acted upon. (3) Finally, words may be treated as independent, mobile agencies with creative powers of their own. I shall return to this idea later.

The first of these attitudes depends on the idea that things have real names which are discovered rather than being purely 'man-made'.[71] The real name is then thought to have the power to call up the thing. It may be noted that this power is typically attributed to the *real* name, and not to *any* reference, however circumlocutory, made to the object. Hence the secrecy attached to 'real' names, particularly one's own, and the taboos on their pronouncement. The belief in the evocative power of names tends to merge into the third attitude – the view of words as active agencies in their own right. Thus the often-quoted belief in a god who creates himself by speaking his own name could be considered an extension, to its logical extreme and beyond, of the idea of creation as the calling up of things by their name out of non-existence. Or the god himself might be considered to be the personification of the primordial word.

But it is the second attitude which is of interest from the point of view of my first question. A sorcerer – Azande believe – goes at night to the threshold of a hut "and calls out into the doorway. A man within answers. The sorcerer takes his words and shuts them up in his medicine and departs. Now the man who has spoken into the medicine is seized by it. The sorcerer having departed the man is left with sickness caused by the medicine, for it strikes him down violently in the night."[72] There is here a combination of two patterns; firstly the usual Zande belief in the efficacy of magical medicines, and secondly the pattern of symbolic identification, by which the medicine, in acting on the words, acts on the man. Another interesting example of a magical act expanded by the use of words as magical symbols is a Caffre rite mentioned by Frazer, which consists of shouting a thief's name "over a boiling kettle of medicated water, then clapping a lid on the kettle and leaving the name to steep in the water for several days", in order, apparently, to 'reform his character' (Frazer 1911, 2: 351; 1957: 326). Here there is a double symbolic element: in the washing of the name as representing the person, and the washing of the person as representing the cleansing of his character.

In my view, then, such magical operations on names are a species of symbolic magic, and imply no belief in the special power, magical or otherwise, of words. The point is simply that, given an objectified view of them, words can be used as appropriate symbols of the objects with which they are in one way or another associated. My account here is diametrically opposed to Horton's, who argues (1970: 90–1):

The magic which is so prominent a feature of African and other pre-industrial cultures turns out in nearly all cases to be an extension of [the] belief in the creative and controlling power of ordinary speech ...Much African magic, it is true, seems to centre on the use of non-verbal symbols...[But] Their function is not to 'say' something that words cannot. Rather, it is to give the ephemeral words of oral speech an increased durability and power of penetration, and hence to increase their creative and magical efficacy.

Actually the opposition made here is a false one. Certainly, symbolic objects do not 'say' anything inexpressible in words – they do not say anything at all. Their function is to *be* something. Horton's thesis, while not actually inconsistent with the use of magical objects other than inscribed words in literate societies, certainly does not explain it: nor does it explain why words other than names are used in magical acts. But the real mistake involved seems to me to be a failure to distinguish between genuine cases of verbal magic (such as that of the Trobriander who breathes his words into his medicine or directly into the goal object) in which words are granted active powers, and those cases in which the words are passively *acted upon*, and which are a special case of the general category of symbolic magic. Once this distinction is clearly made there can I think be no doubt that symbolic magic is not reducible to a belief in the magical power of words.

We must now turn to the second broad link between magic and language: the spell. Here a central distinction was made by Evans-Pritchard between what he called the 'saying' and the 'formula' spell, and it is classically embodied in the contrast between Zande and Trobriand magic (Evans-Pritchard 1929: 625). In the saying spell, it is the content or message which is important: the exact words used may vary. The underlying reason for this is not hard to find: such spells, as in the case of the Azande, are what I have called commanding spells – they follow the logic of giving instructions to a magical agency. The exact words in which the instructions are couched are unimportant, so long as the message is clearly understood. To this, however, one must add a qualification. Sometimes the command may be given in a language which is understood by the magical or demonic agency, but not by the giver. According to Tambiah (1968), for example, sections of the mantra in Sinhalese healing rituals and exorcism ceremonies are phrased in demon language, an "unintelligible polyglot mixture" supposed to be understandable to demons, although it need not be to the exorcist. The idea that such agencies understand only certain kinds of language seems to have been applied in the converse direction by Sinhalese villagers, who until recently spoke a special language, not understood by demons, within the precincts of the threshing room – rather like Russian aristocrats speaking French in front of the servants (Yalman 1968: 524). Now it is evident that, when instructions have to be given in a language which is not understood by the instructor, great attention may have to be paid to the exact form and pronunciation of the utterance. One is reminded of the British tourist of traditional fame, painstakingly following the pronunciation in his phrasebook, in order to tell the garçon to get him a cup of tea. Instructions given in demon language may not have the flexibility of the saying spell, but they still follow the underlying logic of command, and they need imply no belief in the magical powers of the language used – any more than the British tourist thinks of French as a sacred language (except in the sense of ritual avoidance) or of his phrasebook as a compendium of powerful words.

The formula spell, on the other hand, is of considerably greater interest to the student of verbal magic. Trobriand spells require memorising: they often involve unusual or archaic words, and they are usually delivered, according to Malinowski, in a specific kind of sing-song. No doubt these features are to some extent explained by the fact that the spells are handed down verbally from generation to generation. Such verbal transmission, aiming at exact reproduction, is affected at every stage by 'channel noise': as is illustrated in a well-known children's game called Telephone. But Trobriand magic also exemplifies the third of the three ideas on the power of words which I distinguished above. The spell is often believed to be a "primeval text which somehow came into being side by side with animals and plants, with winds and waves" (Malinowski 1935: 218); also, however (p. 216),

in every act the magician's breath is regarded as the medium by which the magical force is carried. The voice...'generates' the power of magic. This force is either directly launched on the earth or the tuber or the growing plant, or else it is indirectly conveyed by the impregnation of a substance, usually herbs, which is then applied to the object to be affected.

Here we have the belief in the active or 'creative' powers of words (embodied in breath) in its pure form.

Magic and operative action

But there is another, extremely interesting, feature of Trobriand formula spells. Although, as Philsooph has pointed out (1971: 186), they often contain commands and instructions, their characteristic kernel nevertheless seems to be either an impersonal present-tense description of the consequences of the magical action, or a first-person present-tense description of what is being done, in terms of its consequences. With this fact in mind Malinowski asserts (1935: 238–9):

> I think that if we stripped all magic to its essentials, we would find simply this fact: a man believed to have mystical powers faces a clear blue sky and repeats: 'It rains; dark clouds forgather, torrents burst forth and drench the parched soil.' Or else he would be facing a black sky and repeats: 'The sun breaks through the clouds; the sun shines.'

(It will be remembered that the word 'spell' itself originally meant a recital or narrative, as in 'gospel'.) If we allow ourselves this degree of idealisation and simplification, then a suggestive comparison emerges between the Trobriand magician and the Catholic priest performing a sacrament. Briefly: (1) In both cases the action consists of a prescribed formula, which takes the declarative form of a first-person (or an impersonal) description of what results are being produced, and is *itself* thought to produce them ("I absolve thee", "I baptise thee"). (2) This is often accompanied, again in both cases, by a symbolic enactment of what is being done. (3) The action is believed to be effective only when performed by certain persons who have the power to perform it. (4) These persons are distinguished, from our point of view, not by their 'natural' characteristics and capacities, but by their 'social' relation to others: namely, by standing in a continuous line of legitimate succession to an original founder who instituted the prescribed form of action which they follow (Christ, or, in the case of the Trobriander, a god, hero or original ancestor). Thus in both cases the power involved is ultimately received by delegation from a divine (or quasi-divine) source – although Trobriand magic is concerned with this-worldly goods, whereas the sacraments are soteriological instruments directed to the next world.

One is of course comparing here actions from very different

cultures, and, necessarily, isolating them from their overall context. The Catholic Church has, as I have pointed out in various places in the last few chapters, devoted a good deal of interpretation to the character and function of the sacraments. That said, however, the similarity of form and function remains striking, and is not, I believe, misleadingly produced by the omission of contextual background which, if supplied, would give the two patterns of action a completely different meaning. Furthermore, it is difficult not to feel some kind of connexion here with those conventionalised operative actions which comprise a set performative utterance ("I declare this road open") with an appropriate 'performative' symbolic action (cutting a ribbon). I earlier argued that the sacraments might plausibly be described as operative acts, despite the fact that the orthodox Catholic view of them is inconsistent with the logic of operative effects. But this interpretation depended on the possibility of 'denaturalising' the orthodox view of their consequences, so that they could be seen as acting directly to create a new pattern of rights and obligations, rather than as producing an ontological change in the soul in virtue of which the new pattern was incurred. Trobriand magic, directed unambiguously to purely natural effects on crops, winds and weather cannot be so treated.

Here we have three patterns of institutionalised behaviour, all of them exhibiting a very similar structure of prescribed actions and words, all effective only when performed by persons with a specific *social* qualification, quite independent of technical capacity or skill. One can be presented as operative action, and is thus interpreted by the performers. Another, although it could be interpreted as operative action, is viewed by its exponents as possessing a creative 'natural' power. The third, similarly seen by the performers, could not, by the very nature of the objectives which it sets for itself, be 'rationally reconstructed' in an operative guise. Is there nevertheless anything of importance to be gleaned from their common form? If the religious logic of prayer and the magical logic of the commanding spell are extensions, beyond human society, of speech acts which presuppose the conditions of a social hierarchy, then are 'formula' spells an extension beyond human society of speech acts which presuppose the social context of operative authority?

There is not much one can do with this question as it stands.

A more promising approach is to ask why, in either case, the specified procedure should take the form it does. In the case of institutionalised operative acts, there were two questions: Why should they usually take the form of performative statements, often accompanied by symbolic enactments? And why should this form be conventionalised and prescribed in a set formula? The answer to the first question was that operative acts take effect on shared systems of rules. Someone who has the authority to change such a system of rules *can only* do it by making it publicly known *that* he is doing it – nor is anything else, by way of causal procedures, required. Hence the way to perform an operative action is to make it publicly clear that one is performing it, and this involves stating it in a performative utterance or in some other way, as by a symbolic enactment. The answer to the second question is in general connected with the usefulness of having a settled and recognised procedure for making clear exactly that is being done. But in addition to this, where operative authority is delegated by a founder who has instituted a procedure through which it should be exercised, then an action which is not carried out in due form takes no effect.

If we can take these points across to the Trobriand 'formula' spell, then its underlying logic emerges as a belief that the magician has a direct creative power over nature which he receives by delegation from a hero or god who has also instituted a procedure by which it should be exercised. The magical power is direct in the sense that it is not thought to reside in an action which itself produces the results aimed at, and could thus be indifferently performed by anyone who knew how to do it: the laid-down procedure is a necessary but not a sufficient condition of magical efficacy. But the power required for its operation is *conferred* on the magician. It is direct also in the sense that, as with an operative action, the only way in which the magician can exercise it is by making it clear that he is doing so, in other words by stating what he is doing. The question then is: Why should this be so? – and it is here that the notion of magical power as being modelled on the analogy of operative authority could come in.

This of course is speculation. It is based, as I have said, on a similarity of form which may be no more than coincidental, and is in any case achieved only after a little idealisation and simplification. And yet it does seem to me that there is something here that would bear thinking about. Two points, however, might come up as objections to any attempt to account for the formula spell along some such lines. In the first place there is the already mentioned Trobriand belief in the creative power of the magical words *themselves*, conceived of as active agencies. Such a belief is not consistent with the magician's supposed underlying view of the spell – as a performative utterance which takes effect through his own quasi-operative power over nature; for *this* idea is in no way dependent on a belief in the magical power of words. There are various ways in which one could try to get round this point. Moving away from the specific case of the Trobrianders, however, a more general difficulty is involved. The symbolic enactments which often accompany magical spells are seen from the point of view of the 'operative theory' as non-verbal ways of saying what is said in the spell. On the identificationist view of symbolic magic, on the other hand, they are seen as ways of acting on the goal-object itself by acting on the symbol which manifests it. The latter theory is more in tune with a wider body of cross-cultural ethnographic material. And we should also remember here a fact noted earlier: namely, that in 'traditional' cultures social statuses and institutions are not seen as constituted by patterns of rules, or rights and obligations; a man's social attributes tend to be seen as consisting in an inward spiritual condition, outwardly marked by ceremony, *in virtue* of which he incurs the rights and obligations which *we* think of as exhaustively constituting the attributes themselves. The installation of a person in a new office or role has a naturally productive character, then, which goes beyond the direct creation of a new rule-pattern. And the ceremonies involved commonly follow the familiar magical patterns of contagious transfer (as in the laying on of hands to pass on authority) or of symbolic identification. So far from serving as the non-magical foundation on which magical actions are by analogy based, they are rather, it seems, themselves conceived in terms of magical instrumentalities.

However even if symbolic magic (as well as contagious transfer) falls outside the range of the proposed 'operative theory', it might still be argued that the identification procedures associated with it, by which the magical symbol is made to manifest the goal object itself, fit the theory rather well. The Malay spell quoted earlier (p. 142) provides a good example. Or consider again the Shilluk investiture ceremony considered in chapter 7 (p. 101). Nyikang's victory over the king-elect is in accord with the normal pattern of symbolic magic. On the other hand, the ceremony in which the effigy is replaced by the king-elect on the royal stool is not itself an enactment in which the magical identification of the symbols is taken as already given, but a process in which the king-elect *becomes* identified with Nyikang. In such examples as these there is scope for the idea of magical action as modelled on operative declaration.

Yet I am by no means sure that the scope of the operative theory, despite the apparent difficulties which I have mentioned, might not after all be shown to be far greater than this. If it is, and if it covers both symbolic identification and contagious transfer, then the interpretation of these which I have suggested would have to be completely revised – with *both* patterns being seen as a way of signalling what is being done and thereby doing it. If this were so, then using 'symbolic' broadly, to mean 'having non-natural meaning', *all* the forms of magical action which we have considered would be 'symbolic'. But neatly comprehensive as this is, the balance of plausibility still seems to me to lie with the account of contagious transfer and symbolic identification given in preceding sections – though I find myself hesitating between the two views.

Concluding notes

The various patterns of thought which I have separately discussed in this chapter are in practice often combined in magical actions, as a number of examples already cited show. Zande magic in general is a good example of this. The main theme is that of a magical object addressed by a commanding spell. On the other hand, the selection of the object, and what is done with it by the magician, often follow the pattern of symbolic identification or contagious transfer. I give an example for each of these. To take the first: a stone is placed on the fork of a tree in order to retard the setting sun. The action is sometimes, but not invariably, accompanied by a spell: "You stone, may the sun not be quick to fall today. You stone, retard the sun on high so that I can arrive

first at that homestead to which I journey, then the sun may set."
As for the second: banana stalks are pricked with a crocodile's
teeth to make them fertile – "Teeth of crocodile are you, I prick
bananas with them, may bananas be prolific like crocodile's
teeth."[73]

There are also, of course, many activities which we could call
magical but which do not fall neatly into the patterns I have
described, even when the patterns are in one way or another
combined. They may be divided into two classes. The first consists
of those counter-examples which look as if they ought to fit, but
do not quite. A typical case here involves what might be called
the problem of the missing symbol. A Dinka way of retarding
the sun, and thus time, is to tie a knot in the grass. This would
seem to be a symbolic binding of the sun, analogous to that of
the symbolically bound ulcer. But nothing is bound in the knot;
no object stands in for or represents the sun. Perhaps we can say
that a tied symbol is created by implication in the act of tying.
Such difficulties can (I hope) be accommodated by refining and
restating the analysis within the main outlines I have proposed.
The second class of activities consists of 'magical' beliefs and
actions which do not even begin to look as if they fit into the
analysis: a belief in the magical power of numbers, for example
(or a special fear of certain numbers as opposed to others), or
the carrying of various kinds of charm. The list of exceptions in
the second class could be greatly multiplied, and there may well
be beliefs or patterns of thought to be elucidated here which will
give them some general shape.

This brings us to the general question, which was raised earlier,
concerning the sense which can be given to the word 'magic', and
the way in which magic is to be demarcated from religion – if it
is to be demarcated at all. It is a mistake to think that a theory
of magic, or of religion, must begin with a definition of what
magic or religion is. If one looks in the anthropological literature
one soon finds a far greater degree of agreement in the way in
which beliefs and actions are in practice classified than in the
definitions which are supposed to establish or systematise this use.
As with the term 'ritual', such definitions are all too often, if taken
strictly, completely off the mark of the author's own usage –
though this matters little, since the part played by the definition
is usually purely ornamental in any case. A more practical

approach is to look for general principles in terms of which what are by rough consensus 'magical' beliefs and patterns of thought can be classified, and to reconsider the question of definitions at the end of this process.

But if there are distinct patterns of thought to be found within the field of 'magical' action, is there any point in grouping them together under one classificatory term at all? The patterns discussed in this chapter do not, as I have said, by any means exhaust the field, but they are sufficiently various to serve as a basis on which this question can be discussed.

Consider first the relation between religion and magic. Actions which rely for their effect purely on symbolic identification, contagious transfer or the creative power of words may or may not play a part in a religious rite; but they are not on any reckoning in themselves distinctively religious. The difficult demarcation concerns those actions which are expected by the actors to produce a result through the mediation of a non-human agency, capable of understanding and action. We must not expect a neatly exhaustive distinction, within this class of actions, between the religious and the magical – unless 'magical action' is to become a catch-all category which sucks in any action in the class which does not fall in the category of a religious rite. The primary idea required here is not the complex notion of religion, with 'magic' as a residual category, but that of a mode of understanding and acting on the world whose fundamental rationalising concept is the notion of *agency*. Such is the explanatory framework of those traditional or primitive cultures which anthropologists have studied. To say this, of course, is not to imply that within such a culture every explanation immediately refers whatever is to be explained back to the action of an agent, human or otherwise. On the contrary, a great mass of everyday explanations link one event or state of affairs with another, without ever moving from the question: Why did it happen? to: Who *did it* or *made it* happen, and why? Within the terms of the underlying conceptual scheme, however, the thinker is naturally led in this direction if he presses for further or deeper understanding.

We can conceive of many agency-based cosmologies which would not constitute a framework of *religious* belief, because they would not allow for the moral and emotional relationships between presumed agencies and believers which must figure, in some form, in anything which we are prepared to call a mode of *religious* life. We can also question whether the belief in cosmological agency is itself an indispensable ingredient of a mode of thought which could properly be called religious.[74] In any case 'religion', like 'magic', should come at the end of the analysis. It cannot serve as a fundamental concept – not because, like 'magic', it is simply a rough-and-ready pre-theoretical term used to invoke a possibly heterogeneous field of behaviour, but for the opposite reason: it has a life of its own in our own culture, in the sense that it is a concept used by believers themselves to signify a complex and changing tradition of thought, feeling and action. Within this tradition there may be changing strands of continuity, of which the consciousness of *being* in a tradition may itself be one.

The aim of analysis is to group together phenomena which share a common explanation. Obviously, therefore, choice of categories must be to some extent interdependent with explanatory theories. That is why the question of what *exact* sense, if any, is to be given to the terms 'religion' or 'magic' must come at the end. Thus for intellectualism the starting point is an agency-based explanatory scheme modelled on human interaction. What we call religion is seen as a specialised development of this, dictated in part by human preoccupations beyond that of purely practical explanation and control. Although these preoccupations can only come into play against the background of an agency-based cosmology, the original cosmocentric emphasis and even the notion of spiritual agency may finally disappear. Whether or not one accepts all the causal dependencies implied by this outline, one implication at least – namely, that 'agency-based' magic should be grouped from the explanatory point of view with traditional religion, and not with the patterns of symbolic identification, or contagious transfer – is convincing enough. Certainly commanding spells are often accompanied by rites based on identification or transference (as in the Zande case), the whole being seen by the magician as a unitary technique. Equally, however, each or all of these techniques can be combined with purely religious actions, or with procedures which the anthropologist would call 'empirical' or 'practical'. But verbal and symbolic magic do have an explanatory factor in common: if I am right, they each in their different ways depend on a lack of differentiation between natural and conventional relations. There might be something to be said for using 'magic' to cover just these patterns of thought; but it should by now be clear that such definitional questions are contingent on further investigation.

Something should finally be said on the other classic demarcation dispute, between 'magical' and 'practical' techniques. If we are to compare like with like, we need to compare 'magical' techniques with other techniques, such as planting seed, which rely on the face of it on 'non-contiguous' causal connexions. Of course, as I have already pointed out, magical thought does seek to supply this desired contiguity of cause and effect, and this is one of its most interesting characteristics. Transference by contiguity is indeed the basic principle of contagious transfer. The case of mimetic identification is more obscure; but again the spatio-temporal distance between goal-event and magical rite is 'cancelled' by their identification. Then the Trobriand magician, it will be remembered, contiguously breathes his powerful words *into* the goal-object, or the magical object he intends to use. In each of these cases, the rite and its effect are not, from the point of view of the actor, spatio-temporally separated after all. With the commanding spell, on the other hand, the spatio-temporal gap between the rite and its effect can be bridged by the magical agency invoked, as with Zande vengeance magic. Here a recourse to theoretical notions makes the connexion. Similarly, 'declarative' or 'operative' magic is often linked with the idea of some kind of *mana*, or magical force, released by the spell. Thus the concept of force is brought in to play a characteristic gap-bridging role.[75]

This brings us to a way of distinguishing between 'empirical' and 'magical' behaviour which stems from Evans-Pritchard. Magical behaviour, on this account, is based on 'mystical' notions; and mystical notions, in Evans-Pritchard's definition, (*a*) attribute to the phenomena 'supra-sensible qualities' which (*b*) they do not possess, where the attribution is (*c*) not based on observation (Evans-Pritchard 1937: 12). The three elements in this definition will obviously have to work together: taken individually, they do not begin to do the required job. Thus, while the term 'supra-sensible' could be discussed at length, it is at least obvious that the 'souls' of magical medicines are neither more nor less supra-sensible than phlogiston or electrons or force-fields. In effect, Evans-Pritchard defines 'mystical notions' as unverified, erroneous theories about the world on which instrumental actions are based.

Now it is quite clear that the class of actions so based is much wider than the class of 'magical' or 'magico-religious' actions could possibly be. In particular, it is perfectly possible for an effective technique to be based on an erroneous, untested theory. (Untested, that is, except in so far as it is put into practice in the successful technique itself.) Thus in the Zande case, planting seed is based on the 'theory' that the soul of the seed is the agency which produces crop growth. On Evans Pritchard's definition, seed-planting would therefore have to be classified as 'ritual behaviour' (behaviour based on mystical notions). Moreover, the successful technique itself, as well as the theory used to account for it, may be untested. Many technical practices in traditional cultures combine (useless) magical methods with (effective) practical techniques. Now if we are to say, on the strength of the fact that the two are never separated and tried out independently, that the *magical* techniques are untested, then we must by the same logic say the same of the *effective* techniques which are used in combination with them. This should be borne in mind by anthropologists who insist on a sharp contrast between hard, empirical techniques which have proved their value in practice over generations, and unverified patterns of magical thought.

A quite different way of drawing the distinction between 'magical' and 'empirical' techniques is to base it on a distinction supposedly made by the actors themselves. Malinowski claimed that the people studied by him distinguished magical techniques from others; Parsons made this into a contrast between two 'systems': of 'rational knowledge and technique', and of 'magical beliefs and practices'.[76] But it certainly does not follow from the fact that the actors draw a distinction, conterminous with ours, between 'magical' techniques and others, that they *mean* the same by their distinction as we mean by ours. (What we mean by ours, as will have emerged by now, is in any case by no means clear.)

What might be meant by the claim that such-and-such a culture distinguishes magical from empirical techniques? It certainly could not mean that it distinguishes the magical techniques *as* ineffective, unverified etc., so long as their instrumental application remains a going concern. It might mean that informants can be made to distinguish between some techniques and others on the questioning of the anthropologist. This might show merely that they see in the techniques thus distinguished *some* common pattern or rationale; similar questioning could elicit from farmers a distinction between techniques which use fertilisers and techniques which do not. It might mean something more interesting: that the culture concerned possesses a generic name which covers roughly that field of behaviour in it which we would call 'magical'. Or it might mean that it also saw in the supposed efficaciousness of magical rites something distinctive, problematic and bizarre. It is with this last point in mind that various writers have denied that a distinction is made, in the society which they have studied, between magical and other techniques (see e.g. Hsu 1952: 87ff.; Thomas 1971: 668).

The traditional European conception of magic as a sacrilegious perversion of religious lore is probably responsible for a number of misconceptions in social anthropology. Setting it aside we see simply a multifarious variety of pre-scientific forms of thought and practice within which some quite noticeable patterns of uniformity can be discerned. There is no obvious reason at all why these modes of behaviour should be lumped with religion, the 'mystical' or the 'sacred', except in so far as traditional religion is itself characteristically cosmocentric and directly concerned with the task of controlling the environment. What is for *us* in the end most striking about magical practices is that they require assumptions which in one way or another run counter to the categorial framework within which we (at least officially) interpret the world: as with the notion of a real identity between symbol and thing symbolised, or of the cosmological power of language, or the treating of objects around one as agencies; or the beliefs that future events can productively affect the present which is implicit in most forms of divination. In this lies their interest, and the strangeness which is from our point of view their common characteristic. But – clearly – this is a characteristic which they can only have from a standpoint *outside* that of the socially shared consciousness in which they play an accepted role.

PART III

THE FRAMEWORK OF BELIEF: INTELLECTUALISM

10

'Ritual' reconsidered

Some social facts...are so to speak demonstrative: it is of their essence that they are conspicuously displayed and hence directly observable. Notoriously, the point of wedding festivities, public trials, ritual confer- ments of office, etc. etc. is to make plain and visible a given social fact.

But equally notoriously, social life has not merely its 'daylight', so to speak, but also its 'night time'.

(Gellner, *Cause and Meaning in the Social Sciences*, p. 190)

The rather far-flung discussion of Part II must now briefly be drawn together. 'Ritual' unites the notions of ceremony, magic and religion in the compendious category of 'symbolic-expressive' action. My main concern has been to question the meaning and usefulness of this unification. In separating out the various ele- ments covered by an over-elastic blanket term, one incurs the inevitable danger of making sketchy remarks on disparate topics. So in this chapter I shall state in outline the overall themes which seem to me to emerge from the discussion, paying attention to boldness of outline rather than to detail.

I have said several times that the essential function of cere- monial is that of marketing out or highlighting what is cere- monialised. This characterisation needs to be narrowed down; the best approach, however, will be to start with the more general category, of which ceremony is the special case. A social universe can be seen as being made up of events and states of affairs which have human significance but no publicly perceptible form other than that which they are conventionally *given* within the culture. They can be publicly known only if they are *made* known; to enter into the social reckoning they must be publicly known. Thus they stand in need of an 'external' or perceptible sign. We can begin therefore with the very general notion of such an event or state of affairs being non-naturally expressed, made perceptible or physically embodied. Within this general field three categories may be singled out, in each of which ceremony can play a part. There is, in the first place, the outward behavioural expression of inward psychological or spiritual states and events. To this category belongs the interaction code. Then there is the publicly perceptible marking or recording of (rule-constituted) social relationships, statuses and states. For example, a fence marks out a property boundary, a uniform signifies a status, lines on a road mark out traffic lanes, a name-board by the side of the road marks out a county boundary. Thirdly, there is the marking of *changes* in the rule-constituted social order. In particular, operative acts effect a change in the pattern of rules by declaring or making it known that there is to be a change: they effect the change they mark. *ex opere operato*

The relation between inner states and external criteria has been very much at the centre of the stage in contemporary philosophy. So also has the relation between meaning and convention, and between convention and the existence of reciprocal layers of belief and intention on the part of those who share the convention. At the same time anthropologists and sociologists influenced by them have been preoccupied with the public expression of social statuses and relationships, most commonly under the heading of 'ritual', or of 'symbolic action'. The philosophical areas of interest can profitably be brought to bear on this concern with 'symbolic action': the effect is to bring out the very different directions of enquiry which are run together within the study of 'ritual'.

People's feelings, attitudes and beliefs can be evinced and recognised at a level below that of full-fledged communication (in the sense discussed in chapter 6); and the reciprocal adjustments of feelings and intentions in an interaction is to a large extent made, by humans and animals, at this level. Among the attitudes and beliefs thus evinced will be those which contain a reference to roles, statuses, norms etc. which, from the point of view of the person involved, shape and govern his social position. The public expression of these socially constitutive rules themselves, however – of the statuses, rights, obligations, prohibitions and so on which they comprise – must *necessarily* take the form of a non-natural sign – since such rules, as opposed to beliefs about and attitudes towards them, are not inner states of which the actor's behaviour can be a natural sign.[77]

Thus if we take the dictum, 'Ritual symbolically expresses the social order', and replace 'symbolically' by 'non-naturally', we seem to have here a domain which fits the saying well. The non-natural expression of social relations and of changes in them, however, involves a wide variety of actions and objects which would not normally be included under the term 'ritual'. A policeman's everyday uniform is not a ritual garment; a notice bearing the words 'Private – No Entry', or a parking badge with a pictorial design on it, are not ritual objects; an armband marking out an official at a public meeting is not a ritual decoration; and the statement "I am the assistant secretary" is not a ritual utterance – but all are non-natural public expressions of a social order. And on the other hand, the dictum excludes actions and objects which normally *would* be included in the category of ritual. It excludes religious and magical activities – I shall come to this in a moment. It also excludes ceremonies of interaction and commemoration. Interaction-code behaviour (and thus interaction ceremony), although it may well testify to a man's *sense* of his social position and of the rights and obligations which that dictates, is not a direct non-natural expression of them: it communicates the actor's feelings towards the other, or his *recognition* of the norms of interaction.

So if the term 'ritual' is to include ceremony in its scope, then not all ritual is a non-natural expression of the social order. Nor, if we are to retain the *specific* notion of ceremony, should 'ritual' be stretched to include *all* 'outward' non-natural signs of the social order or of inner states of the actors – although it is an important fact that what is ceremonialised does always fall into this more general category. Within it we need first to distinguish the more restricted class of events or states which are not merely given outward expression but underscored, set apart or put on record. This setting apart is obviously achieved by comparison with the *normal* degree of stress placed on external signs within a social group; our general

notion for it is that of formality. What is formally marked out
is marked because it is felt to be important that it should be known
to have been done or to obtain: for example, formal interaction-
code behaviour between strangers, a formal appointment, decision or contract.

A formal action is (or is in one of its functions) an external sign,
underscored and set apart, of an inward state, a social order or
a change in a social order. Ceremony is a narrower concept still;
not all formality is ceremonious (e.g. a formal warning). What
is ceremonialised is set apart as something which is in one way
or another special and achieved: it is not merely recorded but
enhanced or embellished with a more or less elaborate *mise en
scène* which is often, although not always, traditionally evolved.
Ceremony says "Look, this is how things should be, this is the
proper, ideal pattern of social life." It gives to the people concerned an image of a harmonious, well-ordered, undisturbed
social universe.

The point of ceremony, why some occasions are ceremonial
and others not, why it takes the form it does, its relation to the
more general categories of formality, of public signs of inner
states and social rules – these are all questions well worth studying, and which to some extent have been studied under the
general heading of 'ritual'.[78] Apart from the important empirical
problems which they raise, they also take one straight to the
conceptual foundations of social science in the analysis of such
notions as *sign, convention, rule, social/non-social, status, institution,
role*. So much should be clear from chapters 6 and 7.

But what now of the connexion between this general field of
enquiry on the one hand and the study of religion and magic
in a traditional culture on the other? At the end of the last
chapter I claimed that the fundamental concept needed for the
latter is that of a cosmology based on agencies responsive to
human communication, and equipped with powers to act on the
world. What then requires study is the variety of ways in which
the agencies which people such a cosmology can be seen by actors
within the culture concerned as extending the membership of
their social field. The logic of the commanding spell is modelled
on the social relationship of authority: but no more is written into
the character of a medicine than is required of an agency capable

of receiving the particular instructions involved and executing them. Other agencies may be attributed a more complex consciousness and freedom of movement without being regarded as members of the extended society of which humans are a part, or they may be thought to be positively alien to it. There are high gods who are so distant and unknown as to invite few rites. There are 'apotropaic' rites, as Evans-Pritchard calls them, whose main object is to turn away the spirits they concern. But the commonest pattern is that of ancestor-spirits, or 'divinities of the middle range', entering into what Malinowski called "the mutual interaction, the intimate collaboration between man and spirit which are the essence of religious cult" (Malinowski 1922: 73).

"No really satisfactory theoretical classification of religious behaviour has yet been made", says Firth (1971: 221), echoing many other writers. There will be no such classification, certainly for traditional culture, until it is clearly recognised that to a large extent religious rites *are* social interactions with authoritative or powerful beings within the actor's social field, and that their special characteristics are in large part due to the special characteristics these beings are thought to have. Interaction ceremonies in particular loom large among religious rites – not surprisingly, when the goal is to establish an equilibrated relationship between man and god. Fortunately the ethnographic literature is quite strong in accounts of this aspect of religious action, allowing a comparison between ceremonial relationships with gods and spirits and ceremonial relationships with chiefs, elders etc. A continuity of ceremonial practice is soon found. In chapter 7 I discussed the case of the Catholic sacrament of Penance; Finnegan has made the point excellently in connexion with Limba prayer, noting that (1969: 550)

the normal word for 'to pray' (*theteke*) is exactly the same as the word for 'plead'. Furthermore it is used in a precisely analogous way. Even if the audience addressed (the dead) is necessarily somewhat different, in other respects when a Limba prays to the ancestors he is performing just the same kind of act as when a man entreats a chief: he is making a formal acknowledgement of his inferiority and dependence and/or a request for aid and forgiveness; at the same time he is expecting that the one(s) addressed will recognise their side of the relationship, 'accept' the plea and answer it; and he is also asserting a continuing relationship between speaker and audience, living and dead . . . In other words prayer and sacrifice need not be explained (or explained away) as being merely 'expressive' or 'symbolic' and thus very different from most everyday speech acts; rather they can be brought under the same heading as such acts as 'announcing', 'saying goodbye' or 'greeting' (terms also, incidentally, used to describe Limba prayer to the dead).

A traditional religious cosmology, then, extends the social field – and thus also the pattern of social relationships – beyond its human members. In doing so it extends the scope of interaction and operative ceremonies. Besides *extending* the social fabric, however, it offers – or so I have suggested – a *conception* of it characteristically different from our own notion of a society as a pattern of relationships between individuals constituted by differentially applicable rules. For the 'traditional thinker', the social characteristics of a person, such as his office, status or roles, are not thus opposed to his natural characteristics, as I have called them. They belong with the general category of his abilities, propensities and inner states, none of which can be read off simply by looking at him, unless they be outwardly marked. His social position is not constituted by rights and obligations; he incurs rights and obligations in virtue of the spiritual state and capacity which characterise the social position he acquires: by being cleansed, or given new powers, or by acquiring knowledge. The social order is a spiritual order immanent in men, and divinely created and underpinned. Therefore what is for us an operative act becomes an action which produces a natural change by a divine dispensation: a 'sacramental rite', as Firth calls it:[79]

Sacramental rites have as their essential feature the notion of some change in the persons performing or attending the ritual...By sacrament in the strict sense is meant a ritual which by its outward forms serves as a visible sign of an inward or spiritual state – a state of grace. In primitive religion the inward state cannot be defined in the same theological terms.

It only needs to be added that the sacramental rite is not *merely* a sign, but is also taken as productive of the spiritual state it signifies.

Here it becomes important to get the division between ceremony and the action which is ceremoniously performed right. The sacramental rite which is highlighted and enhanced by ceremony is an ontologically efficacious magical act, which changes the social world and the characteristics of the persons involved in the change. In our society the symbolic actions which may accompany an operative act, such as cutting a ribbon to open a road, are parts of a conventional procedure which could just as well be replaced by another; and in any case tend to be seen in the 'beautiful and useless' category of ceremonial embellishment, rather than as an integral part of the core action itself. To assimilate sacramental rites (such as the Shilluk investiture mentioned in chapter 7) to this category of the *merely* symbolic is a mistake whose obviousness has not prevented it from being implicitly made time and time again.

Furthermore, sacramental rites are 'sacramental' in that they are referred to a religious framework: they are typically instituted by a god, done in his sight, by his representative (often in a very substantial sense). It is again a peculiarly modern mistake to see in this religious reference nothing more than ceremonious embellishment – that is what is has often become in modern societies. The modern observer has a chronic propensity to misplace the accents of traditional thought: he insists on seeing what is a *religious* action (ceremoniously performed) as a *ceremony* (with an added religious or 'mystical' flavour).

And yet, even if these two mistakes *are* mistakes when what is being aimed at is a descriptive analysis of traditional thought, may there not be something more than *just* a mistake involved in the first of them? In chapter 7 it seemed clear that the Catholic sacraments could be understood only in terms of the framework of theistic belief which gave them their point. But, quite consistent with this, there remained the possibility of interpreting them as operative acts, working within the extended spiritual community postulated by the believer to establish or retrieve his right of eventual participation in the divine life. The interpretation led to a divergence between the orthodox Catholic's view of the logic of the sacramental act, and that of the interpreter. The orthodox Catholic's view was then explained as a misconstruction of the operative character of the sacrament, naturalising it into a causal mechanism for dispensing grace. One can imagine a theory which generalises this approach. First, sacramental rites in general are interpreted as following the logic of operative action – that is, as producing a change in the pattern of rights and obligations by giving a public, non-natural sign *that* such a sign is to take effect.

Then the culture's own understanding of the rites, which assimilates them to the pattern of natural causality, is explained as a naturalising misconception of this underlying logic. Finally, emphasis is laid on the salience of declarative spells and symbolic enactments, not only in sacramental rites which aim to alter social patterns of rights and obligations, but *also* in magical acts aimed at controlling the natural environment; and these magical acts are seen as an attempted extension of the logic of operative action beyond the social domain. Such an approach would be in line with the general 'Durkheimian' intellectualist project (see chapter 11) of showing how conceptions of nature and its workings traditionally are modelled on analogies taken from the social order and social life.

But one can also imagine a theory which goes in the opposite direction. It *begins* with the magic of contagious transfer and of symbolic identification. It then points out that traditional thought naturalises social statuses and relationships; and that it is therefore to be expected that social changes should be brought under the control of magical techniques, such as contagious transfer, as when an office is passed on by the laying on of hands, or of symbolic identification, as when the ownership of land is transferred by the placing of a piece of earth in the new owner's hands. The actions which often feature in operative procedures in our society, and serve merely to 'symbolise' (in the sense of *showing*) what is being done, are then seen as a legacy of these magical techniques. This approach has the advantage of seeking to explain what the other takes for granted as a starting point: that operative acts frequently involve elaborate procedures, often obviously symbolic in character.

In both theories, the claim that traditional thought does not make the distinction which we make between the 'natural' and the 'social' is a central assumption; in other respects, however, the two differ methodologically or philosophically as well as substantively. The first is in the tradition which takes the rite to be prior to the belief, and allows a divergence between the actor's and the observer's descriptions of what is being done. The second adheres closely to the actor's characterisation of his action and the concepts in which this characterisation is phrased. But it can now be seen that the methodological issue, as narrowed down in the contrast between these two theories, turns out to be inseparable from fundamentally empirical questions: questions about the character and relative importance of various patterns of thought within the field of 'magical' action.

Both theories in any case operate within a literalist account of the framework of traditional religious cosmology, and both take for granted the genuinely instrumental character of magical rites. This literalism, which was defended in Part I, is in the end incompatible with the approach which the terminology of 'ritual action' and the associated distinction between instrumental and 'symbolic-expressive' action imply. There cannot be a generic mode of human action of which religion, magic and ceremony are specialised forms. Rather, to characterise an action as 'religious', 'magical' or 'ceremonial' is to characterise it in quite different dimensions. Roughly:

(1) An action, one of the actor's reasons for doing which (or the institutional reasons for doing which) involves some more or less direct reference to the religious beings in which he (or the social group) believes, is a religious action.

(2) An instrumental act whose efficacy is rationalised (by the actor, or institutionally) in terms of one of the patterns of thought discussed in chapter 9 is a magical action.

(3) An action which has the formality and norm-regarding elaborateness discussed above and in previous chapters is a ceremonial action.

These are not definitions: as noted in chapter 9, not everything properly called 'religious' presupposes belief in spiritual beings (e.g. 'demythologised' modern Christianity), and there are patterns of thought which would generally be called 'magical' but which were not discussed in that chapter. However, as sufficient conditions they will do for present purposes – they make it clear that we are dealing with three analytically separate categories: an action's falling under one of them in no way precludes or entails its falling under one or both of the others.

Now consider an ideal-typical 'traditional' world-view. (a) It will rest on an agency-based cosmology which will extend the social order, so to speak, up the hierarchy. (Of course it may also postulate various types of agency, demons, spirits of the bush etc., which are not integrated into the social hierarchy at all.) (b) Its conception of the (rule-constituted) social order will be naturalised and, specifically, 'sacramental'. Consider next an appointment to some important office in this society (law-giver, military leader etc.). This will be an important action, governed by various norms, and requiring publicity; no doubt it will fall under category (3). And, in virtue of (a), the authority to perform it, its efficacy, will be thought of as coming from 'up the hierarchy', from a god; hence the action will fall under category (1). Moreover, in the light of (b), the character of this efficacy will not be thought of as purely operative, bringing about a change purely in the socially constitutive pattern of rules, but will be regarded as achieving an ontological, spiritual change. Thus the action will also fall under category (2).

Let us now suppose a gradual change in our society's conception of nature and society, towards a dereified understanding of the social order as consisting in nothing other than a pattern of rights and obligations obtaining between its members. In accordance with (a), however, this membership will still be taken to extend beyond the empirical human scene. Under these circumstances, the appointment will be seen as a purely operative act, conferring a purely rule-constituted status, and hence will no longer fall under category (2). Nevertheless the authority to perform it will still be regarded as deriving from a god, so the action will continue to fall under category (1).

But consider next an increasing secularisation in our society. There are many possibilities here, but let us suppose that religious belief, rather than being reinterpreted, becomes completely atrophied, at least in its function of providing a rationale for the authority relationships in the society. All religious references in the appointment procedure and the ceremonial surrounding it fade. We are left with a purely secular ceremony, which falls only under category (3). Finally, we can imagine a process of growing bureaucratisation, with the 'beautiful but profitless' activities of ceremonial melting away in the hard sun of cost-effective rationality; the appointment is perhaps now made by an operative formal letter and a public announcement.

This story is not meant to suggest that the various processes involved are empirically independent – they may well not be – but only to bring out the analytical distinctness of our three categories. The term 'ritual' of course commonly covers not only these three categories but also IC behaviour and operative acts which are not *ceremonialised* at all, so long as they follow a relatively stereotyped and preferably non-verbal procedure. What use does a term have which brings together a man shaking hands, a man praying to his god, a man refusing to walk under a ladder, a man clapping at the end of a concert, a man placing medicine on his crops? None at all: these actions have no interesting characteristic in common. Firth remarks (1973: 176): "There can be secular rituals, as there can be secular symbols, rituals varying in the degree of their sacredness. (This is an alternative concept to retention of 'ceremony' which has tended to disappear as a technical term of weight in anthropology.)" I think it a pity that 'ceremony' has tended to disappear. It is a modest word which is nevertheless less unsuited to being a "technical term of weight" than the all-enveloping and super-profound sounding 'ritual'. It makes it quite easy to see that ceremonial need contain no magical or religious elements, and that magical or religious actions may not in any way be ceremonial.

Of course, in a traditional culture the categories 'magical', 'religious' and 'ceremonial' often overlap for the reasons suggested above among others; nevertheless, here too they need to be carefully distinguished. But could we then reintroduce the term 'ceremony' and use 'ritual' in the comparatively narrow sense of 'magico-religious' action? So used it is a convenient enough piece of shorthand, but is still not to be taken seriously as a theoretical term of weight; the two notions 'ritual' and 'magico-religious action' are all too likely to take in each other's washing. For what now is a ritual? A magical or religious action. What is a magical action? A non-religious ritual. This usage can only impede the necessary study of magic in its overall context of 'pre-scientific' techniques and modes of thought. It is moreover an instructive exercise to ask, every time one feels inclined to talk of a 'ritual' danger, a 'ritual' precaution or a 'ritual' prohibition, just what is added by the word – beyond a specious sense of understanding based on the confused idea that 'ritual' dangers etc. are in some profound sense 'Let's pretend' dangers. If the notion of ritual is to be used at all, it is best applied to the *rites* involved in an institutional mode of religious behaviour.

Consider, finally, the equation of 'ritual' with 'symbolic-expressive'. It would be easy but tedious to dwell on the confusions which cluster round the notion of 'symbolic-expressive' action, but there are three persistent equivocations here which need to be mentioned. The first of these is between actions which are expressive in that they intentionally communicate a feeling or attitude, and which may or may not be instrumental, and actions which non-intentionally testify to or evince a feeling or attitude, and which clearly therefore cannot be instrumental *in their character of expressive behaviour*. If Trobriand canoe magic is a ritual which 'stresses the importance of canoe-building for Trobrianders', then presumably running away from a lion is a ritual which expresses the importance of not being eaten for the runner. The second equivocation is between activities which are symbolic in that they consist of an action on a symbolic object which represents some other thing, and those which are symbolic in the sense of being 'merely' symbolic – that is, of having only a token effect, being performed only in order to affirm an attitude (e.g. a symbolic protest against pollution), or serving as no more than a ceremonial embellishment which highlights the occasion (e.g. breaking a bottle of champagne on a ship). Cutting a ribbon to open a road, burning an effigy of the president, are symbolic actions in both senses; the magician who melts his wax effigy is acting symbolically in the first sense but certainly not in the second; a healer who cures by touch acts symbolically in neither sense – the action falls within the pattern of contagious transfer, and not of symbolic magic. Finally, the third equivocation is between actions which are 'expressive' in the sense of being done to 'express oneself' just for the sake of it etc., and which can be opposed to instrumental actions, and those which are 'expressive' in the sense of being designed to 'say' or 'show' something – that is, are communicational – and which can no more be opposed to instrumental actions than red things can be to round ones.

Nevertheless, in making these criticisms of the concept of ritual I do not mean to detract from the real insight which a broadly symbolist approach has often produced in the study of religious rites, magical techniques, ceremonies, interaction codes and so forth in various societies. On the contrary, I have myself tried to show how various types of ceremony, or again various types of action which are themselves often ceremonialised, can be said to 'say something', or to 'do something by saying it'. And I have also suggested that a certain notion of symbolic action is essential in the analysis of magic.

The point, rather, is that this whole investigation needs to be set free from the strait-jacket of 'ritual = sacred = symbolic' versus 'practical = profane = instrumental', and the contortions to which this simple-minded opposition leads. And the second point, which the discussion of Part II has been leading up to, is that when this liberation is effected, it becomes clear that the results of the investigation are in no way incompatible with a literalist conception of religious and magical beliefs in a traditional culture – in fact they presuppose it. In other words, the real contribution of a symbolist-inspired approach, that of focussing attention on important 'symbolic' or 'communicational' aspects of what are nevertheless heterogeneous forms of social action, can be separated from the symbolist conception of the 'context of belief' – indeed, when examined, it turns out to rely precisely on a literalist conception of that context (as in the symbolic account of belief in the efficacy of magic). It is, consequently, perfectly compatible with the intellectualist programme, to which we must finally return in the next three chapters.

11

Intellectualism, 'Frazerian' and 'Durkheimian'

...the part of society in the genesis of logical thought...
(Durkheim, *Elementary Forms*, p. 436)

The philosophical framework: review

Various notions of 'symbolic' or 'expressive' action have been discussed. But what is meant when the cosmology or world-view of a traditional culture is itself described as a 'symbolic' order, universe or system? What is sometimes meant is no more than that it provides a fundamental conceptual scheme and a theory in terms of which the traditional thinker interprets and understands the world around him. Of course in this sense anyone – scientist, traditional thinker or whoever – inhabits a symbolic universe. From this innocuous point, however, the terminology of 'symbolic systems' facilitates a shift to the much stronger, reductive claim that traditional cosmologies are symbolic in that sense which closes off the possibility of a realist account of them. (In philosophy of science the word 'model' has had a similar variability of meaning.) As was noted at the end of Part I, however, this view might still not be fundamentally incompatible with intellectualism in the way that the 'classically' symbolist conception of the meaning of traditional religion is. To bring this out we must distinguish three theses.

(1) The first thesis states that although the doctrines of traditional religion do have a literal face value which is cosmological in character, and may be believed at that level, their real meaning (understanding of which is required for the purposes of sociological explanation) calls for hermeneutic interpretation and turns out not to be cosmological at all. This thesis is denied by the *literalist*.

(2) The second thesis asserts that when traditional beliefs are properly understood they can be seen *not* to rest on any belief in the reality of beings whose actions have effects on the perceptible world but who are not themselves perceptible. Hence, whether or not such beliefs are in some sense hypotheses, they are certainly not *transcendental* hypotheses: they do not postulate an unexperienceable domain in order to explain what *is* experienced. This thesis is denied by the *realist*.

(3) The third thesis is that traditional religious and scientific beliefs have neither a similar (or usefully comparable) logic nor similar (or usefully comparable) functions, and hence, presumably or probably, do not have similar origins. This thesis is denied by the *intellectualist*.

The relations between the three theses are that (2) is independent of (1) and (3), and (1) implies (3). Hence it is in particular possible to reject (1) and accept (2). Literalism of this anti-realist kind is what someone who thought that the cosmological beliefs of a traditional religion constituted a 'symbolic system' might be propounding. Such beliefs would on this view certainly amount to an interpretation, or a way of thinking about, experience, apt for underpinning instrumental action; but the function of 'gods' and 'spirits' and the like within it would be as devices for thinking about the experienced world, not as further unexperienced denizens of it. (Lienhardt 1961 sometimes seems to be interpreting Dinka thought in this way.) The difficulties which result from adopting this view as a descriptive account of the *actual* logic of traditional religious beliefs were summarised in chapter 4. The grounds favouring it are philosophical, and count equally in favour of an identical account of the 'theoretical entities' apparently postulated in many scientific theories.

In fact we encountered *two* kinds of philosophical anti-realism in the discussion in Part I (distinguished in note 34). The first kind, of which anti-realism about theoretical entities in science – 'scientific anti-realism' – and anti-realism about the unobservable beings of traditional thought are particular forms, is a general philosophical thesis to the effect that any apparent reference to unobservable entities made in an area of human discourse which is cognitively respectable/legitimate/meaningful or whatever, must be capable of being paraphrased out without loss of cognitive content. Its application to a given area of discourse (science, or traditional religious thought) is likely to be the result of a positivist philosophical position combined with a desire to endorse the given area as cognitively respectable/legitimate and so forth.

The other kind of anti-realism – 'semantic anti-realism' – is discussed in the appendix. It is based not on directly positivist positions, but on deeper (though related) considerations about the way in which we can attach meaning at all to sentences in a language which we use. Let me now summarise briefly what I have said about the relations between these two kinds of anti-realism and the intellectualist programme. Each is incompatible with *some* of the features of intellectualism in its strongest form; each nevertheless leaves room for an approach which is still recognisably intellectualist, so long as it is uniformly applied *both* to scientific and to traditional religious discourse. To put it another way, intellectualism in its strongest form involves a conception of the status and development of scientific theory which neither kind of anti-realism can accept; but if the intellectualist's basic idea is expressed simply as the thought that *whatever* goes into explaining the origins and functions of (and the changes in) scientific theory *also* goes, by and large, into explaining the origins and functions of (and the changes in) traditional religious cosmologies, then it is not incompatible with either kind of anti-realism. Thus it is argued in the appendix that the conceptual relativism to which semantic anti-realism leads precludes the kind of account of changes from one overall world-view to another which the classical intellectualist approach suggests. But of course that applies as much to changes from one overall scientific theory to another as to changes from 'pre-scientific' to 'scientific' world-views: in each case the change is non-rational, and involves indeed a modification in the criteria of rationality. If the intellectualist's claim is only the weak one that whatever factors underlie change in the one case also, broadly speaking, underlie it in the other, then it survives. This claim *is* indeed very weak – for if the factors involved are in a substantial sense 'non-rational', then there may seem hardly any point in talking about 'intellectualism' in this context at all. But on the other hand, the intellectualist's account of the emergence and functions of a theory, or cosmology, unlike his account of conversion from one such theory to another, remains unaffected by conceptual relativism.

The second kind of 'anti-realism' – the thesis that apparent references to unobservables can always be paraphrased out in legitimate systems of thought – places constraints on intellectualism in another way. One kind of intellectualism (as we shall see below) considers it to be an important point of comparison between scientific theories and traditional religious cosmologies that both seek to explain experience by postulating an unobservable order of things and events which underlies it. Both are, in this sense, transcendental hypotheses. Clearly, from the perspective of the positivist kind of anti-realism, this point of comparison must fall away. Science, on this view, contains no genuinely transcendental element at all. If traditional religious thought *does*, then it is metaphysical non-sense – though it may be enchanted or edifying non-sense, or the kind of non-sense which expresses inexpressible attitudes; it is in any case sharply contrasted with scientific theory in this respect. On the other hand, if one accepts that the spiritual beings of traditional religious cosmologies are in fact 'theoretical fictions', then one can still endorse such cosmologies as legitimate explanatory systems, and still embark on an intellectualist comparison of science and traditional thought.

None of these points of tension arises, of course, between realism and intellectualism – which, indeed, fit together very well. Philosophically the general approach set out in Part I was realist: in the appendix I sketch out how a realist conception of sentence meaning serves to block the move from underdetermination of theory to relativism; and this semantic realism entails either realism or strict reductionism about the status of transcendental hypotheses. I argued for the first option in chapter 4 (see pp. 64–6). Then in Part II I tried to show how some of the true and interesting things to be found in symbolist accounts of 'ritual' can be fitted into a literalist and realist framework (one which denies (1) and (2)). The way in which this has to be done provides one of the strongest arguments against the anti-realist form of literalism (which denies (1) but accepts (2)) and is itself therefore relevant to the issues of Part I. For an essential premise required to make sense of much religious ceremony was that gods and spirits are treated as members of a transcendentally extended social field. Yet this premise is unacceptable to the anti-realist: it is precisely the transcendental element which he rejects. But

the analogy between the magical and the scientific conceptions of the world is close. In both of them the succession of events is [assumed to be] perfectly regular and certain, being determined by immutable laws, the operation of which can be foreseen and calculated precisely... The fatal flaw of magic lies not in its general assumption of a sequence of events determined by law, but in its total misconception of the nature of the particular laws which govern that sequence.[80]

Religion, on the other hand, in postulating imperceptible personal agencies who govern nature from behind the scenes, replaces the ordered universe of the Laws of Sympathy by the intrinsically unpredictable actions of "fickle and wayward" beings (Frazer 1911, I, I: 224; 1957: 67):

if religion involves first, a belief in superhuman beings who rule the world, and second, an attempt to win their favour, it clearly assumes that the course of nature is to some extent elastic or variable, and that we can persuade or induce the mighty beings who control it to deflect, for our benefit, the current of events from the channel in which they would otherwise flow. Now this implied elasticity or variability of nature is directly opposed to the principles of magic as well as of science, both of which assume that the processes of nature are rigid and invariable in their operation.

The comparison, then, is between magic and science; the contrast, between these two and religion. This is linked in Frazer's scheme with a hypothesis of evolution from magic, through disillusion with magic to the sense of dependence on a greater power of religion, and back to the Promethean spirit of science (pp. 234; 72):

man essayed to bend nature to his wishes by the sheer force of spells and enchantments before he strove to coax and mollify a coy, capricious or irascible deity by the soft insinuation of prayer and sacrifice.

What in contrast is Horton's intellectualist scheme? His conception of magic is professedly Tylorean; he sees it as based on a belief in the creative power of words and of symbols as material surrogates for words. Frazer sees science as consisting, in essence, in a systematic structure of laws (pp. 222; 65):

It is therefore a truism, almost a tautology, to say that all magic is necessarily false and barren; for were it ever to become true and fruitful, it would no longer be magic but science.

Horton, however, follows much modern philosophy of science in fixing attention on the transcendental and analogical character of scientific thought. What is for him characteristic of science is its postulation of an unexperienced order to make sense of experience, and its tendency to conceptualise this order in terms of an analogy drawn from everyday experience. This emphasis results in an intellectualist conception quite different from Frazer's: for Horton, the spiritual agencies of traditional religion are simply the theoretical entities of the traditional thinker's transcendental hypothesis. The comparison, then, is between science and the agency-based cosmology of traditional (in Horton's case, African) religions; the contrast, between these two and magic. For magic is not based, as it is for Frazer, on implicitly believed laws, which though they are false might have been true: rather, it is a tendency of thought rooted in the lack of a felt distinction between natural and conventional relations between things – and as such belongs to the contrast between traditional and modern consciousness, not to what they have in common.

One further difference between Frazer and Horton, more methodological than substantive, should be noted. Frazer's primary interest is evolutionary – in the sequential relationships between magic, science and religion, and the likely manner of their emergence. His comparison of the structure and function of magical and scientific beliefs really goes no further than the claim that both involve acceptance of a system of laws, used for purposes of explanation and control. Horton, on the other hand, is primarily interested in the similarities of structure and function between scientific and traditional (religious) thought, his strategy being to push these similarities as far as they will go in order to suggest that both forms of thought are species of a single genus – though they are of course differentiated in important ways which he tries to take into account. The intellectualist interest in origins is still present, for the genus is characterised as forms of thought which originate in an attempt to understand and master the natural world; but Horton's method of approach does not encourage us to suppose that any very precise evolutionary story can be told.

Let us now turn to criticism. Since a cornerstone of Frazer's scheme is his conception of magic, it has to that extent been undermined in the discussion in chapter 9. The view that magic is based on the thought-patterns suggested by the 'Laws of Sympathy' is, quite simply, erroneous. However, for present purposes what is of interest is not so much whether Frazer's particular formulation of the 'laws' of magic is correct, as whether his suggestion (*a*) that magic does rest on generalising beliefs concerning uniformities of nature, beliefs which (*b*) are false but might have been true, is acceptable. Now although I tried to show in chapter 9 that Horton's attempt to reduce all magic to belief in the power of words was mistaken, the account given there of at least certain important types of magical action (symbolic identification, belief in the causal power of words) exemplifies, as does Horton's account, a familiar theme in the study of magic. This is the idea that magic stems, not from empirical error, but from an essentially philosophical unclarity, which fails to recognise the purely non-natural character of the relation between what signifies and what is signified. If this account is correct, (*b*) has to be rejected.

In order to assess (*a*), we must distinguish two possibilities:

(1) Magical actions are rationalised by the belief that certain specific natural uniformities obtain, where this belief is either explicitly formulated or such that the actor would readily recognise, in an explicit formulation of it by an enquirer, *his* belief. However, the generalisations involved (even when formulated by the actors) may be very vague, may be treated unreflectively and unsystematically and so on.

(2) People who perform magical actions expect certain results from them. It is possible for an observer to formulate generalisations or 'laws', linking action and consequence, which will give him some ability to predict, with respect to various types of action, what kind of result magical practitioners are likely to expect or hope for from it. However, these generalisations are not formulated by the actors, nor, when they are put to them, do the actors immediately accept them as their own. Instead, to see their applicability, they must check on their predictive value in a manner very similar to the observer's.

Suppose, first, that (2) describes the actual situation. In this case, Frazer's comparison of magic with science on the score of (*a*) does not get off the ground, even if his account of the underlying logic of magical actions is accepted as correct. Consider, as a partial analogy, a grammatical theorist who concerns himself with the syntax of a language, L. Speakers of L are by and large able to tell whether a given sentence in L is grammatical. The theorist takes these reactions as data and tries to develop a set of grammatical rules for L which will successfully predict them. If he succeeds, he may be inclined to impute these rules to the language-users, claiming that they are in some sense following them in determining whether a sentence is grammatical, and in constructing a grammatical sentence. He may also be inclined to say that in his original learning of L, the language-user in some sense developed a *theory* of L which he, the theorist, has explicitly stated. But saying this still falls a long way short of saying that language-learners are usefully comparable to scientists, or that speaking a language is doing applied linguistics.

Similarly, the theorist of magic may be inclined to impute his generalisations to the magical practitioners he observes, claiming that their expectations about the effects certain types of action will have are in some sense based on them, and that in learning magical techniques they were in some sense learning a 'theory' about the effects of these types of action. But again, given (2), this would in no way justify treating magic as comparable to applied science. In these circumstances, it is probably least misleading to say that (*a*) is simply false.

My tentative impression is that in fact magical consciousness falls somewhere between (1) and (2), but approximates, particularily in pre-literate cultures, (2) rather than (1). Let us suppose, however, that (1) does correctly describe the situation. Obviously Frazer's position is in this case much stronger. The difference, it might now be said, between magic and science is merely that magical beliefs are held unreflectively and uncritically, where science is self-critical, experimental and so on. But this is still superficial – science is essentially more than a set of generalisations, however carefully formulated. Here Horton's estimate of what is important and characteristic in scientific thought – its drive towards a unified and often transcendental conception of the domain to be explained, articulated in the terms of an analogy from familiar experience – is considerably more fertile in suggesting a non-vacuous comparative framework for the intellectualist.

Frazer's conception of magic and science, then, fails on a number of counts. His 'sympathetic' account of magic is incorrect, but even if correct would not support the comparison between science and magic which he wants to make. Nor is his ground for taking religion as the odd-man-out particularily con-

vincing, at least when considered in the light of the characteristically this-wordly preoccupations of a primitive religion. When a
sacrifice fails to achieve its required effect, the sacrificers do not
just put that down to the unpredictability of the god. On the
contrary, they typically expect a predictable reaction from him,
and, when this is not forthcoming, call on a number of standard
explanations to account for this fact.

The intellectualism of Durkheim's Elementary Forms

It is to Horton's very much more compelling presentation of the
intellectualist case that we must now turn. It will again help us
to fix our bearings if we begin by considering Horton's relation
to Durkheim, whose influence on theorists of religion in social
anthropology, of whatever persuasion, is inescapable. The critique of Horton's scheme will then take up the next two chapters.
Horton has himself discussed the 'intellectualism' of Durkheim's
Elementary Forms (Horton 1973a). But before considering this
discussion we must bring in two further elements in Horton's
analysis of traditional religious thought.

(i) As has already been noted, a primary characteristic of
scientific theory – or of any transcendental hypothesis – in Horton's eyes is its exploitation of analogies from everyday experience. Horton uses this basic idea very ingeniously to explain
one of the most obvious differences between modern scientific
theory and the cosmology of a traditional religion: the 'impersonal idiom', as he puts it, of the one against the 'personal idiom'
of the other. For the post-Renaissance West, the paradigm of
order within everyday experience was to be found in the socially
constructed world, in the regularity of simple mechanical arte-
facts. (Naturally, this suggestion implies an initial explanatory
priority of simple technology over pure science – an implication
which Horton does try to defend.) But for the thinker in, say,
traditional Africa the paradigm of order was to be found only
in the social order itself. Hence an impersonal cosmology in the
first case, a personal cosmology in the second.

(ii) Lévy-Bruhl taught that the 'primitive mentality' is 'pre-
logical':[81] not merely as a matter of believing propositions from
which contradictory consequences can be drawn, though the

thinker fails to draw them, but in the sense of believing pro-positions which are in and of themselves ineradicably incoherent. Thus one of the main features of his description of the 'pre-logical mentality' is his claim that it is characteristically willing to identify objects under apparently incompatible descriptions: one and the same thing can be both a stone, or a tree, and a spirit. And yet, as he says, a stone or a tree cannot after all be literally identical with a spirit – they must be two: but they are unified in the 'primitive mentality', in what Lévy-Bruhl calls 'mystical participation'.

Many anthropologists would reject the claim that there is genuine paradox in such beliefs; many, I suspect, would regard Lévy-Bruhl as an awful warning of the weird and wonderful misconceptions about savage thought which one falls into when one treats it in ploddingly literalist spirit. There can be no doubt that many apparent 'mystical participations' are *simply* symbolic identifications: Evans-Pritchard's famous example of the cucumber-ox is a case in point (Evans-Pritchard 1956: 203). The cucumber here seems unambiguously conceived by Nuer as *simply* representing, going proxy for, an ox in the sacrifice: there is no suggestion that it *is*, in any material sense, an ox. But as Evans-Pritchard's whole discussion in the chapter on 'The prob-lem of symbols' makes clear, by no means all, or even most, appar-ent cases of mystical participation are so unproblematic. Again, the discussion of symbolic magic in chapter 9 suggested that what is conceived as mimesis may thereby also be conceived as manifestation. Belief in the efficacy of symbolic enactments rests on a naturalising conception, on the part of the practitioners, of what is in reality a purely symbolic, or conventional, identification.

In any case Horton's approach is very different from that which would explain 'mystical participations' as purely symbolic iden-tifications. Horton, on the contrary, accepts that many, at least, of such beliefs do involve the ineradicable incoherence which Lévy-Bruhl claimed. But – so far from seeing them as contrasting on this account with scientific beliefs – he treats them as a symptom of the anomalousness inescapably generated *whenever* the language of a transcendental hypothesis redescribes (as, to explain, it must) observable phenomena, and which is therefore found in science too – as for example in the mystical participation of Eddington's two tables.

In the first few paragraphs of his book Eddington claims (not altogether seriously) to have sat down to write his lectures at *two* tables – the familiar, coloured and substantial table, and a scientific table which is "mostly emptiness" and in which"sparsely scattered", are "numerous electric charges rushing about with great speed" (Eddington 1928). The problem is that the apparently diverse properties of the familiar table and the scientific table seem to preclude their identification while, on the other hand, they are competing for the same exclusive portion of space. If, furthermore, the scientific table is not the familiar table, then how can it be possible to explain the characteristics of the familiar table in terms of the characteristics of the scientific table? "We may", according to Horton (1973*b*: 279), "have to settle for the reality of both tables, and for a mysterious unity-in-duality which holds between them. The homology with 'mystical participation' could hardly be clearer". "Taking this line implies the admission that the 'is' of correspondence-rule statements...stands for a unity-in-duality uniquely characteristic of the relation between the world of common sense and the world of theory" (Horton 1967: 51).

In his intellectualist interpretation of Durkheim's *Elementary Forms* Horton seeks to being out those themes in Durkheim's conception of primitive religion which are also central to his own views. Of these the most important are claimed to be the following:

(*a*) Durkheim, like Horton, insists that explanation of experience, to be intellectually satisfying, must go beyond experience; and sees in this a common characteristic of scientific and religious thought. To explain, Durkheim says (1915: 237ff.),

is to attach things to each other and to establish relations between them which make them appear as functions of each other and as vibrating sympathetically according to an internal law founded in their nature. But sensations, which see nothing except from the outside, could never make them disclose these relations and internal bonds; the intellect alone can create the notion of them...The great service that religions have rendered to thought is that they have constructed a first representation of what these relationships of kinship between things may be...The essential thing was not to leave the mind enslaved to visible appearances, but to teach it to dominate them and to connect what the senses separated; for from that moment when men have an idea that there are internal connections between things, science and philosophy become possible.

(*b*) Like Horton, Durkheim does not consider the personalistic character of traditional religious thought an essential difference marking it off from the scientific or rational (p. 26):

the fact that religious forces are frequently conceived under the form of spiritual beings or conscious wills, is no proof of their irrationality. The reason has no repugnance *a priori* to admitting that the so-called inanimate bodies should be directed by intelligences, just as the human body is, though contemporary science accommodates itself with difficulty to the hypothesis. When Leibniz proposed to conceive the external world as an immense society of minds, between which there were, and could be, only spiritual relations, he thought he was working as a rationalist, and saw nothing in this universal animism which could be offensive to the intellect.

(*c*) Durkheim, like Horton, seems to locate the difference between science and traditional religious thought not in their structure or functions, but in the institutionalised habits of critical self-analysis and of preparedness for self-refutation which are distinctive of scientific thought (pp. 237–9, 429):

The explanations of contemporary science are surer of being objective because they are more methodical and because they rest on more carefully controlled observations, but they do not differ in nature from those that satisfy primitive thought...in a general way, [science] brings a spirit of criticism into all its doings, which religion ignores...But these perfectionings of method are not enough to differentiate it from religion. In this regard both pursue the same end; scientific thought is only a more perfect form of religious thought.

(*d*) Finally, Horton suggests that Durkheim also stresses, as against Lévy-Bruhl, the *common* source and location of paradox in religious and scientific thought (pp. 238–9):

Today, as formerly, to explain is to show how one thing participates in one or several others...Is not the statement that a man is a kangaroo or the sun a bird, equal to identifying the two with each other? But our manner of thought is no different when we say of heat that it is movement, or of light that it is vibration of the ether, etc. Every time that we unite heterogeneous terms by an internal bond, we forcibly identify contraries...Thus between the logic of religious thought and that of scientific thought there is no abyss. The two are made up of the same elements, though inequally and differently developed.

Of these suggested points of common ground, the last is unconvincing. It is extremely doubtful whether Durkheim had in mind as precise and specific a thesis as Horton advances. For example, the passage from Durkheim just quoted continues:

The special character of the former [religious thought] seems to be its natural taste for immoderate confusions as well as sharp contrasts. It is voluntarily excessive in each direction. When it connects, it confounds; when it distinguishes, it opposes.

One might accordingly draw from Durkheim the view that (1) to identify heat with molecular motion is to "forcibly identify contraries" but that (2) such paradoxical identification is an inherent feature, "today, as formerly", of explanation; or the quite different view that (1) to connect or correlate heat with molecular motion is all that is necessary for explanatory purposes, and that (2) religious thought is "voluntarily excessive" in that "when it connects, it confounds". The most sensible conclusion is probably that Durkheim did not have any such very specific point in mind at all.

The remaining points of similarity are more genuine; it must nevertheless be remembered that they constitute only one strand in Durkheim's thinking about religion. For him, as he specifically asserts (p. 225), religion's

primary object is not to give men a representation of the physical world; for if that were its essential task, we could not understand how it has been able to survive, for, on this side, it is scarcely more than a fabric of errors. Before all, it is a system of ideas with which the individuals represent to themselves the society of which they are members, and the obscure but intimate relations which they have with it. This is its primary function; and though metaphorical and symbolic, this representation is not unfaithful.

It is certainly very difficult to see how this thesis is to be reconciled with (a)–(c), particularily (c): more generally, it is difficult to see how one and the same thing can be *both* an attempt to capture the trans-experiential relations between natural events *and* "a system of ideas with which the individuals represent to themselves the society of which they are members". If this latter claim is taken seriously as a claim about the *meaning* of religious ideas, the two claims are incompatible (see chapter 3): confused talk of 'dual referents' is of no avail.

Now undeniably this tension is present in Durkheim's work. He can only preserve his insistence (a constantly repeated theme in the book) that only his own account preserves the *truth* in religion – that his whole presentation rests on the postulate that millions of believers could not be wrong, the dupes of a tissue of errors – by treating religious doctrines as symbolic statements about society and not literal statements about nature. But to sustain his thesis of the evolution of science and philosophy from religion, he *must* treat them as literal statements about nature. Nor will a historical interpretation according to which what were originally symbolic statements subsequently became literalised and taken seriously as cosmological be compatible with a use of the symbolist interpretation to explain the *survival* of religious ideas.

So where Durkheim's conception of the relation between religious 'representations' and the social order is ultimately of the form 'A symbolises B', Horton's is of the form 'B serves as a model for A'. This is a decisive change, for it then appears as no more true to say that religious ideas are 'really about' society (that is, about empirical human society, rather than the extended spiritual society postulated by the believer) – or that they are simply images of social relationships projected onto a transcendental screeen – than it would be to say of billiard models of atomic interaction that they are 'really' symbolic statements about billiards, and not literal statements about imperceptibly minute objects.

Nevertheless, there are still grounds for calling Horton's form of intellectualism 'Durkheimian'. It is Durkheimian first in its emphasis on the transcendental character of scientific as of religious thought, its creative role in "binding together things which sensation leaves apart from one another". But more specifically, the project of showing how conceptions of nature and its workings are traditionally modelled on analogies taken from the social order, as in Horton's explanation of the 'personal idiom' of traditional cosmology (or, to take another example, not from Horton, as in the idea that operative acts, which produce *social* changes, are taken as models for the magical production of *natural* changes), can with some justice be called 'Durkheimian'. But of course both these points ignore the central symbolist element in Durkheim's work; and for this reason it would be a mistake to take Durkheim himself as unambiguously a 'Durkheimian intellectualist'.

12

'*Traditional*' and '*modern*'

Why the intellectualist needs a contrast between '*traditional*' and '*modern*'; ways of making it

Consideration of Horton's intellectualist account of traditional religious thought breaks down into two questions:

(1) Can the cosmologies of traditional religions be regarded as theories or transcendental hypotheses?

(2) If they can be, how are they differentiated from scientific theory; and on what grounds do we group them – together with modern Christianity – as *religions*?

In this chapter I examine question (2) (leaving (1) for the final chapter): since the subject is vast, I can do no more than survey a ragbag of considerations.

In line with the two parts of question (2), intellectualism requires the contrast between 'traditional' and 'modern' consciousness to serve two purposes: to differentiate between science and traditional religion as species of the genus *explanatory transcendental hypothesis*; and to differentiate between modern and traditional religion as species of the genus *religion*. But now what is meant here by 'traditional' and 'modern'? So far in this book I have been using the term 'traditional' in a rough-and-ready pre-theoretical way to cover broadly the same ground as 'primitive' in 'primitive religion' or 'primitive culture'; where small-scale, often pre-literate, culture-specific 'primitive religions' are contrasted with the 'world religions' such as Christianity, Islam, Buddhism. For the intellectualist, traditional religions are religions which not merely originate in but presently have as their primary function the explanation and control of men's environment; it remains to be seen, however, whether this is to be an empirical result or a definitional truth.

Certainly to use 'traditional' as simply equivalent to something like 'pre-scientific' is to cast the net far too wide for intellectualism: for in this sense all religions, including Christianity, Islam and so forth are or comparatively recently have been 'traditional'. But there is one characteristic which the world religions share and which must presumably count them out from the intellectualist's favoured category of 'traditional religions': their conspicuously other-worldly and soteriological concerns. It is not easy to see how these can be accommodated in any very direct way in the intellectualist's basic pattern of analysis. They are, on the other hand, at the centre of the stage in various well-known and completely non-intellectualist conceptions of religion. Of course the essence of the intellectualist's position is that, in terms of explanatory priority, religion is before it is anything else an agency-based cosmology developing out of a this-worldly search for understanding and control. He can grant that once such a cosmology is accepted it opens up various possibilities of catering for a variety of emotional and social needs – some of which when exploited may eventually result in crucial modifications in the original cosmological starting point itself. But he will not want to include the results of such a process of modification among the 'traditional religions' which are to be, so to speak, his central specimens.

What on the other hand is a 'modern religion'? Here we seem to come down in the end to a single candidate: contemporary Christianity, particularly perhaps in its more 'demythologised' forms. This much at least is therefore clear: that in the field of religion 'traditional' and 'modern' are by no means exhaustive categories. In Horton's case the primary examples of traditional religion are tribe-specific African religions – relatively this-worldly religions which, so to speak, deduce life after death from the existence of ancestor-spirits, rather than deducing the existence of ancestor-spirits from life after death.[82] His starting point is then in the comparative study of three (more or less) definite cases: African traditional religious thought, modern Christianity and modern science. But on this basis he seeks to construct a general inventory of similarities and contrasts between 'traditional' and 'modern thought' (Horton 1967, 1973a, b). In this inventory, and often in other writers' work, the contrast between traditional and modern thought is taken to depend on a *syndrome* of characteristics. (Though, as we shall see, Horton does consider that two key factors underlie this syndrome.) 'Modern' and 'traditional thought' are multi-dimensional concepts and, in a number of dimensions, opposites; they are not exhaustive, but because variations in the dimensions may be uncorrelated, there may be no simple continuum between them.

Let us now begin with two questions. (*a*) What items are being said to be traditional, or modern – belief-systems (world-views, forms of consciousness or thought), cultures, societies, 'predicaments' or men? The primary focus of interest here is on *belief-systems*, specifically on belief-systems which can be said to constitute a cosmology or world-view; I shall also allow myself to talk in an ideal-typical way of the 'traditional thinker' etc. (*b*) Are we interested in a *general* characterisation or inventory of the differences between modern and traditional thought, or are we addressing ourselves specifically to the question of what marks off traditional religious thought from modern science? Our primary interest is in Horton's answer to the more specific question, but I shall begin with some remarks about the more general one.

The criteria which might be used to determine the traditional/modern orientation of a belief-system can be very roughly sorted into three groups.

(i) One could characterise a belief-system as 'modern' or 'traditional' by reference to features of the society in which it is held which are logically (though of course not necessarily causally) independent of the intrinsic properties of the belief-system itself. Such features would centre on, for example, the *technology* (for procuring food, transportation, building places to live, storing and conveying information etc.); the *social structure* (patterns of group affiliation and authority relationships as determined by non-social characteristics such as birth etc., modes of organisation, e.g. for production and consumption); *cultural styles* (art-forms, ceremonial, interaction codes etc., to the extent that these are not internally dependent on the overarching belief-system or world-view itself). Examples of contrasts falling under this category which have been thought relevant to the modern/traditional distinction are: organic/mechanical, industrial/non-industrial, literate/non-literate (this last involves the information-storing know-how of the society).

(ii) Another way of characterising a belief-system as modern or traditional is by reference to the attitudes with which it is held or the manner in which it is institutionalised. A whole cluster of proposed criteria for differentiating between traditional and modern falls under this category – centring on such questions as whether beliefs are (in the sense of Weber) 'traditionally' or 'rationally' legitimated, and whether there is cognitive specialisation (i.e. are some people trained or expected to be especially expert on the belief-system or certain branches or aspects of it?). These will be further considered below.

(iii) Finally, a world-view may be characterised as traditional or modern in terms of its *content*. Obvious bases for contrast here might concern, for example, whether the fundamental organising concepts in the cosmology were of personal beings or of impersonal entities, or what conception was taken of the ontological relationship between the natural, the social and the conventional. This latter issue has already featured in chapters 7–9; it may also serve here as a reminder that contrasts of content may involve not merely clearly and explicitly entrenched concepts and beliefs but also typical tendencies of thought, underlying but influencing and pervasive pictures etc. (A comparison here would be with the Marxist notion of an alienated, 'reifying' consciousness of society.) Ernest Gellner's contrast between 'rational-orderly' and 'meaningful-cosy' pictures of the world (in Gellner 1975 and elsewhere), is a contrast of total atmosphere between, as it were, world-views-as-they-are-lived, but it is clearly based on at least the first of the contrasts of content mentioned above (as well as others, of course).

I am not suggesting that these categories are very clearly demarcated. Consider, for example, a dimension often thought relevant in this area: ritualised/non-ritualised. Do we have here in mind the degree to which social relations or events, whatever these may be taken to be in a society, are ceremonialised? In this case the contrast belongs to category (i). Do we on the other hand have in mind the degree to which the society is secularised? In this case the contrast belongs (in part) to (iii). There can in principle be highly ceremonious secular societies and extremely unceremonious and informal religious ones. A more difficult classificatory nut to crack is posed by Barnes' suggestion "that the occurrence of anomaly within various systems of belief forms the best framework within which to attempt comparison of those systems" (Barnes 1973: 190). The *occurrence* of anomaly in a belief-system – the fact, for example, that it would contain certain contradictions if deductively closed, or that it contains intrinsically obscure or incoherent beliefs – is a matter of content. But its interest for comparative purposes must presumably lie – as Barnes' remark suggests – in the light it throws on the attitudes with which the belief-system is held (or the functions it serves), either through people's reaction to awareness of it or through the fact that they remain *unaware* of it. This issue will be considered at greater length in the next chapter.

Contrasts belonging to category (i) may be useful as a way of fixing the extension of 'traditional religion'. But they cannot answer the original questions, which were: What on the intellectualist view makes traditional religion *religion*, and what differentiates it from science? For no one thinks that what *makes* (conceptually, not causally) a belief-system 'religious' or 'scientific' is the independent features of the society in which it is in fact held. And in any case the natural approach for the sociology of thought is to try to pick out a form of thought in terms of its content and character (in a broad sense which covers considerations falling under both (ii) and (iii)), leaving open for empirical investigation its relation to social determinants.

Horton's account of the contrast

I think one can say without undue simplification that intellectualists (Tylor, Frazer, the 'intellectualist' side of Durkheim) take traditional religion to be religion primarily on grounds from category (iii) – i.e. of content – whereas they distinguish it from science on grounds from category (ii) – i.e. in terms of the attitudes with and institutions in which it is held; and in this Horton follows suit. Furthermore, for Tylor and Frazer, and again in effect for Horton, the specific characteristic which makes such thought 'religious' is its personal idiom: "By religion", Frazer says (1911, 1, 1: 222; 1957: 65–6),

I understand a propitiation and conciliation of powers, superior to man which are believed to direct and control the course of nature and of human life. Thus defined, religion consists of two elements, a theoretical and a practical, namely, a belief in powers higher than man and an attempt to propitiate and please them. Of the two belief clearly comes first, since we must believe in the existence of a divine being before we can attempt to please him.

There is in fact no need for the intellectualist to saddle himself with this as a definition, involving him in problems about whether it should really be taken as stating a necessary condition. It is enough to stipulate the 'two elements' as jointly sufficient: that answers the question of why traditional cosmologies are properly called 'religious'. Thus stated the position seems reasonable to me and I shall not examine it further. I turn instead to the much more contentious question of differentiating between 'traditional religious' and 'scientific' thought.

Here again, as has been noted, Horton follows intellectualist tradition in locating the difference not in content but in attitudes; in particular, though the personal idiom of traditional thought is (on his view) what makes it religious, it is certainly not what marks it off in principle from science. Horton says (1967: 70) that

the difference between non-personal and personalized theories is more than anything else a difference in the idiom of the explanatory quest ...Making the business of personal versus impersonal entities the crux of the difference between tradition and science not only blocks the understanding of tradition. It also draws a red herring across the path of an understanding of science...For the progressive acquisition of knowledge, man needs both the right kind of theories *and* the right attitude to them. But it is only the latter which we call science.

What are these attitudes? For present purposes, Horton's account of the contrasting attitudes of a traditional culture may be summarised under five linked headings.

(*a*) Unreflective. Traditional thought does not reflect on its own conceptual structure and epistemic bases: "there is a sense in which [it] includes among its accomplishments neither Logic nor Philosophy" (p. 162). In contrast a distinctive feature of modern thought is its purifying concern with methodological and epistemological issues raised by its theorising about the world. Often indeed (as in Einstein's work) there is no sharp distinction between these activities and the theorising itself.

(*b*) Unsystematic. The claim here is not that traditional cosmologies cannot be presented as systematic and unified bodies of belief (on the contrary, Horton has stressed the possibility of doing so, for example, in the case of the Kalabari among whom he has worked), but that they are not normally so conceived by the traditional thinker – rather, particular beliefs about spirits and their actions are called in as required to explain particular episodes of sickness and so on. Connectedly, there is no thought of putting the overarching body of beliefs to any kind of experimental test, while it is characteristic of scientific thought that it seeks to find ways of subjecting whole theories to some kind of programme of controlled empirical enquiry, and of absorbing the results of this programme. (It is not being claimed that the only form this absorption can take is that of straightforward falsification.)

Points (*a*) and (*b*) are clearly very closely connected: (*b*) essentially states that there is no *explicit* and *reflective* attempt at systematic formulation and empirical control.

(*c*) Mixed motives. Traditional thought is shaped not only by the "goals of explanation and prediction" but also by other motives and needs. But, in characteristic intellectualist fashion, Horton ascribes logical priority to the explanatory goals, seeing the other motives as contingent on the personalistic cosmology these explanatory goals produce (p. 164):

There is little doubt that because the theoretical entities of traditional thought happen to be people, they give particular scope for the working of emotional and aesthetic motives. Here, perhaps, we do have something about the personal idiom in theory that does militate indirectly against the taking up of a scientific attitude; for where there are powerful emotional and aesthetic loadings on a particular theoretical scheme, these must add to the difficulties of abandoning this scheme when cognitive goals press towards doing so.

With the development of scientific thought, on the other hand (p. 164),

people come to see that if ideas are to be used as efficient tools of explanation and prediction, they must not be allowed to become tools for anything else.

Or, as Ernest Gellner proclaims in nostalgic-censorious vein (Gellner 1964: 211):

We cannot recover those balmy days when our knowledge of the world was so feeble that the objectivity of the world could be prostituted for our edification, when theories could be held true basically because they made sense of our lives and social arrangements.

But it is interesting to note the very different, and non-intellectualist, emphasis of Gellner's passage. (cp. Horton: "...*because* the theoretical entities of traditional thought *happen* to be people...")

(*d*) No (or low) cognitive division of labour. This point is not explicitly made by Horton in his 1967 articles but has been developed from his discussion by others and endorsed by Horton.[83] Traditional thought is not characteristically the product of a specialised group of mind-workers charged with producing theories. In contrast, scientific thought always has been to some degree, and in the contemporary world quite obviously is. However, this point must be treated carefully. It cannot be the claim that scientific thought is the *product* of a minority of intellectuals whereas traditional thought is not; for, for all we know, traditional thought may be. Nor is it quite the claim that scientific thought is the *property* of a minority of intellectuals, whereas traditional thought is common property, though there is truth in this. (Yet of course in both types of culture there is some disparity of knowledge between specialists – scientists, witchdoctors, or 'old men who know', and laymen.) Rather the point is that an *institutionalised* group of specialists become experts in and seek to develop science in modern cultures, whereas there is no comparable institutionalised specialisation in the case of traditional cultures.

There is an important difference between (*a*)–(*c*) and (*d*). The first three may be regarded as *constitutive* of what makes for 'traditional' as opposed to 'scientific' thought. But in an ideal society in which everyone spent more or less the same amount of time on contributing to scientific journals, those journals would not for that very reason cease to be 'scientific'. Specialisation may be one of the social determinants of the essential characteristics of scientific or, more broadly, modern thought, but is not itself one of them.

(*e*) Protective attitude to established beliefs and concepts. Although belief in the efficacy of particular medicines, witchdoctors etc. may often be subject to scepticism, the framework of belief in various types of agency credited with natural powers is never itself questioned by the traditional thinker: it is protected against predictive failures and recalcitrant data by 'secondary elaboration'. In contrast, Horton remarks (1967: 168), "much has been made of the scientist's essential scepticism towards established beliefs; and one must, I think, agree that this above all is what distinguishes him from the traditional thinker". Another aspect of the point, not directly touched on by Horton, might be brought out in terms of the Weberian contrast between *traditional* and *rational* legitimation of belief. Traditional thought gains its authority from "piety for what actually, allegedly, or presumably has always existed" (Weber 1948: 296). Scientific thought, on the other hand, is legitimated by its actual, alleged or presumed power to cope with the relevant facts. In a way, we are led back here to criterion (*a*), for one might think that the characteristic of modern thought is precisely its awareness of the contrast between these modes of legitimation, its rejection of the traditional mode and its consequent epistemological concerns – that is, its interest in the question of what forms justification of claims to knowledge must take.

Horton considers that (*a*)–(*c*) and (*e*), as well as other aspects of traditional thought (for example, belief in the magical power of words), can be explained in terms of two key factors.

(1) The first of these "is that in traditional cultures there is no developed awareness of alternatives to the established body of theoretical tenets" (Horton 1967: 155).

(2) Furthermore, "any challenge to established tenets is a threat of chaos, of the cosmic abyss, and therefore evokes intense anxiety" (p. 156).

One should perhaps first register a slight sense of incompatability between these two points. If the traditional thinker does not *conceive* of the possibility that his traditionally handed-down beliefs are wrong, how can he feel anxious about the possibility that they are wrong? The answer no doubt is that Horton envisages him as being unable to conceive, not the incorrectness of his own picture, but the correctness of any other piecture. This, presumably, is why he thinks (2) follows from (1). For to suppose the incorrectness of one's own theoretical picture is then to suppose the incorrectness of the only possible theoretical picture: that is (apparently) to suppose chaos. Quite what this anxiety-producing supposition is supposed to be, or why it produces anxiety, is perhaps not very clear. But in any case, the idea I shall want to suggest is the opposite of Horton's – to put it in a paradox, the traditional thinker *can* conceive the correctness of other theoretical pictures: what he cannot conceive is the incorrectness of his own.

Let us however remain with point (2) for a moment. What evidence does Horton give for it? The evidence comes down to the facts of taboo: the "reaction of horror and aversion to certain actions or happenings which are seen as monstrous and polluting" (p. 175). The connexion with (2) is made by means of a theory Douglas has proposed, to the effect that abominated objects are abominated because they cut across categories: either falling into a no-man's-land of classificatory incompleteness (showing that classifications which are supposed to be exhaustive are not) or perpetrating classificatory inconsistencies (showing that classifications which are supposed to be exclusive are not). Or to put the point in another way, such objects are exceptions to generalisations which are otherwise (ought always to be?) true: for example, twins are exceptions to 'Human births are never multiple; multiple births are characteristic of animals.'

Methodologically speaking Horton's theory is thus an example of how evidence may be brought to bear on a theory only indirectly, through prior acceptance of another theory. There is nothing wrong with that. But even granting Douglas' proposal, the phenomenon it describes can be explained in other ways. Consider for example the conflation of the moral and conventional order of society with the natural order, which, it has been suggested, is a feature of traditional culture. If the natural order is a moral order, natural laws moral laws, then what infringes on natural order is either above the law – thus, sacred – or a sinner against it, and hence abominated. (Of course the idea of an infringement of natural laws seems coherent only so long as they *are* thought of on the model of moral laws.) Now cross-categorial objects may indeed be sacred rather than abominated (e.g. the pangolin), and this fact is better explained on the current suggestion than on Horton's. For on his account *all* cross-categorial objects should be anxiety-producing abominations. In point of fact the 'anxiety-thesis' does no other real work in Horton's overall scheme than to explain taboo, and can therefore safely be dropped.

Let us now return to (1). First, we must distinguish two theses:

(i) The traditional thinker is unwilling or unable to assimilate alternative 'theoretical tenets' from outside his own culture.

(ii) A traditional culture does not itself autonomously generate theoretical alternatives to its prevailing world-view.

I think one can tentatively say that (i) is on the whole false, and (ii), true. (There would of course have to be qualifications if one were to state these points carefully, as Vansina's independent thinkers (chapter 1) show.) (ii) would be explained by (e), that is, by the traditional mode of legitimation of belief. The interesting thing about (i) on the other hand is the *way* in which new cosmological ideas are assimilated in a traditional culture. Traditional thought tends to the syncretic; scientific thought, to the choosy. The traditional thinker's intellectual toolbox, when he comes into contact with alternative ideas, runs to accumulation, becoming crowded with a collection of methods and ideas which might come in useful. The scientist's is relatively sparser, with wholesale discarding of outworn equipment at regular intervals, rather like what Schumpeter called the 'creative destruction' found in capitalist production.

But this metaphor of toolboxes may be misleading. For, in another sense, when theories are treated only as tools the scientist too tends to retain old stock which has been replaced. But the point is precisely that he treats old theories *simply as tools*: his attitude towards them is instrumentalist, not realist. Thus Newtonian mechanics is retained and used in calculation in various branches of science, but it is no longer treated as a representation of reality. The traditional thinker does not merely have a greater tendency to retain old ideas when new ones come along; he retains them in realist spirit. This is what I had in mind in saying that his inability is not to conceive that other theoretical tenets might be right, but to conceive that his might be wrong. When old ideas are set aside they are not discarded as erroneous models of reality; they are, so to speak, rejected in 'realist spirit': setting them aside tends to take the form of setting aside the reality which they are nevertheless still thought of as capturing. Thus the Tikopia chief converted to Christianity makes farewell offerings to the old gods.[84] A "gentle oracular spirit who lived in the forest by Efon" in Yorubaland in 1927 "told Aladejare, the Alaye, that 'her pot of indigo dye had been broken by the new road, and that she was leaving Efon to return no more' – so the old gods were leaving as the new order advanced" (Peel 1968: 94). The new order does eventually bring about a change of beliefs, but not by directly changing beliefs about what is in the world, with the rejection of some as false. Rather, a story is told about changes taking place in what is in the world itself.

If this account is correct, then what is absent from traditional thought is a clear-cut conception of ideas as no more than *ideas*, about an independent reality, which for that very reason could be, quite simply, *wrong*. (Of course it is unnecessary to stress that 'modern' thinkers' hold on this conception is all too often on the precarious side.) This, apart from thesis (ii), seems to me – so far as I am able to judge – to be the truth in (1), i.e. in Horton's claim about lack of awareness of alternatives in a traditional culture. Yet this unreadiness to reject old ideas as simply *false* need not in any way go with an unreadiness to accept new ideas from outside. Nor does it appear to explain points (*a*)–(*c*) and (*e*). Rather, like (ii), it seems more readily explained *in terms of* (*a*) and (*e*).

Is the suggested contrast of attitudes overdrawn?

We have found no good reason to accept Horton's two claims, (1) and (2), as he states them, nor the suggestion that some single factor of this kind underlies all those characteristics (*a*)–(*c*) and (*e*), which on his view distinguish traditional religious thought from science. But what of this view itself?

It seems to me that Horton is right here – that is, that these characteristics do distinguish traditional religious thought from science, even if nothing else does. (In the next chapter I shall consider the claim that traditional religious cosmologies originate and persist primarily as transcendental hypotheses. If there are grounds for rejecting this claim, then of course there are also much *bigger* differences.) But that they do is one of those big, vague truths which are difficult to see for little, precise qualifications.

These difficulties are particularily great in the case of (*c*). Obviously the most scientific person is influenced in his development or acceptance of theories about the world and society by a variety of emotional pressures and commitments. We normally think nothing of such motives when they influence the development of a new theory (so long as they are combined with a genuine regard for accounting for the data, and do not result in something which from the start is clearly inadequate), but frown on the intrusion of wishful thinking when it comes to its testing. In accordance with this distinction one might say that emotional needs have shaped the content of traditional religious cosmologies, or that emotional needs prevent its abandonment when 'cognitive goals press towards doing so'. On the first of these points it is not at first obvious that – at least on Horton's view – any strong contrast with scientific theory-building emerges. On his account emotional needs do not enter into determining the personalistic character of traditional cosmology – he has a quite different explanation of that. The suggestion must instead be that *particular* developments of belief within this overall scheme are significantly more influenced by emotional or ideological imperatives than in the case of scientific thought. To me this suggestion is convincing. The second point is in essence that the traditional thinker has a more protective attitude towards his beliefs than the scientist because he has a greater need to believe in them or is more influenced by this attitude. Whether or not this more protective attitude exists will be discussed in connexion with (*e*). Granting that it does, I am not sure how one could tell that a greater need to believe is the cause of it – rather than, say, the fact that beliefs are traditionally legitimated and thus not to be put into question.

But the real dispute is likely to come on (*a*), (*b*) and (*e*). The objection here tends to be not that the traditional thinker is more critical, reflective and less conservative than Horton makes him out to be, but that the scientist is *less* critical etc., and *more* conservative, than Horton claims; and these points are made on Kuhnian grounds (see Barnes 1973; Marwick 1974).

Here we need to separate points (*a*) and (*b*) on the one hand and (*e*) on the other. A person or social group may be notably prone towards replacing beliefs at regular intervals, but at the same time quite unreflective, unsystematic and unexperimental in the way he or it holds them. The converse situation is also possible: mediaeval scholastic thought about theology, philosophy and science appears highly reflective, analytical and systematic, but certainly has a strongly protective attitude towards fundamental theoretical tenets, and a respect for arguments from traditional authority. To think that Kuhn's work gives cause for qualifying the contrast between science and traditional religious thought on the score of (*a*) and (*b*) is to misunderstand it: his claim is not that the scientist is less methodologically self-conscious, analytical or systematic than has been thought. Kuhn's account does however become relevant with respect to (*e*): on his view, in a period of normal science a paradigm is developed in a programme of experimental enquiry, anomalies being defused by auxiliary hypotheses or even put on the shelf. But is this not – at a more disciplined, systematic level – identical with the traditional thinker's process of 'secondary elaboration' as described for example by Evans-Pritchard in the case of the Azande?

In chapter 1 I distinguished between structural and attitudinal blocks to falsifiability. *Any* generalising system of beliefs about experience has structural resources which can be used to preserve given beliefs against experience by the generation of alternative auxiliary hypotheses. This reflection, combined with an anti-realist conception of meaning, leads to the relativism discussed in the appendix. There I argue against this form of relativism on realist grounds. The question for present purposes is therefore simply whether traditional thought exploits such structural resources to a significantly greater degree than scientific thought does – well beyond the point, in Lakatos' phrase, at which the 'research programme' enters onto a 'degenerating problem shift'.[85] Now consider the rough claim that traditional cosmological thought is more stable, less prone to change than scientific thought. Here again various elucidations, about the level in the respective belief-systems at which the comparison is being made and so forth, would have to be made; nevertheless the claim seems to me to contain obvious truth. What then are the logically possible explanations of this fact?

(i) Traditional religious thought is not, contrary to appearances, cosmological at all: it does not seek to provide a representation and explanation of experience. The question of experience's coming into conflict with it therefore does not arise.

(ii) It does indeed contain cosmological theory; this theory is simply better than the theories which have been discarded in the West – any apparent conflicts with experience it engenders are merely the result of human error or are otherwise trivially explicable. There is therefore no need to change the theory.

(iii) Traditional cosmologies do contain important anomalies and in particular do lead to genuine conflicts with experience, but these anomalies and conflicts are not noticed or registered by the traditional thinker.

(iv) They are noticed; nevertheless, for one reason or another, nothing is done about them.

(v) People in a traditional culture exploit the structural resources for conservatism built into their system of belief to a far greater degree than scientists use the resources built into theirs.

Explanation (i) has already been rejected; its falsity is in any case presupposed by all parties to the present debate. Note also that the fact that, when (i) has been rejected, (ii) remains as a possible explanation, shows the erroneousness of the often-made claim that the truth-value of beliefs under study by the sociologist is irrelevant as far as explanation of why they are held goes. (Curiously enough, one author makes this claim in the very same paper in which he advances the thesis that "the occurrence and treatment of anomaly within various systems of belief forms the best framework within which to attempt comparison of those systems" (Barnes 1973: 190). He does not explain how one recognises anomaly – inconsistency – in a set of beliefs while remaining neutral on the question of their truth-value.) Of course to reject the view that the truth-value of a set of beliefs is irrelevant for purposes of sociological explanation is in no way to accept the equally incorrect view that true beliefs stand in no need of sociological explanation.

In any case anyone who explains the relative stability of traditional thought exclusively in terms of one or more of (iii)–(v) is implicitly or explicitly rejecting (ii). Here I do so explicitly. It should be noted that of the remaining factors (iv) poses some potential danger for the intellectualist. For when a system of belief is recognised as being in conflict with experience, or in other ways anomalous, but nothing is done about it, this must tend to cast doubt on the view that it originated and continues to function as an explanation of experience. I shall return to this point in the next chapter.[86]

If (v) is rejected, one has to explain the greater stability of traditional thought exclusively in terms of (iii) and (iv). But, while there is no doubt truth in both, exclusive concentration on them is unconvincing. It is far more plausible to recognise (v) as a significant factor. This does not *entail* that 'the traditional thinker' is less prone to changing *his own views* than the scientist. Nevertheless, the touchingly humble claim (in the mouth of the social scientist) that the average scientist is no readier to change his own views than the average tribesman strikes me as being on the fanciful side. Science contains as a strongly institutionalised element in its ideology the ideal of the scientist open-mindedly changing his theories in the light of experience, as well as the ideal of the scientist battling on with his own theory against apparent initial set-backs; and this must have some effect. But I need not press this point, even while adhering to (v). For even if no scientist ever rejected his own theories, he could still reject theories handed on to him from others, refusing in their case to indulge in 'secondary elaboration'. This in itself would provide the mechanism for a regular turn-over of ideas. The stuff of scientific debate is controversy – in general most academics probably spend most of their time criticising other people's ideas (and perhaps sometimes changing their own); nor does such disagreement always occur within a shared paradigm – it can also involve a clash of paradigms.

The traditional thinker is, precisely, traditional: this is not directly a matter of being unwilling to reject one's own theories, but of unwillingness to reject traditionally handed-down ones – of "piety for what actually, allegedly, or presumably has always existed". It is a consequence of the contrast between 'traditional' and 'rational' legitimation of belief that a mode of thought which is in this sense traditional will, given equally recalcitrant experience, exploit its structural resources for conservatism to a far greater degree than one which is, in this sense, rational.

Science no doubt contains 'traditional' elements of legitimation (arguments from the views of important historical ancestors etc.); nevertheless, in terms of the Weberian terminology, it is a 'rational' rather than a 'traditional' mode of thought. In short, Horton's account of the syndrome of attitudes which differentiate traditional religious and scientific thought seems broadly acceptable (even if the suggestion that a single key factor underlies them is rejected). Hence if the two forms of thought have the same structure and functions, then the intellectualist is in a position to argue that *only* these attitudes distinguish them in principle. It is to this question, of similarity of structure and function, that we must now turn.

13

Paradox and explanation

Structure and function of traditional cosmologies

It has repeatedly been noted that intellectualism contrasts science and traditional cosmological thought on grounds of attitude, and compares them on grounds of structure and explanatory function. But the distinction invoked here can of course be no more than a rule of thumb: and when such significant differences of attitude exist between science and traditional religious thought as those conceded in the last chapter, one might legitimately wonder whether they can be regarded *merely* as differences of attitude. In this context a *mere* difference of attitude is one whose existence can be consistently accepted with the view that both systems of thought have essentially the same primary function – that of explanation and control – and essentially the same origins – as theories developed to serve these functions. But it is not clear for example whether the general sketch, given in the last chapter (pp. 199ff.), of the way cosmological beliefs change in a traditional culture and old beliefs are discarded can, if correct, be regarded as a mere difference of attitude. For if the point were developed it might throw doubt on the intellectualist's account of change in such beliefs – according to which rival sets of belief are in effect compared, and one is preferred, on grounds of explanatory force. Such an account seems to suppose that the traditional thinker can be depicted as treating rival beliefs *as* rival representations of reality. This possibility has sometimes been attacked on relativist grounds (though of course, if correct, the attack would work equally well against the parallel account of scientific theory-change). The present difficulties are less philo-sophically heavyweight and more soberly empirical; they would work differentially to suggest that the traditional thinker (unlike the scientist) does not approach changes of belief in anything like the way suggested by intellectualism.

I shall not follow this point up here; but another difficulty which I shall consider concerns believers' attitude (or lack of it) towards anomalies or apparent paradoxes which exist in their system of beliefs. Here again a 'difference of attitude' may begin to seem much more than a *mere* difference of attitude. But let us first examine what similarities between the two modes of thought, in point of structure and function, the intellectualist can point to.

On a literalist approach it does become clear that, as the intellectualist claims, in traditional cultures religious beliefs are often brought in in contexts of prediction and explanation, and religious actions are often performed with the aim of controlling natural events. Of course it does not follow that explanation, prediction and control are the primary or primitive functions of religious belief and action. As for structure, the overarching proposal is that traditional religious thought, like any attempt to get beyond the observable regularities and absences of regularity to a more coherent underlying order, conceives of unobservable entities and characterises their behaviour in terms of some systematic pattern of laws. Again it would be fallacious simply to conclude that traditional thought, where it makes reference to unobservables, as theory does, must also be the result of a quest for a 'hidden' explanatory order, as theory is. But the conclusion becomes considerably more plausible if the structural comparisons with science can be made sufficiently detailed. Here one naturally turns to the comparisons Horton has sought to draw between Western science and African traditional thought (Horton 1967, 1973*b*).

The Lévy-Bruhlian anomalies and the comparison with science

In his project of providing a general characterisation of 'traditional thought', Horton is very aware of the precedents set by Lévy-Bruhl, who discussed the general characteristics of the 'primitive' or 'pre-logical' mentality. Horton's attitude towards the Lévy-Bruhlian thesis that certain distinctive types of paradox characterise 'pre-logical' thought, is by no means one of whole-sale rejection. Nevertheless he does regard many of the para-doxes Lévy-Bruhl claimed to detect as merely apparent; and – this is the important point – that they are merely apparent becomes clear, on his view, only when the relevant aspects of traditional thought are set in their correct comparative context: namely, with scientific thought.

Thus the gods of traditional thought are often thought of as identifiable with a number of godlings, or other beings or things, which are nevertheless not identified with each other. This apparent many–one nature of the gods is regarded by Lévy-Bruhl as a characteristic area of anomaly. Horton, on the other hand, offers an explanation designed to show that comparison with science dispels the appearance of paradox. An applied scientist may use (where it is convenient) a local theory covering a specialised domain, and switch to a more fundamental general theory only as it becomes necessary. Similarly, Horton argues (1967: 62), in traditional thought "the spirits provide the means of setting an event within a relatively limited causal context", whereas "the supreme being...provides a means of setting an event within the widest possible context". Thus

the relation between the many spirits and the one God loses much of its aura of mystery...it is essentially the same as the relation between the homogeneous atoms and planetary systems of fundamental particles in the thinking of our chemist...it is a by-product of certain very general features of the way theories are used in explanation.

Is this an adequate account? Consider an ideal-typical traditional cosmology in which diverse spirits govern or underpin diverse areas of experience, and the high god ultimately controls all (such as is discussed in Horton 1971: 101). The relation between spirits and high god may then be comparable, according to Horton, either to that between a general theory and special theories reducible to it or to that between special theories and a general theory which supersedes them. Take the first alternative. In this case the situation may be that the spirits govern events and God governs the spirits. Or the spirits initiate sequences of events and God – while perhaps acting occasionally as 'first cause' – sustains the efficacy of causal connexions in the sequence. But now suppose our cosmology *identifies* the lower spirits as personae of the high god. Why should it do that? Why not be satisfied with an ontologically articulate and puzzle-free hierarchy of high god and lower spirits? The many–one identification is not explained, and so the 'aura of mystery' remains.

Now take the second alternative. If Horton's chemist is equally committed to the view that an atom is a planetary system of fundamental particles *and* to the view that it is homogeneous no matter how small the parts of it that may be considered, then he is certainly in trouble. But this is where one of Horton's *contrasts* between science and traditional cosmologies is illuminating – the scientist envisages as a matter of course the possibility that a range of incompatible theories may fit a domain of facts to reasonable degrees of approximation. There is therefore room for alternative conceptualisations of a given problem. Scientific thought includes the notion of 'can be usefully thought of for present purposes as', as well as 'actually is'. Thus, to take another example, a man who accepts that Einsteinian physics has superseded Newtonian physics, and is strictly speaking incompatible with it, may nevertheless quite consistently think through a practical problem in terms of classical mechanics; for the theory is correct to a far higher degree of approximation than his figures are. Similarly the relation between homogeneous and planetary-system atoms in the chemist's thought is roughly an intrumentalist– realist relation.[87] This is the relation which is, I think, at the back of Horton's mind when he says that the relation between spirits and god is 'essentially the same'. But explicit reflection on the nature of that relation shows that this cannot be right. It is certainly tempting to say that just as the homogeneous atom is 'really' a planetary system of particles, so the spirits are 'really' God, thus apparently resolving the obscure relation of multiplicity-in-unity between them. But the chemist's thinking involves not two different levels of theory, but two different cognitive attitudes towards incompatible theories. There is nothing to suggest that the traditional thinker, regards, say, the spirits as useful fictions and the high god as the real thing. He is equally convinced of the existence of both (?) kinds of personal being, like a chemist who believes atoms to be both homogeneous *and* planetary systems of particles. So the mystery remains undispelled.

Pursuing his structural comparison between science and traditional thought, Horton goes on to make two further points. The 'spirituality' of the beings postulated in traditional cosmologies consists, he suggests, in their lack of personal or social characteristics. And the reason why traditional thought does not supply them with these characteristics is just the same as the reason why science does not predicate colour of molecules or temperature of electrons: although both take their theoretical models from analogies with everyday experience, they select only certain characteristics of these everyday analogies – those in respect of which the analogy serves as a representation of the 'theoretical calculus'. In reply to this argument one can make, I think, at least three points.

Firstly, the non-physical nature of the gods, their extraordinary logical characteristics, and their great powers, give them a sufficiently 'spiritual' aura, however, detailed and vividly described might be their personal and social life. Secondly, scientific thought normally itself supplies the reasons why certain aspects of the everyday analogy, colour and temperature, say, cannot be carried over to the theoretical model. This goes also for the unobservability of theoretical entities (they are too small etc.). Traditional thought, on the other hand, in general explains neither why the gods should lack the characteristics it fails to supply, nor why they should be unobservable at all. And thirdly, it has often been pointed out that models can have a heuristic value in science, for those characteristics of the everyday analogy which do not initially interpret the theory may suggest ways of expanding the theoretical model beyond the demands of the calculus, and thus may suggest further theoretical questions. This would of course be particularly true of a theoretical model conceived in terms of personal beings with cosmological powers. In general the scientist, having committed himself in introducing a theory to the existence of certain types of theoretical entity, will naturally seek to discover further characteristics of these entities beyond those specified by the initial theoretical context. But in fact it is debatable whether any analogues to this process can be found in traditional cosmologies.

The second of the points Horton goes on to make is that a structural comparison with scientific theory can throw light on the bizarreness of the characteristics attributed to the spirits. Just as a theoretical model can become increasingly modified, sometimes in *ad hoc* fashion, as it absorbs a wider range of data, so

8-2

the spirits acquire characteristics to suit their developing functions which are not wholly consonant with the original analogy with human beings. Horton (1967) gives two examples, from Lugbara and Kalabari societies, each intended to show how the bizarre features of spirits can be thought of as growing out of their explanatory functions. They are analysed in the table below.

Type of spirit	Theoretical function	Bizarre characteristic explained
	KALABARI	
1. Ancestors	Defend and sustain lineage values	—
2. Heroes	Defend and sustain communal values, back up men in their struggle against nature	Come from outside community, disappear without death or burial, leave no descendants
3. Water spirits	Control important natural forces, back up man in his natural, non-social aspect	"Like men and also like pythons"
	LUGBARA	
1. Ancestors	Defend and sustain lineage-based social order	—
2. *Adro* spirits	Powers of the bush and of extra-social human activities	Cannibalistic, incestuous, walk upside down

NOTE: The ancestors are listed since the work of other types of spirit gets much of its point from the contrast with theirs.

The characteristics of the Kalabari heroes are designed to exhibit their lack of lineage or kinship ties, and hence their interest in nonlineage values. And those of the Lugbara *adro* spirits "serve as a graphic expression of their general perversity" (Horton 1967: 68). But there is an important point to notice here. It is the ascribed *functions* of the spirits which give them their explanatory role. Thus the link between the breaking of lineage norms and subsequent illness is made via an ancestor spirit because that spirit has the power to inflict illness, and because it has the function (goal) of sustaining lineage values. Propitiation of a water spirit can have the required effects on weather, water and fish only because these are *controlled* by water spirits. In no case does explanation involve any essential reference at all to the bizarre characteristics of the spirits. These characteristics, rather, serve to *symbolize* their roles. Horton's own explanation approaches them in this way: the *adro* spirits' characteristics are "graphic *expressions* of their general perversity".[88] There is here no obvious comparison with science. Scientific thought may ascribe properties to its theoretical entities for causal-explanatory reasons, but to assign them properties which symbolically express their character is a procedure quite alien to it.

Mystical participation and theoretical identification

The detailed structural comparisons which have been considered so far, then, are unconvincing, and might indeed be thought to argue against Horton's general approach rather than for it. But there is, according to Horton, another structural similarity between science and traditional African thought, which we have not yet examined. It is, in a way, the *pièce de résistance*, though it is not brought out in Horton's 1967 paper at great length (he discusses it more fully in 1973a, b). This allegedly common feature has been set out in chapter 11 (pp. 183–5) and again involves the areas of anomaly which Lévy-Bruhl claimed to be characteristic of traditional ('pre-logical') thought. It concerns in particular what Lévy-Bruhl called 'mystical participations' – identifications of observable phenomena (trees, rain, thunder, crocodiles) as being Spirit. As we saw, Lévy-Bruhl took the tendency to think in terms of mystical participations as a distinctive feature setting off primitive from modern thought. Horton's approach is very different. For him, on the contrary, 'mystical participations' are unavoidably generated *whenever* experience is interpreted in terms of a theoretical explanation – which postulates a domain going beyond the experienced (Horton 1973a: 232):

the sciences are full of Lévy-Bruhlian associations of unity-in-duality and identity of discernibles. These assertions occur whenever observable entities are identified with theoretical entities... I shall argue, not only that they are irreducibly paradoxical, but also that their paradoxicality is integral to their role in the process of explanation.

Thus Horton has two ways of dealing with the 'Lévy-Bruhlian' material, both based on a comparative reference to science. (1) Some of the apparent paradoxes in traditional thought he treats as merely apparent – they dissolve when the theoretical functions of the statements are properly understood. (2) Others, however, he recognises as genuinely anomalous – but these paradoxes, on his view, are not gratuitous features of traditional thought; they are, rather, integral elements in any process of theoretical explanation. If these claims, particularly (2), are correct, they constitute an extremely strong argument for intellectualism. For it would follow that the intellectualist approach is uniquely able to explain the presence of certain genuine and striking paradoxes in traditional thought.

We have found some reason already to doubt (1). But a proper critique of (2) requires a quite extended argument: an analysis of the logic of theoretical identities in science, of Lévy-Bruhlian paradoxes in traditional thought, and of certain anomalous doctrines in Western Christian (or rather in particular in Catholic) thought.[89]

What is perhaps the crucial issue centres on the nature of theoretical identities in science, such as 'Heat is the motion of molecules', 'A crystal is a lattice of atoms', 'A lightning flash is a stream of electrons' etc. On what grounds does Horton think such identifications to be irreducibly paradoxical? He bases his argument on a remark of Heisenberg's, who says that

it is impossible to explain rationally the perceptible qualities of matter except by tracing these back to the behaviour of entities which themselves no longer possess these qualities. If atoms are really to explain the origins of colour and smell of visible material bodies, then they cannot possess properties like colour and smell.[90]

Bridge laws which relate theoretical and observational language are indispensable in explaining why everyday objects have the observable properties they do have. The properties of a table, for example, are explained by reference to the properties of a theoretically described object: namely, an organised collection of molecules. Surely then, if Heisenberg is right, this organised whole cannot itself have the observable properties which it is supposed to explain. But if the bridging-statement linking it with the table is an identity-statement it must have them – for if this table simply *is* a certain collection of molecules, then it has a certain property if and only if the collection of molecules has that property. Now the properties of the collection of molecules explain the properties of the table only if the collection of molecules *is* the table. But the properties of the table are explained (for the reasons given by Heisenberg) only if they are *not* the properties of the collection of molecules, and thus (by the indiscernability of identicals) only if the collection of molecules is *not* the table. The explanatory function of the bridging-statement imposes both the view that the table is the collection of molecules and the view that it is not. Horton (in my view, correctly) rejects a solution which proposes an anti-realist view of molecules or an anti-realist view of tables. And so he concludes that a Lévy-Bruhlian mystical participation is inevitably generated by the project of theoretical explanation.

Nevertheless, the paradox is only apparent. To see this we must distinguish carefully between the properties of parts and those of wholes. It may be true that atoms are not to be thought of as having properties such as colour, temperature, solidity, smell, if they are to explain why macroscopic objects have them. But, for example, the fact that temperature cannot be predicated of individual gas molecules does not show that it cannot be predicated of *organised collections* of them. Heisenberg's account of theoretical explanation, if it is correct, shows only that the *micro-objects* postulated to explain perceptible qualities cannot themselves have those qualities. His point can thus be accepted quite consistently with the ascription of temperature to *collections* of such objects. There is therefore no paradox in accepting that, for example, the temperature of a volume of gas is explained precisely by identifying the gas as a collection of molecules and identifying the property of having a certain temperature with the property of having a certain mean kinetic energy.[91]

Now, if I am right in thinking that no paradox of a Lévy-Bruhlian kind is generated by the application of scientific theory to everyday experience then an important prop for Horton's position falls away. For it follows that Horton is wrong in thinking that such paradox is the inevitable result of *any* recourse to theoretically postulated entities in the explanation of observable phenomena, and hence wrong in thinking that the paradoxes of traditional religious cosmology follow inevitably from the fact that it resorts to a theory of imperceptible beings in its understanding of experience. The argument for intellectualism, that it alone could account for the presence of 'mystical participations' in traditional thought, is correspondingly weakened.

The Lévy-Bruhlian anomalies and the comparison with Christian doctrines

Let us consider one example which Horton gives (1973a: 292). For him the Nuer statement "Rain is Spirit" is a paradoxical identification generated by the explanatory application of theory to experience. But what is here being explained – the fact that it rains and the origin of rain, or again the nature of rain? If we take the Nuer to be concerned with explaining why it rains and where rain comes from then the idea that rain is sent by *kwoth* does perfectly well: to bring in the irreducibly obscure notion that rain actually is *kwoth* is gratuitous from the purely explanatory point of view. Horton ingeniously suggests that the Nuer's hesitation between concepts of causality ('sent by') and identity ('is') in characterising the relation between *kwoth* and rain (or thunder) is an instance of a more general oscillation between these respective notions which is also frequently found in scientists' thought about the relationship between an observable state or event and its theoretical *explanans*. As an empirical claim, this suggestion about scientists' thought may be true; but if Horton is right the unclarity must be ineradicable: neither concept – causality or identity – *can* furnish a coherent account. In fact, however, each of them can do so, depending upon the particular case in question. Heat (as opposed to sensations of heat) cannot be conceived of as *caused* by molecular motion except at the expense of paradox or at least ontological excess; but if I am right it can quite unparadoxically be conceived of as just *being* molecular motion. Rain, on the other hand, cannot without obscurity be conceived of as simply *being* Spirit; but it can quite unproblematically be conceived of as caused by (sent by) it.

Horton does not give his reasons for thinking causality an inadequate concept in the second case. I think he implicitly assimilates the second case to the first. But there can be more than one kind of transcendental hypothesis. One kind, familiar from modern science, transcends experience by postulating micro-constituents of perceptible objects too small to be themselves perceived: causality cannot be the concept which captures the relationship between these entities and the perceptible realm. Not all theoretical notions transcend experience in this way, however. The fundamental 'theoretical' concept of traditional cosmologies in Africa is that of agency; and spiritual agency is conceived of as an imperceptible extension of the phenomenal world, not as constituting its imperceptibly minute structure. The relation between 'theoretical entities' and experience can therefore be quite coherently captured by the notion of (agent) causality.

It may be suggested that Nuer are concerned to explain not merely what causes rain but what rain *is*: the identification of rain with Spirit stems from *this* explanatory interest. But with this suggestion we move away from the neat economy of Horton's theory, which saw the paradox as springing from the very business of explanation itself. For to explain what rain is in this way is to opt for just one among indefinitely many other, non-paradoxical ways.

When rain is described as being sent by *kwoth* the notion *kwoth* is deployed within a conceptually transparent cosmology in just the explanatory function which Horton and others of an intellectualist bent have stressed. But when rain is identified with Spirit, when in a storm Nuer pray to God to come to earth gently, or when they speak of Him as being in the lightning or thunder, then religious concepts seem to figure in what one is strongly inclined to describe as a mythically or mystically heightened apprehension of the world. Here, one then feels, comparisons with scientific theory have little to offer.

This suggests that the apparent conceptual anomalies to be found, for example, in a number of African traditional religions might be more profitably approached within a very different comparative framework: that another "area of English discourse" might serve as a more "adequate instrument of translation" than scientific thought provides (Horton 1972: 22). A refreshing glimpse of the obvious leads us to the thought that African religious ideas might usefully be compared with Western *religious* ideas.

I shall concentrate here on the Catholic doctrinal tradition. Catholic doctrine contains certain areas of apparent or real conceptual paradox which (or at least some of which) I shall be brash enough to summarise in the table below. Some of these conceptual puzzles may be soluble (3*b*, for example); in any case all of them have puzzled Catholic theologians. There are however a number of significant differences between the paradoxes grouped under (1) and (2) and those under (3) and (4). First, all of the paradoxes in the former group are in one way or another paradoxes of identity. Secondly, and connected with this, they have a recognisable 'Lévy-Bruhlian' character – I have put in parenthesis the Lévy-Bruhlian categories under which they appear to fall. The third point, again connected with the first two, is that the paradoxes under (3) and (4) are recondite in a way in which those under (1) and (2) are not. The anomalies in (3) and (4) arise as contradictory consequences which can apparently be drawn by putting various parts of Church teaching together. In (1) and (2), on the other hand, we are concerned with doctrines which seem unintelligible in themselves, rather than being inconsistent with other parts of Church teaching. Thus one might expect, *ceteris paribus*, the 'Lévy-Bruhlian' paradoxes to strike the believer as such simply as a result of his attempt to grasp what it is that he is to believe, and consequently to lead him to some kind of conscious reflection on its content; whereas one would expect him to become aware of the other paradoxes only *as a result of* reflective scrutiny of his beliefs.

When we turn to the comparison with African religions we find a further point of difference between the areas of paradox under (1) and (2) and those under (3) and (4). I shall suggest that areas of paradox significantly similar to those found in the former group can be found also in a number of African religions. This does not seem to me to be the case, however, in the case of (3) and (4). There are probably a variety of reasons for this, among which I myself would number the following. In the first place, life after death is, in traditional African religious thought, far less clearly conceived and emotionally salient than in orthodox Christian faith; in particular, deserts are generally speaking expected in this life rather than in the next. Secondly, the supreme being is not normally unambiguously benevolent nor does it combine benevolence with the omnisciently omnipotent interest in this world of the Christian God. Thirdly, the conflict between destiny (if not divine precognition) and human freedom

(1) The nature of God	Doctrine of the Trinity	How can God be one being and yet three persons? (unity-in-diversity)
(2) God's relation to the world	(a) The Eucharist (b) The Incarnation	(a) How can a piece of bread be the whole Christ? (mystical participation) How can more than one Host be identical with the whole Christ? (multi-presence, unity-in-diversity) (b) What is the relation between Christ's divine and his human nature? (mystical participation)
(3) The perfections of God versus the imperfections of creation	(a) The problem of evil (b) Man's freedom of will	(a) If God is omniscient, omnipotent and benevolent, how can evil exist? (b) If God is omniscient, how can man be free?
(4) Life after death	(a) Paradise (b) Hell	(a) How can finite creatures "share in the Divine life"? (b) How can a perfectly just God ordain an infinite punishment?

is often resolvable in ingenious ways. For example, the Tallensi say that a child before birth is with *Naawan* (the supreme being). Its destiny in life (*Nuor-Yin* – literally, 'spoken destiny') is determined by its wishes, declared at that time, to *Naawan*. Thus the individual's destiny is itself reduced to his choice – an ultimate act of existential choice, one might say, for the "Tale notion of the Pre-natal Destiny designates what, in more abstract language, could be best described as an innate diposition that can be realized either for good or ill" (Fortes 1959: 68).

A comparison of Christian and African religious thought in respect of the Lévy-Bruhlian anomalies will naturally raise the question of how believers react to their awareness (if any) of the anomalous features of their beliefs. Here the important point in the Catholic case is that the Church *recognises* the paradoxical character of such doctrines as the Trinity, the Eucharist and the Incarnation. These doctrines are accepted as 'supernatural mysteries in the strict sense': an expression which has since at least Vatican Council I had a technical use. In a nutshell, a 'mystery' is a doctrine whose truth cannot be demonstrated but must be taken on faith; a mystery 'in the strict sense' is a doctrine such that not merely the fact that it is true, but also the fact that it has a definite, coherent sense, must be taken on faith.[92] In other words the Church accepts that no human being, however much logical ingenuity he may apply to the task, can succeed in showing how a strict supernatural mystery, such as the doctrine of the Eucharist, given the concepts it deploys, and the use made of them, can avoid strictly logical incoherence. Nevertheless it regards such doctrines as literally – and certainly not metaphorically or symbolically – true.

One does not need to insist that no scientific theory ever has any conceptually anomalous features, or that scientists will never put up for a moment with incoherence or anomaly, however peripheral, in an otherwise usable theory. The key point is that a theory is not accepted as *true*, when it is simultaneously accepted that no amount of ingenuity could show how it avoids logical incoherence. If anything is distinctive of the demands placed on *scientific* theory it is that theory should be intelligible – intelligible *to us*. For it is to a *human* understanding that what we are ready to call 'science' seeks to present the world. What the doctrine of mysteries in the strict sense in contrast does is to open a fundamental breach between the significance of a proposition and its intelligibility, or at least human intelligibility; for in the case of the strict mysteries these become, so to speak, parallel lines which meet only in the mind of God. There is a real and important difference between a system of thought in which the recognition of logical paradox among accepted beliefs about the world generates attempts to replace the affected parts by new theories at the first-order level, and one in which paradoxical beliefs can be defused by a second-order, or philosophical, reinterpretation of the relationship between meaningfulness and intelligibility. And thus there is a real and important difference between the two 'areas of English discourse' which we are presently considering as candidates for comparison with the African material to which we now turn.

In a number of African religions areas of paradox of the kind discussed by Lévy-Bruhl can be found which seem structurally analogous to the paradoxes involved in the Catholic doctrines listed under (1) and (2). One could classify these areas of paradox under such headings as 'unity-in-diversity' – where a number of distinct spiritual beings or godlings are nevertheless thought to be identical with a single supreme being or god; 'multi-presence' – where a spirit is thought to be present, in a quasi-corporeal way, in more than one place at a time; and 'manifestations or materialisations' – where perceptible phenomena (sculptures, rain, lights over marshes) are thought to be or to become spiritual beings. The analogy, in the logical character of these anomalies, with the Trinity, Eucharist and Incarnation is clear.

In Skorupski 1973 I discuss monographs on Nuer, Dinka, Kalabari and Lugbara religious thought which illustrate these points, and also briefly consider the methodological difficulties which may be thought to attend a scheme of translation which implies the existence of logical anomaly in the 'translated' culture's beliefs. I shall not recapitulate the illustrative material here, nor discuss how apparent methodological difficulties can be answered – since my disagreement with Horton is not over whether the existence of such specific areas of obscurity in traditional African thought can in principle or practice be established. We both agree it can. In crude summary, spirits and gods in traditional African religions and in Christianity are a kind of being which can be many distinct persons and yet one, which can be in many determinate places at the same time or in no determinate place, and which can turn itself into, or enter into a pre-existing, creature or thing. Horton's proposal is, in essence, that these anomalous characteristics of the spirits in African thought are best explained by treating them as theoretical entities whose characteristics can then be explained in terms of features of the 'model-building process' familiar from Western scientific theory. I on the other hand suggest that the comparison with analogous paradoxes in Western Christianity is far more useful in identifying the right questions to ask.

Suppose we accept, as a working assumption, what Horton also assumes: namely, that where areas of paradox similar in their nature and location are to be found in separate, but in their overall cultural functions, similar, belief-systems and traditions, there is a prima facie expectation that the explanation of them will in each case share some significant common ingredient. A number of points can then be made. In the first place, it becomes implausible to suggest that the paradoxes of spiritual identity originate or persist in African religious thought because of the traditional African thinker's practical concerns, and his conse-quent lack of interest in the theoretical and reflective business of taking his beliefs to their conclusions and searching them out for incoherences. I distinguished earlier between (i) paradoxes in a belief-system which one would expect to strike the believer simply by virtue of leaving it unclear *what it is* that he is to believe, and which might therefore lead him to critical reflection, and (ii) paradoxes which only become apparent when implicitly contra-dictory consequences are drawn out. The persistence of para-doxes of the latter kind, especially when they are marginal, or require thinking through one's beliefs in an unusual direction, might be explained by reference to the practical, non-reflective (etc.) concerns of the thinker. The explanation is considerably less plausible in the case of category (i) yet it is into this category that the paradoxes of spiritual identity fall. But the comparison with Catholic doctrinal tradition makes the explanation even more implausible. For there we find a reflectively intellectual and penetratingly logical tradition which, far from speedily eliminat-ing the analogous paradoxes, gives them an official epistemolo-gical status all to themselves.

Now I have also argued that the paradoxical character of the spirits and their relation to the world cannot actually be *accounted* for in the way Horton suggests, by treating the religious cosmo-logies in which they figure as explanatory theories. This leaves, as the only explanation available to the intellectualist of the source and persistence of such paradoxes, an appeal to the untheoretical, occasion-bound orientation of the traditional thinker. But this is precisely the line of thought which has just been dismissed as unacceptable. What is more, a tradition of thought (Catholicism) which presumably, in this respect, should have been just another case in point for the intellectualist -- of paradoxes persisting as a result of the unreflective and unsyste-matic orientation of the believers -- in fact provides a definite counter-example to it.

This point should be pressed further. It was noted earlier that an essential goal of science was that of making the world intelligible *to us*. This is not simply a feature of such particular explanatory systems as we are prepared to call 'scientific', incidental to the general explanatory objectives they share with others. On the contrary: in the delimited sense of 'explanation' which is required if intellectualism is to preserve substantive content, it is surely a way of expressing the explanatory objective itself. The more purely a shared set of beliefs is designed for the *explanation* of a given domain of experience, the more one expects a premium to be placed on an intelligibly articulated structure – hence expulsion of what is perceived as paradoxical rather than recourse to the second-order tactics of allowing for doctrines having a meaning which is nevertheless humanly incomprehensible.

The 'Lévy-Bruhlian' character of religious thought remains unaccounted for by intellecualism: the classic issues of interpretation and explanation it poses remain wide open.

Concluding remarks

We have now completed our survey of Horton's intellectualist treatment of African religious thought. It is, at the moment, the most detailed and sustained exploration of intellectualism's interpretative possibilities. Obviously, when we are considering an overall framework for analysis such as the intellectualist programme represents, we should not in general expect to be able to bring more than inclining reasons *directly* to bear on it; moreover, in considering Horton's argument, I have naturally concentrated on those of its aspects which are of greatest interest to the philosopher. I have not examined at all, for example, his 'Durkheimian' explanation of the personalistic concepts of traditional cosmology as against the impersonal concepts of scientific theory, with its implied thesis of the priority of technology over pure science. This is a suggestion which calls for the skills of a historian of science. Nevertheless, I hope to have shown that even in the restricted area which has been considered, inclining reasons can work quite strongly for or against. Had the detailed structural comparisons which Horton seeks to draw worked, they would have added up to a close-to-compelling case for intellectualism, at least in respect of traditional African thought. If on the other hand they fail, and fail in the ways I have suggested, they leave instead important and distinctive areas of traditional African thought which cannot be explained on the intellectualist approach.

In Part II of this book I tried to show how some of the most interesting material concerning ceremony and magical or religious action, which symbolist anthropologists have stressed, can be accommodated within a literalist account of the framework of belief. Of course, I do not claim that the whole symbolist approach can be accommodated in this way: as Part I shows, I think, much of it – and much of what for a variety of domestic cultural reasons makes it most attractive – is plainly incompatible with a straightforward literalist approach. Now the acceptance of a literalist interpretation, or 'translation' of traditional thought at once sets up a definite momentum towards the intellectualist scheme of analysis. Nevertheless, for reasons given in these last two chapters, the case for intellectualism seems to me to be at best unproven. On the other hand, given literalism, what other overall programme of explanation, at this level, is there? A clear alternative remains to be worked out.

Embracing programmes are not a bad but a good thing – in practice, probably indispensable in suggesting lines of empirical enquiry and questions for the field worker to address himself to. One can, for example, see the effects of Lévy-Bruhl's grand speculations on Evans-Pritchard's work among the Azande and the Nuer. One can see even more clearly the effect of functionalist and symbolist perspectives on anthropologists' investigations of 'ritual'. They have had many good effects, but it is very noticeable that they have also left unexplored various types of empirical data about traditional beliefs, and systematic ways of presenting those data, which one suddenly wants to know about if one is interested in intellectualism. Fieldwork inspired by the intellectualist perspective (or, as in the comparable case of Lévy-Bruhl and Evans-Pritchard, by a specifically anti-intellecualist perspective) is, in the kind of detail it goes for and the form of presentation it adopts, likely to have a refreshingly different look. It will require some comparative familiarity with history/philosophy/sociology of science, and this may pose a certain difficulty. But on the whole one would expect it, even if in the end it does nothing else, to round off very considerably our understanding of traditional conceptions of the world and society. For these reasons I applaud the intellectualist project even though its case seems to me to be unproven.

Turning to the philosophical side, the status of intellectualism is of interest to philosophy in that broad sense of 'philosophy' in which such large questions as the nature of science, of religion and of magic, fall within the philosophical domain. More narrowly, as I have several times suggested, the dispute between literalist and symbolist views of religious belief, though not identical with the philosophically more familiar disputes between realist and anti-realist views of it, has tended at various points and in various ways to be intertwined with them. More narrowly still – specifically for the philosophy of social science – the debate about intellectualism has always been in considerable part methodological and philosophical, focussing on difficulties involved in the 'translating' or 'understanding' of other cultures' beliefs. The problems here can to some extent be separated from the broader questions mentioned above; they range from the far-reaching philosophical issue of relativism to particular methodological difficulties about translation which I have not gone into to any great extent.

In social anthropology very general theories or conceptions of religion have never been lost sight of, even when the grander projects of its founding fathers – of Tylor or Frazer, Durkheim or Lévy-Bruhl – have been abandoned. This ambitiousness gives the subject its philosophical interest: partly for the philosophy of social science, because of the methodological issues raised, but more generally because it has inspired reflection on questions with which philosophy of science and religion also deal, but which in social anthropology are nourished by a very different 'diet of examples'.

Relativism and rational belief

The thesis that experience underdetermines theory; a further step required to relativism

The second pair of blocks to falsifiability mentioned by Tylor, although specifically offered by him as explaining the persistence of magico-religious beliefs in a traditional culture, are in fact perfectly general in their application: they are structural features of any system of explanation and not merely of magico-religious beliefs, or of beliefs in a traditional culture. Consider a scientific law which asserts that y is a given function of x under conditions $C_1, \ldots, C_n$. Suppose an experiment to test its validity, in which the variable x is determined at a given value, and y is then measured; and suppose that the results are on the face of it incompatible with the law. The scientist can always claim, to take the first of Tylor's blocks, that the experiment was not properly conducted, that the readings were not taken properly etc.; or, to take the second, that the conditions $C_1, \ldots, C_n$ were not constant at the assumed values, or indeed that further conditions not explicitly specified in the law but assumed to be invariant had altered.

The theme, when developed and more generally stated, is that a theory can always be defended from apparently falsifying experimental data by the production of auxiliary hypotheses. This point has been dwelt on by philosophers of science. Scientists sometimes accept such defences and sometimes reject them, depending on how plausible they seem to them to be. But what determines these assessments of plausibility? May they not be an amalgam of preconceptions, personal predilections and so forth, from which no rational basis for choice can be disentangled? The conceptual, as opposed to the empirical, side of the question is: Can criteria in principle be specified which will distinguish those cases in which it is rational to accept an auxiliary hypothesis which defends a theory from an apparent clash with empirical data, from those cases in which the theory should be regarded as falsified? Or is any decision between the two alternatives a matter of scientific 'nous' for which no rules can be stated? And if the latter, then can such decisions properly be spoken of as 'rational' or 'irrational' at all?

The fundamental point involved here can be summed up as the thesis that theory is underdetermined by experience – not just *actual* experience but all possible experience. This follows from the claim that any statement in a theory can be defended against any possible experience by suitable amendments in the rest of the theory. For then, with the choice of different statements to be defended come what may, can come different theories, all of which may be stated in such a way as to be falsifiable, but between which experience cannot discriminate: it falsifies one if and only if it falsifies all. Now given that any statement in a theory *can* be preserved against experience, how *does* such a statement get falsified? For experience to score a direct, disconfirming hit on a particular target, there must be a theoretical framework, not itself in question, which sets the target firmly in place. From this a further step takes us to a relativist position: the truth-value (truth or falsity) of the statement is itself relativised to the theoretical framework within which it is assessed.

That this *is* a further step can be seen in a number of ways. In the first place, it does not follow from the fact that, whenever a statement is subject to experiential test, there must be *some* background of unquestioned statements which is not itself subject to test, that one and the same set of statements within a theory is always presupposed in *any* test, and can never itself be subject to test. In the now trite analogy, we must stand on some part of the raft to mend another part, but it may still be that there is no part on which we *must* stand, and which we cannot mend. Let us waive this point for the moment, however, because a much more fundamental one is involved.

Even given the structuring of a theory into a framework and a set of hypotheses within the framework, the fact that *the method by which we determine* the truth-value of a hypothesis within the framework *presupposes the truth* of the statements making up the framework does not at first sight entail that the *truth-value* of the hypothesis is itself relative to (the 'truth' of) the statements within the framework. The conditional character of our knowledge does not obviously entail the relativity of its object. The one is an epistemological matter, concerning the inferential relations of various parts of our knowledge, the other is an ontological matter, concerning the status of what is known.

Relevance of relativism to the intellectualist programme

This point will be taken up at greater length in a moment. But let us first see why the issue is relevant to intellectualism. It is argued by the relativist that in the absence of a framework which includes as a part, in Wittgenstein's phrase, 'propositions which have the form of empirical propositions', experience underdetermines belief – and, it seems to follow, rational considerations cannot lead us determinately to the acceptance or rejection of a hypothesis. So these apparently empirical propositions which have been firmed up into the framework of theory set the scene for the determinate rational assessment of beliefs, and given the scene are not themselves objects of rational assessment at all. They function rather as *criteria* of rationality; for since truth within the theory is relativised to the framework, there can be no activity of rationally assessing the truth-value of this framework itself – it enters into the procedure by which the truth-value of a statement within it is determined. But, as we have seen, there is an indefinite number of possible frameworks within which experience can in principle be satisfactorily interpreted, and with this an indefinite variation in criteria of rationality. (This remains the case even if some specific criteria are a universal feature of any workable theoretical framework).

It now begins to look as if choices *between* overall frameworks of belief are not themselves to be counted rational or irrational at all. For (to apply the point in a familiar type of way) the overall framework provides the indispensable, culturally shared categories within which a person understands his world, and in terms of which rationality is exercised: the acceptance or rejection of the framework itself, therefore, must be determined by social and psychological factors which run deeper than, and are presupposed by, the possibility of any application of the procedures whereby beliefs within it can be rationally assessed.

This conclusion looks unpalatable to the intellectualist since it is precisely such an overall framework of belief (the agency-based cosmology of traditional religious thought) that intellectualism seeks to explain – and it explains it as an intellectual reaction: an application of reason, at a given level of inherited knowledge, to experience. Furthermore, it is a natural extension of this approach that the transition from, say, traditional magico-religious curing to modern Western medicine, is capable of being explained at least in part as a the result of a more or less reasonable assessment of their comparative effectiveness. Hence if the conclusion is to be that moves between overall cognitive frameworks are intrinsically non-rational, the whole programme seems undermined.

On formulating the relativist thesis

Let us then consider more closely the step from the underdetermination of theory to relativism. To simplify the discussion I shall begin by making two very large idealisations in my use of the term 'theory': (1) I shall include all assertoric sentences which a person or a social group would accept as expressing truths about the world in his or its 'theory'; (2) I shall assume that every such 'theory' contains a subset of 'paradigm' sentences which constitute its 'theoretical framework', and which are not put in question. Theories are numbered by their paradigms: change the paradigm and you change the theory, but an alteration in a non-paradigm sentence just gives a different version of the theory.

As to (1), the relativist argument is restricted in scope but not altered in logic – barring a qualification to be discussed later – if we distinguish between theoretical and observational sentences, with observational sentences determined by experience but underdetermining the theoretical sentences. We can therefore discuss the general case. As to (2), if we drop the idea of a sharp class distinction as regards proneness to revision between paradigm sentences and others, and replace it by a completely classless society, or a hierarchical continuum of tenure, we make the relativist's life more difficult in that change of opinion, where the conditions to which truth is relativised remain constant, becomes difficult to separate from a change of those conditions. At the classless extreme, there seems no difference between moves in a theory and changes of theory, and hence it becomes difficult to see how, on a relativist view, any pair of opinions could ever be inconsistent: by the very fact of their being different, their truth-value would be relativised to different theories. It is at least arguable, however, that a fairly clearly marked distinction between sentences constitutive of a framework or 'paradigm' and sentences within it provides a more realistic picture of our actual systems of belief; in any case I want to consider the relativist argument on its most favourable ground. As a final point it may be noted that an exclusive concentration on *sentences* ignores what many people, whether Kuhnian or Wittgensteinian, regard as vital constituents of a 'paradigm' or 'language-game' – angles of vision, ways of doing things, felt priorities etc. (These will make some slight reappearance in later sections of this appendix.)

Having cleared the stage almost completely of its props we can now pay undivided attention to the central outlines of the relativist scene. Many philosophers seek to catch relativism in a trivial-or-obviously-false dilemma. On the one hand, the would-be relativist may be telling us no more than that Eskimo have lots of words for snow and Tuareg have lots of words for sand. This is an interesting fact but has no philosophical consequence. On the other hand, he may be committing himself to the absurd view that the holders of different theories genuinely construct and inhabit different worlds. Of course this way of speaking is common enough in the social sciences, but it almost always testifies not to idealism but to idealist rhetoric ('The child's construction of reality', 'The social construction of reality' etc.).[93] The genuine relativist, however, is presumed to take it literally.

For example, Ayer glosses a passage in Wittgenstein's *On Certainty* (paras. 214, 215) thus: "I take it that what he means... is that it is only in the light of certain assumptions that the notion of agreement with reality comes into play. The assumptions themselves neither agree nor disagree with reality. They determine the nature of the reality with which agreement is sought" (Ayer 1974: 233-4). If these words are taken literally they commit Wittgenstein (on Ayer's account) to a type of empirical idealism.

People make certain *assumptions*; and these *determine* the nature
of reality. To this the reply is easy: one can assume and assume,
without making an iota of difference to what one is making
assumptions about. And if this is not sufficiently obvious, one only
needs to point to the absurd consequences which flow from the
position – how could one 'travel' from one such thought-
determined world to another, or learn its language? It may be
that some relativists have been led into some such view, or have
confused it with the trivial point about differences in concepts,
perhaps helped along by the idealist-sounding rhetoric noted
above. But a more careful relativist can pass between the horns
of this supposed dilemma.

His view is not that reality is in any way affected by the
adoption of a theoretical framework – it is that reality is what
is indifferently describable by the true sentences relative to total
theory 1 (T_1), the true sentences relative to total theory 2 (T_2) . . .
the true sentences relative to total theory n (T_n). The relativism
of this position might initially be encapsulated in these two theses:

(*a*) A sentence may be true-in-T_i, false-in-T_j

(*b*) The paradigm sentences of $T_1, . . . , T_n$ cannot be said to be
true (except in an honorific sense) or *false* at all.

This formulation is, however, open to trivialisation. For there
is nothing out of the way in the point that one and the same
(syntactically characterised) sentence can be true in one theory,
false in another, if it changes its *meaning* as between them. So
we must amend (*a*):

(a_1) If S_i and S_j are sentences in T_i and T_j (S_i may be S_j), and
S_i is synonymous with S_j, then S_i may be true/false-in-T_i and S_j
may be false/true-in-T_j.

Consequently the relativist needs a conception of meanng
which will show how sentences can be compared in meaning
across total theories. He needs this for another reason, which
stems from his supposition that there can be more than one total
theory. The identity-conditions for theories have been given in
terms of the identity of paradigm sentences. But do T_i and T_j
differ if their paradigm sentences, as syntactically characterised,
differ? Not necessarily, surely. For if these syntactically different
sentences have the same meaning, then T_i is T_j. So we must now
say, more exactly, that the identity of theories turns on whether
their paradigm sentences differ *in meaning*.

Step from underdetermination to relativism underpinned by verificationist (anti-realist) theory of meaning

The kind of theory of meaning which can produce the results the relativist wants is verificationist in its general tendency. The meaning of a sentence, on this view, is determined by the possible experiences (and, if necessary, inferential procedures) which would establish its truth and the possible experiences (etc.) which would establish its falsity. It might now be thought that S_i and S_j have the same meaning if and only if the same sets of experiences (and perhaps inferential procedures) respectively determine their truth and their falsity. Furthermore, since different such sets of experiences may become associated with a sentence when there is a change in the paradigm sentences, it looks as though the meaning of a sentence will depend upon its theoretical context.

However, these conclusions would be misconceived because the assertion of S_i and S_j does not place constraints on experience categorically, in and of itself, but only conditionally, on acceptance of some set of paradigm sentences which in the case of S_i and S_j differ *ex hypothesi* in meaning. Where one has two conditionals such that the same sets of possible experiences justify their assertion, and whose antecedents differ in meaning, one cannot conclude that the consequents have the same meaning.

But, on the other hand, on what grounds could we establish that the paradigm sentences of T_i and the paradigm sentences of T_j differ in meaning? Paradigm sentences of various theories are alike in being accepted come what may. They are thus limiting cases: one can either refrain from saying that any experience would *establish* their truth, or one can say that *any* experience does. In either case, there seems no possibility of distinguishing between paradigm sentences in respect of meaning and hence no possibility of distinguishing between theories in the way we have just adopted.

To avoid this conclusion we must amend the verificationist theory of meaning towards verisimilitude by splitting it into two levels. Let us for brevity's sake call the sets of experiences which respectively justify assertion or denial of a sentence its *assertability conditions*. Then:

(1) The meaning of a sentence is a function of the meaning of its constituent expressions.

(2) The meaning of a constituent expression is its contribution to determining the assertability conditions of all the sentences in which it appears.

We can now say that paradigm sentences, and generally any sentences with the same assertability conditions, may nevertheless differ in meaning by dint of differing in their semantic structure (where the semantic structure of a sentence consists in the semantically simple units which compose it and the way it is built up out of them).

However, this revised approach still needs to take serious account of the underdetermination of theory: a sentence on its own does not have determinate assertability conditions – it has them only in the context of a theoretical framework. Therefore a constituent expression can make a determinate contribution to the assertability conditions of a sentence in which it appears only in the context of a theoretical framework. One way of drawing the moral of this is to say, as Quine has said, that while Frege was right in pointing out that the unit of meaning is not a word, he should have gone further than he did – and taken as the basic unit of meaning not the sentence but the theory. In the context of verificationism the unit of meaning is that which has assertability conditions. Frege's doctrine of asking for the meaning of a word only in the framework of a sentence is expressed in (2). But now that the unit of meaning has shifted up from sentence to theory we must apply this approach to sentences themselves. More exactly, on my use of 'theory', it is a given *version* of a theory which has assertability conditions – where versions are identical if they consist of the same set of sentences. So we finally arrive at a holistic version of verificationism:

(1a) The meaning of a given version of theory is a function of the meaning of its constituent sentences.

(2a) The meaning of a sentence is its contribution to determining the assertability conditions of all the particular versions of theories in which it appears; and this contribution in turn is a function of the meanings of its constituent expressions.

(3a) The meaning of a constituent expression is the systematic part it plays, for any sentence in which it appears, in determining the contribution of that sentence to the assertability conditions of the particular versions of theories in which that sentence appears.

This, as far as I can see, is the position which is required to yield the relativism formulated in (a_1) and (*b*). For a sentence now preserves a definite meaning through the various theories in which it appears, just as an (unambiguous) word preserves a definite meaning through all the sentences in which it appears. At the same time, however, while preserving its meaning, a sentence may be true in one theory, false in another, and perhaps paradigmatically true in a third.[94] But the important point to hold on to is that we have not deduced this relativist conclusion from the thesis that belief is empirically underdetermined alone. We have conjoined that thesis with a verificationist theory of meaning. It is this conjunction which leads to holism about meaning and relativism about truth.[95]

When verificationism is replaced by semantic realism, the step to relativism fails

To see the importance of verificationism here let us see what happens when we replace it by its classical alternative in semantics – realism. On a realist view, there is for any assertoric sentence, a set of possible states of affairs such that if one of them obtains the sentence is true, and a set of possible states of affairs such that if one of them obtains the sentence is false. These respective (possibly empty) sets constitute the *truth-conditions* of the sentence. The realist's conception of sentence meaning is then (1) together with:

(2*b*) The meaning of a constituent expression is its contribution to the determination of the truth-conditions of all the sentences in which it appears.

The underdetermination of theory does not now drive us to holism. For the realist the question of whether a sentence is true or false is determined by whether or not the states of affairs which make it so obtain, quite independent of whether we are in a position to find out that they obtain. The fact that we *can* consistently preserve a sentence in the face of any possible experience does not in any way affect the fact that that sentence is, taken on its own, true or false depending on how the world is. In particular, that we decide to treat a statement as true, come what may, is quite compatible for the realist with its being false. The realist does not accept, as does the verificationist, that a sentence for which such a decision has been made is true 'by convention'. Of course he does accept that, given a hitherto uninterpreted term, a partial account of its meaning can be given by (consistently) stipulating that certain sentences in which it occurs are true. What he rejects is the idea that, given a sentence which already has meaning in the language, we can by a stipulative convention make it – without inducing a change of meaning and thus truth-conditions – (paradigmatically) true. If it already has meaning, then its truth-value is already determined by how the world is, and there is no room left for stipulative convention. In short what is conventionally determined for him is always meaning, and never directly truth. We can at most conventionally *take* a sentence to be true – its actual truth-value is unaffected by this. (Even here there may be problems, analogous to those raised, in the case of a single person, by the idea of 'choosing to believe'.)

That a sentence has determinate truth-conditions on its own is thus unaffected by the fact that we can preserve our belief, that its truth conditions obtain, against any experience – by making suitable adjustments in our other beliefs. What *this* shows is no more than that we can preserve a false belief against disconfirmation on pain of holding other false beliefs. Connectedly, relativism does not follow from the empirical underdetermination of theory on the realist account. Underdetermination shows at most that there must be a choice; it does not show that the choice is arbitrary, nor that the question of whether the choice is correct – in the specific sense of whether the framework chosen is *true* – is senseless. The realist says: "We are taking P as true (though it may be false) and, given that framework and the experimental experience, we must accept that Q is true (though it may be false)." The verificationist cannot accept the possibilities parenthesised – for the realist, on the other hand, the problem which threatens is that of providing a convincing answer to scepticism.

For the verificationist, the paradigm sentences of a theory do indeed function in a substantial sense as 'criteria of rationality' within that theory: they play an essential role in the procedures by which hypotheses within the theory are rationally to be assessed, and one cannot significantly ask of them (as a move in the game, as opposed to a change in the game played) whether they may not themselves be false. Once it has been established that a certain belief is, in the light of experience, inconsistent with them, one cannot rationally put into question the claim that that belief has been proved false. The relativism which has been set out here, then, carries with it a relativism about criteria of rationality. For the realist, on the other hand, paradigm sentences are no more the criteria for, rather than the objects of, rational assessment than are any other sentences of the theory. (This does not include, for a realist who draws a fundamental distinction between logical and empirical truths, the logical truths of a theory.)

The move from the thesis that theory is empirically under-determined to relativism requires, then, a particular conception of meaning as an additional premise. What I have tried to show so far is that we can go a certain distance in describing what form this conception must take – it will have to be holistic and verificationist. I am not suggesting that this conception can be worked out coherently – I suspect, on the contrary, that it cannot be. However the incoherence is not immediately specifiable, and to that extent a relativism based on this conception is not as easily refutable as many philosophers have thought relativism to be. The main difficulty for it is likely to stem from its holistic charac-ter – that is, from the fact that it takes the 'theory' rather than the 'sentence' as the prime bearer of assertability conditions. What is puzzling is how, on this account, it is possible for a language to be learnt.[96] The normal (realist) picture is that we learn the truth-conditions of a sample of sentences, taking them at this stage as syntactically unanalysed blocks, then break them up and hypothesise constituent meaning and syntactic structure, achieving in this way a compositional understanding of the old sentences and of new ones whose truth-conditions we have not directly learnt. If the view that the prime unit of meaning is the theory is taken seriously, it would seem to imply that what must be learnt *en bloc*, as the initial step in learning a language, are the assertability conditions, of sample *theories*: but this seems an unintelligible project. It might however be suggested that this difficulty would be considerably lessened if a distinction was drawn between theoretical and observational sentences, with observational sentences taken as having independent assertability conditions, but underdetermining theory – so that the account of meaning outlined above applied to theoretical sentences alone. This would involve a relativism which applied not to beliefs as a whole, but only to theories; and would presuppose the possibility of drawing a distinction of the kind required, between theoretical and observational sentences.

What constraints would be placed on intellectualism by the truth of the relativist thesis?

However I shall not pursue this suggestion; I want to turn instead to examining more concretely how relativist objections to the intellectualist programme, objections which can now be seen as stemming from verificationist premises, are countered by realist replies. (It will be clear in what follows that I find the realist conception of meaning much the more plausible, not to say intelligible, of the two: here again, however, as with my sketch of the Wittgensteinian position in chapter 1, we cannot explore the contrasting implications very deeply if the discussion is to be kept within reasonable bounds.) As a preliminary, let us consider how much of intellectualism can survive if a relativist framework is *accepted.*

In the first place then, relativism of the kind described here is quite compatible with a literalist account of traditional thought; for this merely asserts that traditional religious thought does constitute a framework of belief within which people seek to understand and control the world. It says nothing about how this framework evolved or about its rational comparability with other frameworks. When we consider the intellectualist account of how the traditional framework is evolved, however, the situation is more complex. Rationality in the 'context of discovery' is a different matter from rationality in the 'context of validation'. This is well recognised by intellectualism, at least in the contemporary version of it which was discussed in Part III. The fundamental notion that traditional religious cosmologies are the products of rational theory-building is in this version maintained but the kinds of factor which are taken as counting towards the *rationality* of a process of theory development,– an interest in accounting for experience in an economical, simple, consistent way, in terms of a basic analogy which is familiar and well understood and so on – can apparently be accepted as playing a role in the development of a theory, consistently with a relativist view of the theory itself. To this extent, then, it seems that intellectualism is compatible with relativism. On the other hand, I noted earlier that it is a natural part of intellectualism to suppose that the change in, say, an African culture from traditional magico-religious curing to Western medicine can be seen as resulting from a rational assessment of their comparative effectiveness. Now here rationality is involved in the context of a comparative evaluation of frameworks which compete at about as fundamental a level as one could find; it is therefore at least unclear that relativism could accommodate such an explanation of the change from one framework to the other even as an *a priori* possibility.

The overall picture then is that philosophical relativism does impose some cutbacks on the full-blown intellectualist project, but that a pretty substantial part of it could survive – much more, perhaps, than has often been thought; while a realist conception of what it is for a sentence to have meaning blocks the path from underdetermination of theory to relativism, and consequently allows intellectualism its full scope.

Rational belief: criteria and judgement

Let us call the choice of whether to retain, accept or reject a belief a *retention choice*. It is easy to see that not all such choices can be settled by the application of specifiable *criteria* which effectively determine what choice should be made. For any such criterion would have to take the form: 'Retain if and only if *p*'. But whether it is or is not the case that *p* could itself independently come up as an issue requiring a retention choice. (Even the limiting case of a criterion which took the form of a straightforward stipulation as to what beliefs should be retained would not be an exception to this. For if the stipulative criterion was embodied in a publicly specified list of statements to be retained, then the claim that the belief *was* expressed by one of the statements on the list could always itself come up for a retention choice. But suppose on the other hand that the stipulation consisted of a *private* list which was *not* in some way perceivably specified or embodied independently of the stipulative decision itself. Then even if we allow that the question of whether such-and-such a belief should be retained could be genuinely separated by the believer from the question of whether it was indeed one of the beliefs which he had previously decided to retain, the latter belief, concerning what decision he had in the past made, could always itself come up for a retention choice.) So the applicability of an effective retention-choice guiding criterion can in every case itself be subject to a retention choice, and from this it follows that some retention choices are not made by the application of any such criterion. The point is a general one, not dependent on a particular epistemological view: a believer cannot modify his beliefs by a purely rule-guided procedure which does not itself presuppose an acceptance of *some* beliefs on his part. If we now apply it to empirical beliefs, the special case of a purely stipulative criterion for retention choices drops out; for an *empirical* belief is a belief whose acceptance or rejection is in some more or less direct way responsive to the believer's experience.

Let us call the faculty exercised when a man makes a choice, which is not effectively governed by criteria, as to the retention or acceptance of an empirical belief, *judgement* – obviously judgement is always exercised in the light of a given range of experience and in the context of an already received framework of beliefs. It is then clear that some empirical beliefs must be founded on judgement and not on the application of criteria – though there can be discussion about the scope for rule-constituted decision-procedures, and about the degree to which the necessary base of judgement can be narrowed down.

The same point can be approached in another way. I have previously spoken of experience as consistent or inconsistent with a set of beliefs – but what notion of consistency is involved here? Consistency is a relation between bearers of truth value: A and B are inconsistent if not both can be *true*. Experience however is neither true nor false – it is just experience. The inconsistency must therefore be between a set of beliefs and the judgement a believer is inclined to make on his incoming experience. A pre-given propensity to make certain judgements is presupposed.

A fortiori, if rational belief about the world is possible, then it too must include judgementally based beliefs. Criteria of rationality float on a sea of judgement. They must therefore be conceived as necessary conditions which rational belief aims to meet: there cannot possibly be criteria which effectively determine, with respect to every belief, whether it is rational to accept or reject it. This type of point is in no way new;[97] yet when the existence of 'criteria of rationality' is brought up as a defence against sceptical doubts about the possibility of rational belief, it can easily get obscured. But a position which more or less covertly interprets rational beliefs as beliefs which are or could be uniquely arrived at by the application of criteria of rationality, lays itself open to the sceptical attacks which it is designed to rebut. For the sceptic can then correctly argue that it is not in principle possible for all beliefs to be rational in this way. A proper counter to this scepticism must therefore begin by recognising the fundamental place of judgementally based beliefs, and it must defend the notion of rational judgement.

Relativism: two modes of application and the realist's reply

The above distinction between the application of criteria and the exercise of judgement serves to distinguish two forms which the relativist critique of intellectualism can assume.

In one of these a distinction is made between 'contextually provided' and 'universal' criteria of rational retention choice.[98] If the criteria which (constitutively) determine or constrain a rational retention choice are at least in part given within the context of an overall theoretical framework, then it follows that rationality and rational belief are themselves context-bound notions. This thesis must be distinguished clearly from a weaker view: namely, that what beliefs it would be rational for a person to accept or reject varies with the overall background of beliefs against which he makes his assessment. Any application of criteria of rational belief necessarily presupposes, as we have seen, some corpus of beliefs which are accepted for the purpose of the application. When these vary then the same criteria will pick out varying ranges of belief as rational. But to argue that a varying background of overarching beliefs produces, not just varying results with an application of the same criteria, but varying results through a variation in what criteria are applicable, is to make a much stronger claim. (An analogous point is often made about moral relativism.) Leaving aside, then, any criteria of rational belief which may be accepted on all sides as 'universal', we are left with the question of what sense can be given to the notion of a contextually provided criterion. That a fairly clear sense can be given, and that it presupposes a verificationist framework in the theory of meaning, was shown above. How do the verificationist's claim, and the realist's reply, work out in specific cases?

A theoretical statement which is treated as a complete or partial 'definition' can be seen as the limiting case of a set of priorities which dictates an order in which statements in a theory can come up for rejection when inconsistency looms. Now where such priorities are specifiable they can certainly be seen as contextually provided criteria of retention choice. But there is no reason to regard them as constitutive of the *rationality* of such a choice. In the Zande system of witchcraft, oracles and magic, events are allowed to show the dishonesty or incompetence of a witchdoctor, or the relatively greater reliability of one man's rubbing-board over another's. But no events are allowed to show the unreliability of the poison oracle, when it is properly consulted. In any actual case where its predictions and subsequent events come into clear enough conflict, auxiliary hypotheses are brought in to save the day. The rule for resolving conflicts *between* Zande oracles is that rubbing-boards are more reliable than witchdoctors, termites more reliable than rubbing-boards, and the poison oracle takes precedence over all (see Evans-Pritchard 1937, pt. III, chs. 1–5). These beliefs and practices may be said to evidence a contextually provided criterion for choice in such conflicts. But on what grounds do we make the stronger claim: that the rationality of Zande belief *consists* (among other things) in the degree to which it meets this internally given criterion?

Certainly it is not unreasonable for individual Azande to accept the validity of the principle on testimony; and there may be good reasons advanced within the overall framework of beliefs for accepting it – for example, Azande point out that witchdoctors and rubbing-boards are more open to human hanky-panky than the other oracles. But the point is precisely that it makes sense to ask whether the rule is a rational one or not, in the sense in which one could question whether some of the intra-theoretical procedures of phlogiston theorists or Ptolemaic scientists were rational. And this is a general point, which could be applied to any contextually given criterion for retention choices: it might always be asked, with respect to any such criterion, whether it is rational to follow it, in given circumstances, or not. This is the realist's point again – the criterion itself could always become the object rather than the tool of assessment. Indeed (for the realist) so long as we are talking about beliefs of a fundamentally factual kind about the world – and on the intellectualist thesis, that is what magico-religious beliefs in a traditional culture are – then there cannot in any non-trivial sense be contextually provided criteria of rational belief.[99] All that is true is that within any such framework certain overarching beliefs are not questioned, and are used to assess the acceptability of other intra-theoretical beliefs; and that the beliefs which it is rational to accept or reject vary, in accordance with *universal* criteria of rationality, between different overall frameworks of already accepted belief.

In its second form the relativist's critique begins by pointing out – perfectly correctly, as we have seen – that 'rational belief' cannot be characterised solely in terms of the application of 'criteria of rationality': there must, in particular, be room for the notion of a rational belief based purely on judgement. It then places the notion of a *trained* judgement at the centre of the stage. Judgement, it is pointed out, is always exercised within an overall framework of belief; and, as a person is trained within such a framework, his judgement – his whole way of interpreting his experience – is modified. Now if this acquired judgement is an essential condition for the rational assessment of beliefs, and if it can only be acquired within a particular framework or paradigm, then again it begins to seem that a choice between frameworks, and hence any transition from one to another, must be non-rational.

There are no specifiable rules underlying the art historian's identifications of the origins of a picture, or the wine connoisseur's of the origin of a wine. The idea that, in a somewhat similar way, the ability to make rational retention choices in a scientific discipline involves the acquiring of a specialist's 'feel' or judgement going beyond specifiable criteria, lies behind Kuhn's appeal to the group of trained, competent scientists as arbiters of rational progress.[100] Again the question here is whether the shared decision of the group of scientists is being appealed to as *constitutive*, within the paradigm, of the notion of rational choice. For as in the case of the Zande thought-system, it follows for the realist, from the fact that theory aims to provide a description and explanation of experience, that it must always make sense to question the correctness of a decision made by any particular group of scientists – in a way in which it would not make sense if such decisions were constitutive of 'scientific rationality'.[101]

Moreover, the picture of a conceptual asymmetry between, on the one hand, the acceptance of an overall framework of beliefs – allegedly presupposed by the exercise of rational judgement – and, on the other, the acceptance or rejection of beliefs within the framework – with respect to which rational judgement can be exercised – is a false one. A cultural framework of ideas, used for jobs of description and explanation, is not acquired by a kind of primary imprinting on the mind which requires no critical or creative participation on the part of the person involved. It is *learnt*: but learning of this kind is itself a process in which experience is interpreted by judgement, and it makes sense to ask whether this judgement is rationally exercised. For a language and thus a system of thought to be learnable, there must be (as Wittgenstein pointed out) some shared interpretation of experience among language-users and learners on which the learner can build. This shared interpretation presupposes an agreement of judgement (I mean here the process as well as the result). Hence trained judgement should be seen as the product, rationally exercised or otherwise, of a cultural framework of beliefs extending and modifying, as well as being modified by, a disposition which must be pre-culturally shared by those who can share a common culture. (This last point gives us a clue to Tylor's and Frazer's insistence on the 'psychic unity of mankind' as a fundamental assumption of the intellectualist approach.)

How does the realist position I have outlined in the foregoing sections bear on intellectualism? It is evident that Tylor's second two blocks to falsifiability, since they are necessarily incurred in *any* explanatory framework, cannot be used to explain why traditional magico-religious cosmologies should be relatively *more* difficult to break out of than scientific theories are. If the Azande are 'enmeshed' in their 'web of belief' simply by reason of the structure of the web itself, then so is the scientist enmeshed in his. Now this can cut in one of two ways. On the one hand it can be argued that in both cases rational thought is indeed imprisoned within an overall framework of beliefs; so that while the Zande thinker or the scientist can reason cogently and critically within the framework, changes in the framework can be produced only by social and psychological forces of a more fundamental kind. But if, as I have argued, this conceptual asymmetry is a false one, so that both beliefs within the framework and the beliefs which constitute it can be rationally assessed then the point again applies equally to the scientist and the Zande thinker.

There is, then, nothing in the logical structure of traditional magico-religious beliefs – whether specific to them, or general to all experience-ordering systems of theory – which in principle rules out the intellectualist's mode of explanation. The essential feature of intellectualism is that it traces both the origins and (what is in some ways more relevant for present-day studies of religion in traditional small-sale societies) the causes of subsequent changes in magical and religious beliefs to rational attempts at explanation. This applies not merely to modifications within the traditional cosmological framework, but also, for example, to the loosened hold of traditional ideas linking illness with spirit-possession, witchcraft or sorcery, when they come into contact with techniques of modern medicine. The intellectualist sees in the transition from one set of beliefs to the other a more or less rational reaction to experience, and regards the attempted syntheses of modern and traditional therapeutic techniques which anthropologists often report as halfway houses along this road. Such a transition most certainly represents a 'paradigm-shift', but the intellectualist's view of it cannot be excluded simply on that account – an additional premise is required, if he is to be faced by *a priori* difficulties of a relativist kind here, and this premise involves an extremely problematic position in the theory of meaning.

Notes

1 See for example Horton 1962, 1964, 1967, 1973a, b; Jarvie 1964; Jarvie & Agassi 1967; Peel 1969; Spiro 1966. Both Horton and Jarvie acknowledge the influence of Popper, particularly, perhaps, of his 1949 article. Jarvie and particularly Horton would be willing to go farthest along the intellectualist path described in this chapter.

2 See Evans-Pritchard 1933. Horton, however, sees it also as a neglected theme in Durkheim's *Elementary Forms* – see Horton 1973b; and Peel 1968, 1969 looks to Weber's sociology of religion.

3 Evans-Pritchard 1965 provides a brief intellectual history.

4 Tylor does not separate out these four points himself. I am highlighting them because of their intrinsic philosophical interest – which will be discussed in what follows – and also because of their subsequent importance in discussions of the persistence of magical and traditional forms of thought. It should also be noted that Tylor is discussing, in the passages I have quoted, magical rather than religious practices: "intellectual conditions accounting for the persistence of magic". He would not however see any significant difference between traditional instrumentally oriented religious practices and magical practices in this respect.

5 Evans-Pritchard 1937: 475. Cp., with Tylor's first reason, Evans-Pritchard's (13); with Tylor's second, Evans-Pritchard's (11) and (5); and with Tylor's fourth, Evans-Pritchard's (10).

6 Thus Keith Thomas remarks (1971: 645): "The Azande of Central Africa, whose magical beliefs form the subject of Evans-Pritchard's classic anthropological study, are said to be 'not experimentally inclined'. The leading [seventeenth-century] English opponents of magical beliefs, by contrast, were conspicuous for their self-conscious insistence on the need to test old opinions and to reject untenable dogmas." But he follows Evans-Pritchard, and thus indirectly Tylor, in taking the 'structural' blocks to falsifiability in thought-systems such as astrology as reasons for their persistence; see e.g. pp. 335ff.

7 Naturally, then, he would reject this remark: "Oracular revelations [among the Azande] are not treated as hypotheses and, since their sense derives from the way they are treated in their context, they therefore *are not* hypotheses" (Winch 1972: 20).

8 The former have been studied from an intellectualist point of view in Jarvie 1964.

9 Ross (1971) uses this term to cover more or less the same distinction.

10 See Kneale 1949. I am here building a realist conception of theory into the intellectualist account.

11 I am abstracting here from another dimension of Wittgensteinian philosophy of language – its anti-realism. As a conception of meaning this receives some attention in the appendix to this book.

12 Apart from the paper by Winch already cited (1972), see also Wittgenstein 1971, Phillips (forthcoming), and, for a sympathetically critical view, Mounce 1973.

13 It is interesting that this line of thought seems to be accepted also by Goody (1961), who otherwise argues for a literalist approach to religion.

14 Leach shows himself a Durkheimian not least in this casuistry, which is of a kind of which Durkheim was particularly fond. Cp. the argument Durkheim uses in a discussion of his views on religion: "a rational interpretation of religion could not be thoroughly irreligious, since an irreligious interpretation of religion would be one which denied the very fact it sought to explain" (reported in Lukes 1973*b*: 516). "This ingenious remark", Lukes adds, "met with applause."

15 See e.g. Jarvie 1964, Leach 1954, Geertz 1966, Gluckman & Eggan 1966, Peel 1968, Spiro 1966.

16 For African religions, see e.g. Evans-Pritchard 1956, Horton 1962, Lienhardt 1961, Middleton 1960, Turner 1962. For English religious beliefs, see Thomas 1971.

17 Though, as Thomas (1971) shows, the degree to which the mediaeval Christian world-view was homogeneously accepted and understood by ordinary laymen should not be overestimated.

18 Though even this seemingly indispensable foundation for a distinctively *Christian* faith is increasingly subject to revision.

19 Is a diminished sense of the multiplicity of God's roles related to a diminished sense of the diversity of the *persons* of God? An answer to this could bear on the question of what the reasons are for the unity-in-diversity of gods in African religious thought. See ch. 13.

20 'Positivism' is a label which has acquired an indefinite spectrum of connotations. Any reasonably definite formulation will therefore be to some degree stipulative. It will be noted that mine in no way commits positivism to e.g. an anti-theoretical 'fact-collecting' stance, or to a doctrine of the methodological unity of the sciences. While the second of these is historically connected with the positivist tradition, the former results from no more than a misunderstanding.

The three positivist theses I have stated are, respectively, epistemological, ontological and semantic. Philosophically, the last of these requires comment. It may well be the case that some philosophers who have felt allegiance to logical positivism have simply combined the epistemological and ontological theses with a straightforwardly realist (truth-conditions) notion of meaning. Nevertheless it is normally accepted that the distinctive feature of logical positivism is the semantic foundation of its attack on metaphysics. Thus, for example, the anti-realist tenor of the Schlick slogan I have used. So here I am taking the logical positivists' conception of meaning as at least cognate to the verificationism discussed in the appendix.

21 Parsons expresses a kind of 'what we cannot speak of we must consign to symbols' attitude towards religious thought; Malinowski sometimes tends to an emotivist view of religion and magic.

22 Durkheim 1915: 2, 417. Durkheim's arguments for the postulate are remarkably poor ones. "How could a vain fantasy have been able to fashion the human consciousness so strongly and so durably?", he asks (p. 70). One might ask a similar question about the belief that the earth is flat. Or again: "Surely it ought to be a principle of the science of religions that religion expresses nothing which does not exist in nature [i.e. in reality]; for there are sciences only of natural phenomena... What sort of science is it whose principal discovery is that the subject of which it treats does not exist?" (p. 70). Clearly the fallacy here lies in confusing the reality of religious beliefs with the reality of their objects. If Durkheim's argument were valid there could be no science of false beliefs.

23 For Durkheim the difference between his own theory and historical materialism is that he does not regard religion as a mere epiphenomenon of society (see Durkheim 1915: 423-4). This is true of his work on religion as a whole. But if one takes the distinctively symbolist element in it seriously, he is in no better a position to give religion a degree of relative autonomy than Marx is – a less good one, in fact.

24 Jarvie & Agassi (1967: 73n.25) take Beattie up on this point. Beattie replies by stressing that it was a capacity for second-order "systematic and analytic thinking *about concepts*" which he had in mind (Beattie 1970: 252n.2). In that case however it is difficult to see why the lack of this capacity should explain the resort to symbolic modes of expression at the *first-order* level of discourse about society. Are we to suppose that the concepts required to discuss society and social relationships cannot emerge without second-order analytical thinking? This evidently could not be true of first-order discourse in general. Special considerations are therefore required to support it in this case.

25 Leach 1966: 39. (Other examples can be found in Radcliffe-Brown 1952, ch. 7, 'Taboo'.) A good part of Leach's ethnographic evidence consists of the observations of various ethnographers, which have led them to conclude that Trobrianders or Tully River Blacks do not all fully believe the relevant religious doctrines, do not believe them all the time, or act in ways and make statements which are inconsistent with them. But even if this shows that they do not really believe, or take seriously, what they say, it is a long step from this to the conclusion that what they say must have some other, symbolic meaning which does express their beliefs. Indeed if they really were expressing symbolically the statements about social relationships which Leach imputes to them, there would be no possible reason for the disagree-

ment and doubt which Leach starts with as evidence. Incisive criticisms of the whole article are made by Spiro (1968) – one obvious point being, of course, that the symbolic message seems to presuppose "ignorance of physiological paternity" after all.

26 Pareto 1935, II: para. 1008. (Another writer often invoked in this context by anthropologists is Robertson Smith.) Pareto's argument is criticised by Winch (1958: 103–11) from a philosophical position different from that argued for here (though the emphasis on the primacy of that description of an action under which it is done by the agent is shared).

27 This point appears to be recognised by Leach (1976: 11).

28 Lienhardt 1961: 169. Cp.: "I have described [the powers] for the most part as the Dinka themselves understand them; but in this chapter I try to give a different account of them, not now as ultra-human 'beings' which might form the subject matter of Dinka theology, but as representations (or as I here prefer to call them, 'images') evoked by certain configurations of experience contingent upon the Dinkas' reaction to their particular physical and social environment" (p. 147).

29 "The fact that in traditional African religion many events are believed to be due to the activity of 'personalised' spirits certainly provides an explanation of these events, and this explanation involves an analogy with the experienced human world; these propositions have never been denied" (Beattie 1973: 8–9).

30 Winch 1972: 41. Winch himself accepts that Zande magic involves notions of 'causal influence'. But see the following discussion.

31 The same point is made in Peel 1969. It seems that insight into the uselessness of their own practices can be acquired by ritualists at a very early age: "The child, even *before he is fully responsive to verbalizations*, begins to get a picture of experience as potentially menacing. He sees his parents, and other elders, *confess their impotence* to deal with various matters by technological and other rational means in that they resort to exotic prayers, songs and 'magical' observances, and to esoteric rites" (my italics; Kluckhohn 1970: 218).

32 Beattie is insufficiently clear about the difference between the the two and so fails to see the force of Jarvie & Agassi's claim that they are incompatible (Beattie 1970: 247–8). It is one thing to say that rituals are symbolic imitations of control, which help to reduce the frustrations of felt powerlessness and *lack* of control; it is another to see them as mimetic dramas, believed by the actor to have a cosmological power which *gives* him control. For the same reason Beattie thinks his own and Horton's views on magic to be closer than they really are (p. 265).

33 In particular, if the Azande *are* concerned with "understanding the world", then the European cannot be "committing a category mistake" in "pressing Zande thought where it would not naturally go – to a contradiction" (Winch 1972: 26). Else what could we say to a *Zande* who tried to follow the logic of the beliefs accepted in his culture in an unaccustomed direction – "You are making a category mistake: the kind of understanding of the world offered by these

doctrines is quite compatible with the derivability of a contradiction from them"? (Cp. Gellner 1968: 402.) It follows from the aim of understanding the world that the pointing out of inconsistency cannot be an *irrelevant* activity.

34 To explain my use of these philosophical labels: By 'realism' (correspondingly, by 'anti-realism') here I mean what might be called 'scientific realism'; i.e. the view that the apparent reference made to unobservable entities in theoretical discourse is genuine, so that in espousing a theory one commits oneself to the existence of such entities. This should be distinguished from the 'semantic' realism and anti-realism (verificationism) discussed in the appendix. The two are related as follows:

(1) If one is a semantic realist about both theoretical and observational language, then one must be either a scientific realist, or a reductionist in the strict sense of thinking theoretical statements to be translateable into observational statements.

(2) Alternatively, one may be a semantic realist about observational language alone. Then one might take an 'instrumentalist' view of theoretical 'statements', according to which they would not have truth-value at all. That, like reductionism, would be a form of scientific anti-realism.

(3) Again, one might combine (semantic) anti-realism about theoretical language with semantic realism about observational language – what might be called 'scientific constructivism' and has been called 'operationalism'. The position is not readily classifiable in terms of the notion of 'scientific realism'.

(4) Finally we have a position of *general* semantic anti-realism. A person holding this view might call himself a scientific realist in as much as he could think that theoretical entities *exist* in just the sense in which observable entities do. (Statements referring to them are assertable.) Something like this might be thought to be the position of Quine. Cp. e.g. Boorse 1975.

35 An example already mentioned is Beattie's theory that magic flows from a belief, on the part of the actor, in the efficacy of symbolic enactments. This thesis will be examined in ch. 9.

36 The "totem is 'sacred' as Durkheim says, or is an object of ritual attitude, as I prefer to say" (Radcliffe-Brown 1952, ch. 6, 'The sociological theory of totemism': 125).

37 Cp. e.g. Horton 1962: 204: the Kalabari say "*tomi oru beremare*" – "It is people who make the *oru* important." See also Beattie & Middleton 1969, 'Introduction': xxii.

38 Whether or not an action is a means to a further end of course depends at least in part on the level at which it is described. But the finer complexities which this point suggests can be kept to one side, I think, as far as the broad issues involved here are concerned.

39 The popularity of this association could be extensively documented. Apart from the authors already cited, consider e.g. Douglas, who takes ritualism "to signify heightened appreciation of symbolic action", and

assures us that "ritual is pre-eminently a form of communication" (1970b: 8) – although she also remarks that ritual is for the anthropologist "action and beliefs in the symbolic order *without reference to the commitment or non-commitment of the actors*" (my italics; p. 2). Or Raymond Firth: "Ritual may be defined as a kind of patterned activity oriented towards control of human affairs, primarily symbolic in character with a non-empirical referent, and as a rule socially sanctioned" (1971, ch. 7, 'Ritual in social reality': 222).

40 I have in mind here what Goffman (1972) calls 'interaction ritual' (see esp. 'On face-work', 4–47). But I shall argue that it is important to distinguish the code in general from interaction ceremonies in particular.

41 I use the word 'non-intentional' because such alternatives as 'unintentional', 'involuntary', 'uncontrolled' etc. all have misleading implications.

42 Connectedly, whereas with a case 2 smile a good performance is required, in case 3 this is no longer important.

In the foregoing paragraph I have drawn on Grice's account of "utterer's meaning" (Grice 1957). His analyses have become increasingly complicated to cope with counter-examples (see Grice 1968, 1969). These complications – in particular, the question of the precise object of communicative intentions – go beyond the scope of the argument of this chapter. In his 1969 article Grice remarks (p. 177): "I see some ground for hoping that, by paying serious attention to the relation between non-natural and natural meaning, one might be able...to show that any human institution, the function of which is to provide artificial substitutes for natural signs, must embody, as its key-concept, a concept possessing approximately the features which I ascribe to the concept of utterer's occasion-meaning." I take the interaction code to be just such an institution.

I have also gained, here and particularly in ch. 7, from Lewis 1969, from Bennett 1973 and from Austin 1962.

43 See the essays in Hinde (ed.) 1972. The same point is there made by Mackay, and by Lyons. They however would include case 2 behaviour in the communicative category.

44 A greeting/apology etc. is a piece of IC behaviour which in certain circumstances is normatively laid down. To say "I greet you/apologise" is to say one is performing such an act: to do so simply by saying one is doing it. This can work only because in such cases overt acknowledgement that an obligation applies can sometimes discharge it. There are however difficulties in taking overt acknowledgement of the relevant norms to be the standard *communicative* intention of a person who says "I apologise/greet you" etc. – at least if such a standard intention in some way determines the sense of the utterance.

45 As Goffman tends to. Of course 'code of behaviour' usually has just this meaning, of laying down how one *ought* to behave to others. However I am using the word 'code' not in this sense but in the sense of 'system of communication'.

46 What I say about the social boundary and condition-marking character of ceremony is influenced by Mary Douglas' suggestive remarks (Douglas 1970a).

47 In connection with the last few (very sketchy) remarks I would again draw the reader's attention to Mary Douglas' discussion of order, pollution and dirt (Douglas 1970a).

48 My distinction between 'social' and 'non-social' runs along somewhat similar lines to that made in Anscombe 1958 between 'brute' and 'institutional' facts; and along very similar lines to Searle's in Searle 1969: 50ff. I agree with Searle in seeing 'social' facts as constituted by systems of rules, but not with his view of the rules involved.

49 The obligation created by the rule must be very weak for the regularity to remain conventional. See Lewis 1969. (I am indebted in this paragraph to a conversation with Jane Heal.)

50 Cp. e.g. the 'hot food' ritual of the Tikopia (Firth 1971, ch. 7, 'Religion in social reality': 227-32), or Kalabari sculpture rituals (Horton 1965). I say 'has the appearance of', because the Church has been careful to formulate its own teaching on this question of 'localisation', or 'binding': "We should think of [Christ] as present whole and entire, but without the limitations of dimensions, place or movement...He is present there but not 'as in a place' – not confined, or held, or bound" (O'Shea 1966: 107).

51 Obligative acts, which have been distinguished from operative acts (see pp. 99-100), are also often ceremonialised. They do not have the theoretical interest in connexion with the analysis of magic which operative acts have and will not be separately considered henceforth.

52 Turner (1967: 30): "The basic unit of ritual, the dominant symbol, incapsulates the major properties of the total ritual process...[it] brings the ethical and juridical norms into close contact with strong emotional stimuli...norms and values, on the one hand, become saturated with emotion, while the gross and basic emotions become saturated through contact with social values." And Whitehead, one of the philosophical gurus of the symbol, proclaims (1928: 104): "Those societies which cannot combine reverence to their symbols with freedom of revision, must ultimately decay either from anarchy, or from the slow atrophy of a life stifled by useless shadows."

On the soberer level of analysis of types of symbolism, an article that has been influential is Sapir 1933. Sapir has some very interesting examples, but his distinction between 'condensed' and 'referential' symbolism is obscure, and difficult to reconcile with them. The main element involved in it seems to be the contrast between emotional and purely cognitive meaning. This (quite apart from Sapir's influence) is one of the two main contrasts commonly made between signs (purely cognitive, and artificial, arbitrary or unmotivated) and symbols (emotive, and natural, non-arbitrary or motivated). See e.g. Bastide 1968; Bastide builds this opposition into a contrast between the West (a civilisation of the sign) and Africa (négritude – the civilisation of the symbol); see also Sperber 1975: 23ff.

53 Beattie 1964: 69. Cp. also Turner: "The symbol is the smallest unit of ritual which still retains the specific properties of ritual behaviour" (Turner 1967, 'Symbols in Ndembu ritual': 19).

54 See Grice 1957. The distinction between natural and non-natural meaning is related to the contrast I drew in the last chapter between natural (non-social) and social characteristics or facts. That something has (Gricean) natural meaning is always a natural (i.e. non-social) fact. That it has non-natural meaning is always a social fact.

55 Stebbing 1930, however, uses the contrast between 'natural' and 'conventional' signs to cover the same distinction as Beattie's contrast between symbols and signs.

56 The above characterisation seems to me to point to a common and useful sense of 'symbol'. It is however still too wide. E.g. a dummy representing a human being in a simulated car accident would on this usage be a (variable) symbol. (I owe the example to J. E. J. Altham.) Something probably needs to be added about the function of the representation. But for present purposes this complication can be ignored.

57 I here follow the description given in Horton 1965: 11.

58 Believers in a generalised magical power commonly think of it as stemming from gods or original heroes, as Philsooph (1971) points out. Cp. the Catholic notion of grace.

59 For (1) see Douglas 1970a, ch. 5, 'Primitive worlds'; and Philsooph 1971. (2) is a background concept occasionally brought into play by a wide variety of authors, from Malinowski and Evans-Pritchard to Leach.

60 Evans-Pritchard 1929, 1937. Cp. Douglas 1970a; Tambiah 1968, 1973; Philsooph 1971.

61 See Philsooph 1971. And see the account of Sinhalese healing rituals in Tambiah 1968.

62 See e.g. Yalman 1968: 524; Nadel 1954: 158-9; Thomas 1971: 493.

63 As e.g. by Mauss 1972: 21. He uses the same argument as I have used to show that a religious rite may contain magical elements, to conclude: "Sympathetic rites may be either magical or religious." On this approach it must ultimately be impossible to give any clear sense to the term 'magic' at all.

64 Frazer confusedly notices it himself, however: "in practice the two branches are often combined; or to be more exact, while homoeopathic or imitative magic may be practised by itself, contagious magic will generally be found to involve an application of the homoeopathic or imitative principle" (1911, 1, 1: 54; 1957: 15).

65 In lectures given by Horton on Tylor's view of magic at Ile-Ife (1972).

66 Frazer 1911, 1, 1: 57; 1957: 17. Such rituals are taken not merely as mimesis but as manifestation: when Nadel (see 1954: 190-1) offered food to a dancer wearing the mask of the *ndakó gboyá*, he was ridiculed and told that "spirits do not eat": once sacrifice has been performed over the masks, he tells us, "they are no longer merely a material object, but the thing itself which they signify" (p. 191).

67 "representation is originally the creation of substitutes out of a given material" (Gombrich 1963: 8).

68 I owe a great deal to discussions with Robin Horton which vividly made me aware of the importance of the distinction between 'nature' and 'convention' for the study of magic.

69 The "new significance and purpose of the *sign* comes from the fact that it contains, by virtue of transubstantiation, a new ontic reality" (my italics; *Sacra. Mundi* 1970, II: 263).

70 Evans-Pritchard 1956: 134. The general drift of this chapter in *Nuer Religion* however is to argue against Lévy-Bruhl's account of magico-religious paradoxes of identity.

71 When the pagan Maximus of Madaura asserted that men called God by many names, since no man knows the true one, Origen replied that that correctness of certain names is proved by their superior efficacy in spells and exorcisms (Dodds 1965: 118n.4). Or, in the words of Ogden & Richards' proverb, "The Divine is rightly so-called."

72 Zande text from Mgr Lagae, quoted in Evans-Pritchard 1937: 393.

73 Evans-Pritchard 1937: 469, 450. The two examples are cited in Tambiah 1973 – in an analysis which differs considerably from that given here – as an example of the contrast between the magical, or "conventional-persuasive" use of analogy, and the "scientific-predictive" use.

74 I am in agreement with Goody (1961: 157): "religious beliefs are present when non-human agencies are propitiated on the human model" – if this is taken as highlighting both the belief in non-human agencies *and* the presence of moral and emotional attitudes towards them. Goody's remark takes the form of a sufficient condition for religious belief: this also seems correct – the condition could not be regarded as necessary. Generally, I favour the Weberian view that the 'definitional problem', and indeed the question of whether the theoretical terms of the sociology of religion should ultimately include the term 'religion' at all, should come at a later stage and not, as in the Durkheimian approach, be used as a starting point. Cp. Peel 1968: 1; also Runciman 1969.

75 *Mana* is conceived of course as a constituent of the universe, and not in any sense as a reducible theoretical concept.

76 Parsons 1964, ch. 10, 'The theoretical development of the sociology of religion': 202–5. On this point cp. Goody 1961: 151.

77 'Natural sign' is being used here in the sense of Grice's contrast between 'natural' and 'non-natural' meaning.

78 Gluckman's interesting essay (1962) on rituals and the articulation of roles is an example, and can readily be understood in terms of the notions of interaction and operative ceremonies.

79 Firth 1971: 223. Turner remarks that rites of passage in a traditional culture, and the knowledge and 'ritual' objects they involve, are felt "to have ontological efficacy. They recreate or transform those to whom they are shown or told and alter the capacity of the initiand so that he becomes capable of performing the tasks of the new status

ahead of him...without the ontological aspect the initiand would be 'lost'; he would not be able to perform even the physical acts appropriate to this new status nor to fulfil the ritual component of this new status. For example, unless a girl has been ritually 'grown' into a woman, as the Bemba put it...many aspects of sexuality will present dangers for her" (Turner 1968: 577).

80 Frazer 1911, I, I: 221; 1957: 64–5. (The phrase which I place in square brackets occurs only in 1957 edn.)

81 In his earlier work. See for example Lévy-Bruhl 1910: 76ff.

82 The this-wordly/other worldly dimension of religion should not be confused with the question of whether the gods or high god are in the world or beyond and perhaps unknown to it, nor of course with the 'transcendental' character of religious thought in my sense – that in which a thought-system is transcendental if it conceives of entities which are not experienceable.

83 See Barnes 1973; Gellner 1973a; Horton 1973b; Finnegan & Horton 1973, 'Introduction'.

84 Firth 1967: 471. I owe this reference to J. B. Loudon.

85 Of course if, as Lakatos claims (1970: 119). "there is no falsification before the emergence of a better theory", and if traditional thought does *not* generate its own theoretical alternatives, then the conservatism of the traditional thinker (in the absence of stimulation from outside his own culture) might be explained. My own view, however, is that failure to generate alternatives is itself to be explained in terms of the traditional mode of legitimation of belief.

86 For an interesting discussion connected with it see Sperber 1975, ch. 4, 'Symbolism and knowledge'.

87 This is assuming the chemist to be working, for the sake of argument, in the period before the planetary model of the atom was itself superseded.

88 The same criticism is made by Beattie 1970: 262–3.

89 I have set the argument out at some length in a paper to which Horton has replied, and for a full account I refer the reader to them (Skorupski 1973, Horton 1973a, Skorupski 1975). Here I shall merely summarise the leading points of disagreement involved.

90 Heisenberg 1952: 54–5. See also Hanson 1963: 42–9 for a useful discussion.

91 See Putnam 1976a, I. Another thing which has puzzled people about theoretical identities is why, if such statements really are plain identities, they must be empirically discovered, and how they can give us new information about the world. In Skorupski 1973 I tried to answer such puzzles in terms of the claim that identity-statements of this kind are contingent. I now think this is quite wrong (for the reasons given in Kripke 1971, 1972). 'Heat is the motion of molecules', 'A flash of lightning is a stream of electrons' are, if true, necessary truths. The proper answer to the puzzle requires a distinction between necessity and aprioricity: theoretical identities are necessary truths, but are nevertheless known only *a posteriori*.

92 For further detail and background on this point see Skorupski 1973, pt. II.

93 "The selections offered here draw out of sociological theory of knowledge a certain thread. The theme goes back to Hegel and Marx; that reality is socially constructed. Every thinking sociologist would now agree [to] it in principle. But how far dare they follow it?" (Douglas 1973: 9–10). I call this idealist rhetoric because it no doubt boils down in the end to the not-so-daring idea that *conceptions* of reality are socially constructed.

94 For a sentence to be true-in-T is for it to be a member of some correctly assertable version of T.

95 Readers familiar with the field will recognise the authors I draw on in discussing the relation between relativism and the underdetermination of theory. I am not claiming to give a picture of the views of any one of them. The purpose of this appendix is to outline as plausible a version of relativism as possible, in order to consider its bearing on intellectualism. However, readers who want to follow up the issues discussed on pp. 228–36 might consult: Feyerabend, e.g. (among his many papers on these subjects) 1970a, b; Kuhn 1962, 1970; Quine 1953, 1969, 1970; Wittgenstein 1974. Discussion of some of these views may be found in Lakatos 1970, esp. the appendix; an important but difficult piece (to which I am particularly indebted) on Quine's philosophy of language is Dummett 1973, ch. 17; a generally realist critique of some of the above writers can be found in Putnam's papers, e.g. Putnam 1976a, b.

I am not suggesting that underdetermination of belief is the only source for relativism. It is however the source which bears on discussions of intellectualism, since further analyses of Tylor's blocks to falsifiability have led naturally to it.

96 Another difficulty which faces the relativist lies in the task of spelling out his crucial notion, viz. that of a sentence making a *determinate* contribution to the assertability conditions of a theory: a point made to me by Mr John McDowell.

97 That rules stand in need of judgement for their application is a crucial theme in Wittgenstein's later work – connected with his insistence that the "limits of empiricism are not assumptions unguaranteed, intuitively known to be correct, they are ways in which we make comparisons and in which we act" (Wittgenstein 1967, pt. v, sec. 18). Cp. also: "General logic contains, and can contain, no rules for judgement. For since general logic abstracts from all content of knowledge, the sole task that remains to it is to give an analytical exposition of the forms of knowledge [as expressed] in concepts, in judgements, and in inferences, and so to obtain formal rules for all employment of understanding. If it sought to give general instructions how we are to subsume under rules, that is, to distinguish whether something does or does not come under them, that could only be by means of another rule. This in turn, for the very reason that it is a rule, again demands guidance from judgement" (Kant 1968, A133, B172).

98 I take these terms from Lukes 1967; he argues against relativism in this paper. However the admission that *some* criteria of rationality are context-dependent already implies a relativist position. To say that the totality of 'criteria of rationality' varies from context A to context B is to say that it picks out different sets of beliefs as rational under identical experiential conditions in A and B. That just is relativism about rationality; and it is difficult to see how it could be held without relativism about truth.

In general Lukes (in 1967, 1973a) too readily assumes that demonstrating the universality of 'criteria of logic' would be an adequate defence against relativism. The kind of relativism I have been discussing could perfectly well accept that certain sentences (those expressing truths of logic) are never rejected in the light of experience, but appear in every theory. Truth could still be relativised to a theory, and choice between theories would still be non-rational.

99 Here, then, we are talking about varying 'theories', 'language-games' etc., all of which share the aims of explanation and control. The question of whether other 'forms of life' with quite different aims involve different notions or 'criteria' of rationality is a separate one. Thus e.g. Winch's view that Zande magic involves its own 'criteria' of rationality and should not be judged by the criteria of Western science, need not be taken as a form of the relativism I have been discussing, but may be seen rather as stemming from his claim that the aims of this form of life have little if anything to do with explanation and control.

100 See Kuhn 1972. Of course, the art historian's or wine taster's judgement may be checked 'against the facts', whereas the scientist's retention choice comes at a more fundamental level – involving a judgement as to what facts experience should be allowed to establish.

101 Kuhn himself has stated that his appeal to the shared decision of a scientific group is descriptive and not stipulative, but still in his 1972 article draws the conclusions justified only by taking the appeal as stipulative.

References

Anscombe, G. E. M. 1958. 'On brute facts', *Analysis*, XVIII, no. 3, 69–72

Aristotle, 1954. *The Nichomachean Ethics of Aristotle*, tr. D. Ross, London

Austin, J. L. 1962. *How to Do Things with Words*, Oxford

Ayer, A. J. 1974. 'Wittgenstein on certainty', in G. Vesey (ed.), *Understanding Wittgenstein*, London, 226–45

Banton, M. (ed.) 1966. *Anthropological Approaches to the Study of Religion*, London

Barnes, B. 1973. 'The comparison of belief-systems: anomaly versus falsehood', in Finnegan & Horton (eds.), *Modes of Thought*, London, 182–98

Bastide, R. 1968. 'Réligions Africaines et structures de civilisation', *Présence Africaine*, no. 66, 2ème trimestre, 98–111

Beattie, J. H. M. 1964. *Other Cultures*, London

    1966. 'Ritual and social change', *Man*, N.S., I, 60–74

    1970. 'On understanding ritual', in B. Wilson (ed.), *Rationality*, Oxford, 240–68

    1973. 'Understanding traditional African religion: a comment on Horton', *Second Order*, II, 3–11

Beattie, J. H. M. & Middleton, J. (eds.) 1969. *Spirit Mediumship and Society in Africa*, London

Benedict, R. 1933. 'Magic', in *The Encyclopedia of the Social Sciences*, New York, X, 39–44

Bennett, J. 1973. 'The meaning-nominalist strategy', *Foundations of Language*, X, 141–68

Boorse, C. 1975. 'The origins of the indeterminacy thesis', *Journal of Philosophy*, LXXII, 369–87

Catholic Dictionary of Theology 1967. London, 4 vols.

Dodds, E. R. 1965. *Pagan and Christian in an Age of Anxiety*, Cambridge

Douglas, M. 1970a. *Purity and Danger*, Harmondsworth

    1970b. *Natural Symbols*, London

Douglas, M. (ed.). 1973. *Rules and Meanings*, Harmondsworth

Dummett, M. 1973. *Frege: Philosophy of Language*, London

Durkheim, E. 1915. *The Elementary Forms of the Religious Life*, London

Eddington, A. S. 1928. *The Nature of the Physical World*, Cambridge

Evans-Pritchard, E. E. 1929. 'The morphology and function of magic', *American Anthropologist*, XXXI, 619–41

1933. 'The intellectualist (English) interpretation of magic', *Bulletin of the Faculty of Arts*, Egyptian University (Cairo), I, 282–311

1937. *Witchcraft, Oracles and Magic among the Azande*, Oxford

1956. *Nuer Religion*, Oxford

1962. 'The divine kingship of the Shilluk of the Nilotic Sudan', in Evans-Pritchard, *Essays in Social Anthropology*, London, 66–86

1965. *Theories of Primitive Religion*, Oxford

Feuerbach, L. 1967. *Lectures on the Essence of Religion*, tr. by R. Manheim, London

Feyerabend, P. K. 1970a. 'Against method', *Minnesota Studies in the Philosophy of Science*, IV, 17–130

1970b. 'Consolations for the specialist', in I. Lakatos & A. Musgrave (eds.), *Criticism and the Growth of Knowledge*, Cambridge, 197–230

Finnegan, R. 1969. 'How to do things with words: performative utterances among the Limba of Sierra Leone', *Man*, N.S., IV, 537–52

Finnegan, R. & Horton, W. R. G. (eds.) 1973. *Modes of Thought*, London

Firth, R. W. 1967. *The Work of the Gods in Tikopia*, 2nd edn, London

1971. *Elements of Social Organisation*, London

1973. *Symbols Public and Private*, London

Fortes, M. 1959. *Oedipus and Job in West African Religion*, Cambridge

Frazer, J. G. 1911. *The Golden Bough*, 3rd edn, London, 12 vols; pt. 1 (vols. I-II), *The Magic Art and the Evolution of Kings*; pt. 2 (vol. III), *Taboo and the Perils of the Soul*

1957. *The Golden Bough*, abridged edn., London

Geertz, C. 1966. 'Religion as a cultural system', in M. Banton (ed.), *Anthropological Approaches to the Study of Religion*, London, 1–46

Gellner, E. 1964. *Thought and Change*, London

1968. 'The new idealism', in I. Lakatos & A. Musgrave (eds.), *Problems in the Philosophy of Science*, Amsterdam, 377–406

1973a. 'The savage and the modern mind', in R. Finnegan & W. R. G. Horton (eds.), *Modes of Thought*, London, 162–81

1973b. *Cause and Meaning in the Social Sciences*, ed. I. C. Jarvie & J. Agassi, London

1975. *The Legitimation of Belief*, Cambridge

Gluckman, M. 1962. 'Les rites de passage', in Gluckman (ed.), *Essays on the Ritual of Social Relations*, Manchester, 1–52

Gluckman, M. & Eggan, F. 1966. 'Introduction', in M. Banton (ed.), *Anthropological Approaches to the Study of Religion*, London, xi–xlii

Goffman, E. 1972. *Interaction Ritual*, London

Gombrich, E. H. 1963. *Meditations on an Hobby Horse*, London

Goody, J. 1961. 'Religion and ritual: the definitional problem', *British Journal of Sociology*, XII, 142–64

Grice, H. P. 1957. 'Meaning', *Philosophical Review*, LXVI, 377–88

1968. 'Utterer's meaning, sentence meaning, and word meaning', *Foundations of Language*, IV, 1–18

1969. 'Utterer's meaning and intentions', *Philosophical Review*, LXXVIII, 147–77

Hanson, N. R. 1963. *The Concept of the Positron*, Cambridge

REFERENCES

Hegel, G. 1931. *The Phenomenology of Mind*, 2nd edn, tr. and with intro. and notes by J. B. Baillie, London

Heisenberg, W. 1952. *Philosophical Problems of Nuclear Science*, London

Hinde, R. A. (ed.) 1972. *Non-Verbal Communication*, Cambridge

Horton, W. R. G. 1962. 'The Kalabari world-view: an outline and interpretation', *Africa*, XXXII, 197–219

   1964. 'Ritual man in Africa', *Africa*, XXXIV, 85–104

   1965. *Kalabari Sculpture*, Lagos

   1967. 'African traditional thought and Western science', *Africa*, XXXVII, no. 1, 50–71, no. 2, 155–87; reprinted (abridged) in B. Wilson (ed.), *Rationality*, Oxford, 1970, 131–71

   1970. 'The romantic illusion: Roger Bastide on Africa and the West', *Odu, A Journal of West African Studies*, N.S., III, 87–115

   1971. 'African conversion', *Africa*, XLI, 85–108

   1972. 'Spiritual beings and elementary particles: a reply to Mr Pratt', *Second Order*, I, 21–33

   1973a. 'Paradox and explanation: a reply to Mr Skorupski', *Philosophy of the Social Sciences*, III, no. 3, 231–56, no. 4, 289–314

   1973b. 'Lévy-Bruhl, Durkheim and the scientific revolution', in R. Finnegan & W. R. G. Horton (eds.), *Modes of Thought*, London, 249–305

Hsu, F. L. K. 1952. *Religion, Society and Human Crises*, London

Jarvie, I. C. 1964. *The Revolution in Anthropology*, London

Jarvie, I. C. & Agassi, J. 1967. 'The problem of the rationality of magic', *British Journal of Sociology*, XVIII, 55–74; reprinted in B. Wilson (ed.), *Rationality*, Oxford, 1970, 172–93

Kant, I. 1968. *Immanuel Kant's Critique of Pure Reason*, tr. by N. K. Smith, London

Kluckhohn, C. 1970. *Navaho Witchcraft* [excerpts from] in M. Marwick (ed.), *Witchcraft and Sorcery*, Harmondsworth, 217–36; from Kluckhohn, *Navaho Witchcraft*, Boston, 1962, 67–121

Kneale, W. M. 1949. *Probability and Induction*, Oxford

Kripke, S. 1971. 'Identity and necessity', in M. K. Munitz (ed.), *Identity and Individuation*, New York, 135–64

   1972. 'Naming and necessity', in D. Davidson & G. Harman (eds.), *Semantics of Natural Language*, Dordrecht, 253–355 (addenda, 763–9)

Kuhn, T. S. 1962. *The Structure of Scientific Revolutions*, Chicago

   1970. 'Reflections on my critics', in I. Lakatos & A. Musgrave (eds.), *Criticism and the Growth of Knowledge*, Cambridge, 231–78

Lakatos, I. 1970. 'Falsification and the methodology of scientific research programmes', in I. Lakatos and A. Musgrave (eds.), *Criticism and the Growth of Knowledge*. Cambridge, 91–196

Lakatos, I. & Musgrave, A. (eds.) 1970. *Criticism and the Growth of Knowledge*, Cambridge

Leach, E. R. 1954. *Political Systems of Highland Burma*, London

   1966. 'Virgin birth', *Proceedings of the Royal Anthropological Institute*, London, 39–50

   1968. 'Ritual', in *The International Encyclopedia of the Social Sciences*, New York, XIII, 520–6

REFERENCES

1972. 'The influence of cultural context on non-verbal communication in man', in R. A. Hinde (ed.), *Non-Verbal Communication*, Cambridge, 315–44

1976. *Culture and Communication: The Logic by which Symbols are Connected*, Cambridge

Lévy-Bruhl, L. 1910. *Les Fonctions mentales dans les sociétés inférieures*, Paris

Lewis, D. K. 1969. *Convention*, Cambridge, Mass.

Lienhardt, G. 1961. *Divinity and Experience: The Religion of the Dinka*, Oxford

Lukes, S. 1967. 'Some problems about rationality', *Archives Européenes de Sociologie*, VIII, 247–64; reprinted in B. Wilson (ed.), *Rationality*, Oxford, 1970, 194–213

1973a. 'The social determination of truth', in R. Finnegan & W. R. G. Horton (eds.), *Modes of Thought*, London, 230–48

1973b. *Emile Durkheim, His Life and Work*, London

MacIntyre, A. 1970. 'Is understanding religion compatible with believing?', in B. Wilson (ed.), *Rationality*, Oxford, 62–77; orig. publ. in J. Hick (ed.), *Faith and the Philosophers*, London, 1964, 115–33

Malinowski, B. 1922. *Argonauts of the Western Pacific*, London

1935. *Coral Gardens and their Magic*, London, vol. II, *The Language of Magic and Gardening*

1949. 'The problem of meaning in primitive languages', Suppl. I in C. K. Ogden & I. A. Richards, *The Meaning of Meaning*, London, 296–336

Marwick, M. 1974. 'Witchcraft and the epistemology of science', Presidential Address to Section N of the British Association of Science, 1974 Meeting, held at the University of Stirling

Marwick, M. (ed.) 1970. *Witchcraft and Sorcery*, Harmondsworth

Marx, K. 1968. 'Theses on Feuerbach', in *Karl Marx and Frederick Engels: Selected Works*, Progress Publishers, Moscow (eds.), London, 28–30

Mauss, M. 1972. *A General Theory of Magic*, London

Middleton, J. 1960. *Lugbara Religion*, Oxford

Mounce, H. O. 1973. 'Understanding a primitive society', *Philosophy*, XLVIII, 347–62

Nadel, S. F. 1954. *Nupe Religion*, London

The New Catholic Encyclopedia 1967. Washington, D.C., 15 vols.

Ogden, C. K. & Richards, I. A. 1949. *The Meaning of Meaning*, London

O'Shea, W. J. 1966. *Sacraments of Initiation*, Englewood Cliffs, N.J.

Pareto, V. 1935. *The Mind and Society*, New York, 4 vols.

Parsons, T. 1964. *Essays in Sociological Theory*, New York

1968. *The Structure of Social Action*, London

Peel, J. D. Y. 1968. *Aladura: Religious Movements Among the Yoruba*, Oxford

1969. 'Understanding alien thought systems', *British Journal of Sociology*, XX, 69–84

Phillips, D. Z. (forthcoming). *Philosophy and Religion*

Philsooph, H. 1971. 'Primitive magic and mana', *Man*, VI, 182–203

REFERENCES

Popper, K. 1949. 'Towards a rational theory of tradition', *The Rationalist Annual*, 36–55; reprinted in Popper, *Conjectures and Refutations*, London, 1963, 120–35

Price, H. H. 1969. *Thinking and Experience*, London

Putnam, H. 1976a. *Philosophical Papers*, Cambridge; vol. I, *Mathematics, Matter and Method*; vol. II, *Mind, Language and Reality*
   1976b. 'What is "realism"?', *Proceedings of the Aristotelian Society*, LXXVI, 177–94

Quine, W. V. O. 1953. 'Two dogmas of empiricism', in Quine, *From a Logical Point of View*, New York, 20–47
   1969. 'Epistemology naturalised', in Quine, *Ontological Relativity and Other Essays*, New York, 69–90
   1970. 'On the reasons for the indeterminacy of translation', *Journal of Philosophy*, LXVII, 178–83

Radcliffe-Brown, A. R. 1952. *Structure and Function in Primitive Society*, London

Ross, G. 1971. 'Neo-Tylorianism – a reassessment', *Man*, VI, 105–16

Runciman, W. G. 1969. 'The sociological explanation of "religious" beliefs', *Archives Européennes de Sociologie*, X, 149–91

Sacramentum Mundi 1970. New York, 6 vols.

Sapir, E. 1933. 'Symbolism', in *The Encyclopedia of the Social Sciences*, New York, XIV, 492–5

Searle, J. R. 1969. *Speech Acts*, Cambridge

Skorupski, J. 1973. 'Science and traditional religious thought', pts. I–II, III–IV, *Philosophy of the Social Sciences*, III, no. 2, 97–116, no. 3, 209–31
   1975. 'Comment on Prof. Horton's "Paradox and explanation"', *Philosophy of the Social Sciences*, V, 63–70

Sperber, D. 1975. *Rethinking Symbolism*, Cambridge

Spiro, M. E. 1966. 'Religion: problems of definition and explanation', in M. Banton (ed.), *Anthropological Approaches to the Study of Religion*, London, 85–126
   1968. 'Virgin birth, parthenogenesis and physiological paternity: an essay in cultural interpretation', *Man*, N.S., III, 242–61

Stebbing, S. 1930. *Modern Introduction to Logic*, London

Tambiah, S. J. 1968. 'The magical power of words', *Man*, N.S., III, 175–208
   1973. 'The form and meaning of magical acts', in R. Finnegan & W. R. G. Horton (eds.), *Modes of Thought*, London, 199–228

Thomas, K. 1971. *Religion and the Decline of Magic*, London

Turner, V. 1962. 'Chihamba: the White Spirit', *Rhodes-Livingstone Papers*, no. 33
   1967. *The Forest of Symbols*, New York
   1968. 'Myth and symbol', in *The International Encyclopedia of the Social Sciences*, New York, X, 576–82

Tylor, E. B. 1866. 'The religion of savages', *Fortnightly Review*, VI, 71–86
   1891. *Primitive Culture*, 3rd edn., London, 2 vols.

Weber, Max 1948. *From Max Weber*, ed. H. H. Gerth & C. Wright Mills, London

Whitehead, A. N. 1928. *Symbolism, Its Meaning and Effect*, Cambridge

Wilson, B. (ed.) 1970. *Rationality*, Oxford

Winch, P. G. 1958. *The Idea of a Social Science and its Relation to Philosophy*, London

  1972. 'Understanding a primitive society', in Winch, *Ethics and Action*, London, 8–49; also in B. Wilson (ed.), *Rationality*, Oxford, 1970, 78–111

Wittgenstein, L. 1958. *Philosophical Investigations*, 2nd edn., Oxford

  1967. *Remarks on the Foundations of Mathematics*, Oxford

  1971. 'Remarks on Frazer's "Golden Bough"', ed. R. Rhees, *The Human World*, III, 18–41

  1974. *On Certainty*, Oxford

Yalman, N. 1968. 'Magic', in *The International Encyclopedia of the Social Sciences*, New York, IX, 521–8

Index of names

INDEX OF NAMES